A TRAVELER'S GUIDE
to the
PLANTS *of* MEXICO

M. WALTER PESMAN *and* STEVE CHADDE

Dedicated to
THE PEOPLE OF MEXICO
lovers of flowers
from time immemorial

A TRAVELER'S GUIDE TO THE PLANTS OF MEXICO
M. Walter Pesman and Steve Chadde

ISBN: 978-1-951682-87-3

A Pathfinder Field Guide
Published by Orchard Innovations
Mountain View, Arkansas

The author may be contacted at: steve@orchardinnovations.com

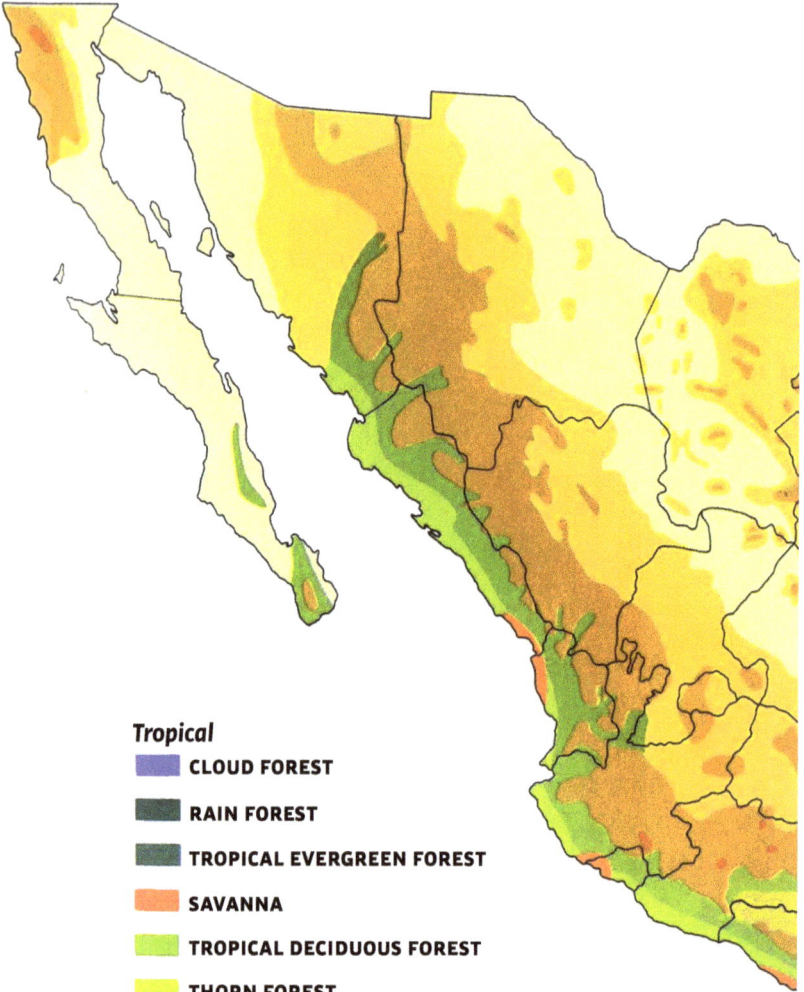

Tropical

- CLOUD FOREST
- RAIN FOREST
- TROPICAL EVERGREEN FOREST
- SAVANNA
- TROPICAL DECIDUOUS FOREST
- THORN FOREST
- ARID TROPICAL SHRUB

Mexico's Vegetation Zones

Adapted from Leopold, 1959.

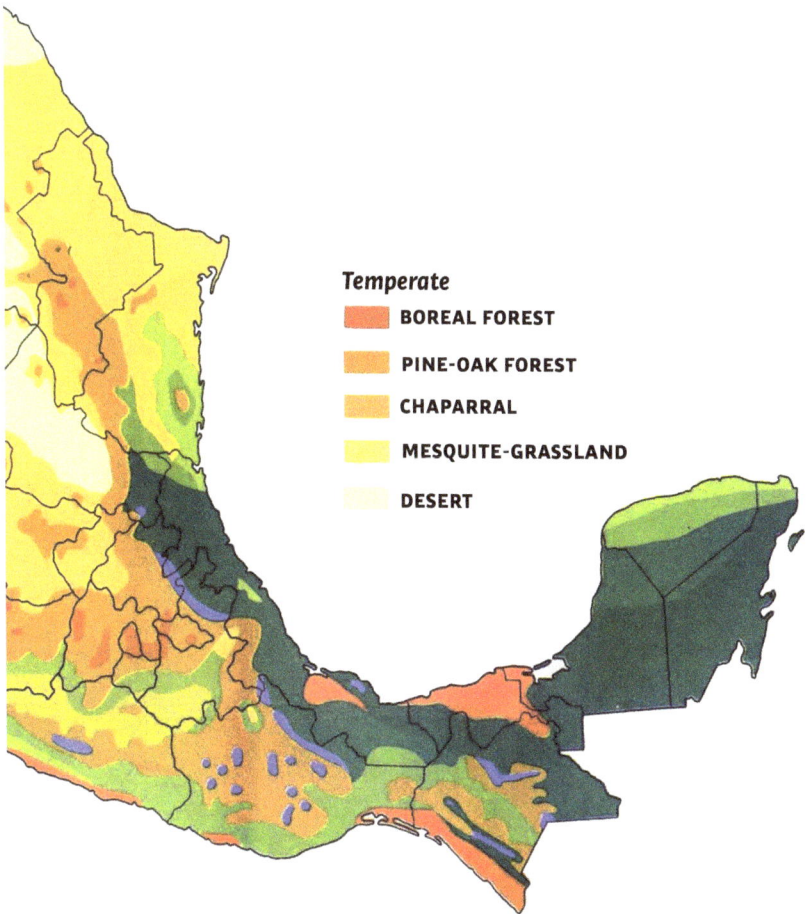

Temperate

- BOREAL FOREST
- PINE-OAK FOREST
- CHAPARRAL
- MESQUITE-GRASSLAND
- DESERT

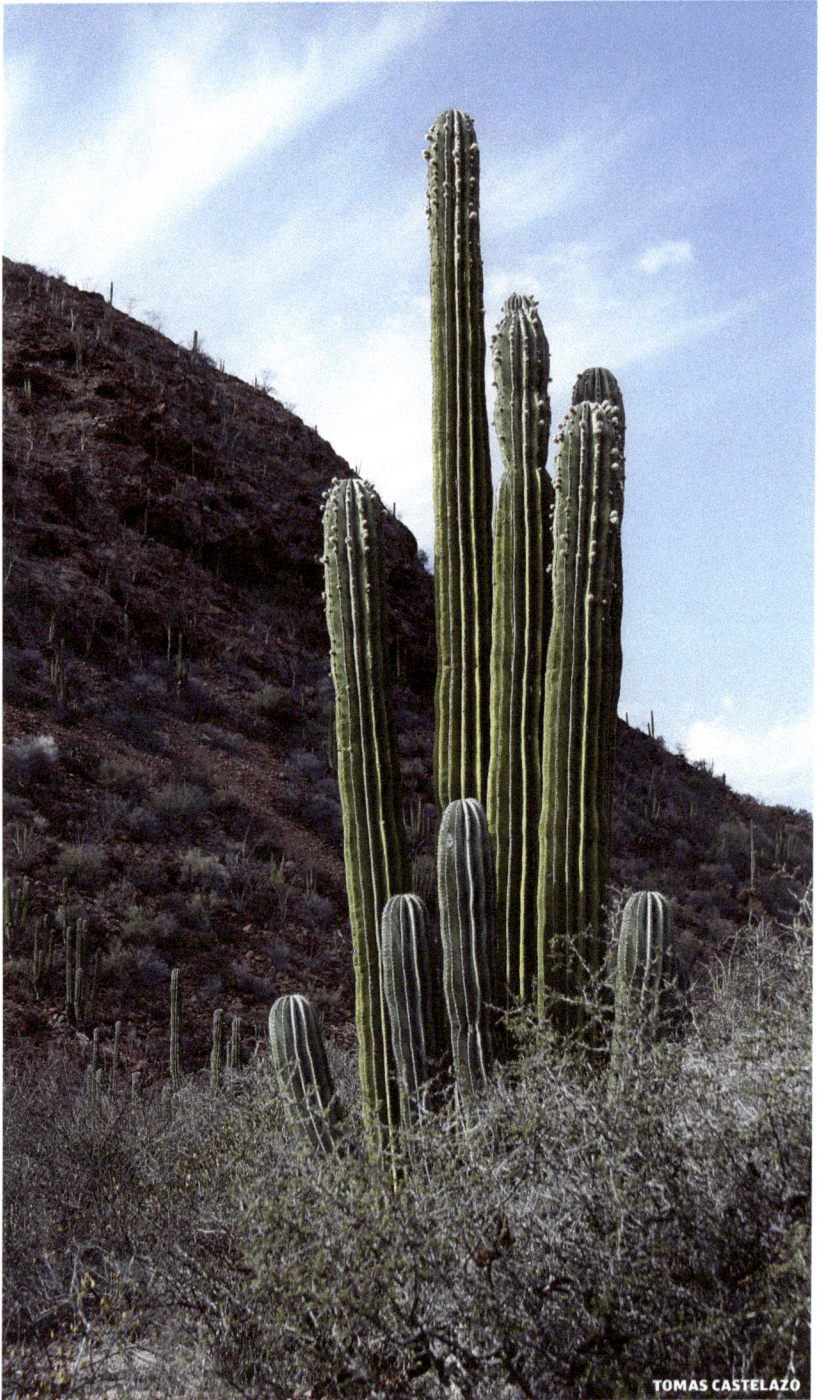

CARDÓN, *Pachycereus pringlei,* in the Sonoran Desert, Sonora, Mexico.

A *Traveler's Guide to the Plants of Mexico* was first published in 1962 as *Meet Flora Mexicana*, and subtitled: *An easy way to recognize some of the more frequently met plants of Mexico as seen from the main highways.*

This pioneering work, illustrated with many line drawings remains one of the few non-technical guides to the common plants of Mexico, both native to the country and introduced from elsewhere. Even today, I was unable to locate a comparable work suitable for anyone interested in the country's flora.

The book is also unique in that it is *ecologically based*, that is, plants of the major vegetation zones found in Mexico — for example, desert, thorn forest, tropical rainforest, etc. — are grouped together, narrowing down the large flora of Mexico into something more manageable. This arrangement is more useful to the traveler, as once the vegetation zone is identified, the important plants of that zone can be more easily determined.

Further, within each vegetation zone, I have arranged the plants in family order (alphabetically by the scientific family name) so that closely related plants are in close proximity to one another. I have found that once you can place a plant within its family by sight, for example into the Aster or Pea families, identification to the genus and species level becomes much easier.

Travelers are sure to note the many cultivated or landscape and garden trees, shrubs, and herbaceous plants so common in Mexico. Many of these are introduced from elsewhere, and are treated in the final two chapters.

With the passing of more than 60 years, our knowledge of the Mexican flora has improved and numerous changes in the arrangement (or taxonomy) of plants has occurred. To this end, I have updated all scientific names and family assignments in this work to follow those presented by the **Plants of the World Online**, a massive, authoritative database of the world's plants maintained by the Royal Botanic Gardens, Kew, England (see *https://powo.science.kew.org*).

In addition to each plant's scientific name, common names, while not standardized, are given that reflect one or more of the most widely used popular names. Importantly, the local name, in Spanish or in Nahuatl (one of Mexico's original languages at the time of the Conquest) is also given.

This new edition replaces the original book's line drawings with color photographs, and over 300 plant species are illustrated. Acknowledgment must be given to the numerous photographers who have made their work available under commercial-use Creative Commons licenses (the photograher's name is provided with each photograph). Photographs were chosen that illustrate a diagnostic part of the plant for aiding in its identification, often flowers, fruit, or leaves.

Additional details are provided in the written descriptions: the plant's growth form (tree, shrub, herb, liana, cactus, etc.), habitat, and range, both in Mexico and worldwide. Of note are the many references to cultural uses for the majority of the plants described.

The writings of Walter Pesman are largely retained in the introductory chapters that follow, with only slight editorial revisions and updates (for example, he estimated the number of vascular plant species known from Mexico to be about 12,000; today it is considered to be between 23,500 to 26,500).

My hope is that this book will serve as an introduction to the amazingly diverse flora of Mexico, provide a better understanding of its vegetation and lifezones, and further enrich your travels, no matter where you are in the country.

— STEVE CHADDE

ALEXIS LÓPEZ HERNÁNDEZ

YELLOWSILK SHELLSEED, *Cochlospermum vitifolium*

Perhaps you have had a similar experience to mine in regard to Mexico's amazing flora. Information is so scarce and so difficult to find! Here is an example. For three successive trips into Mexico I was thrilled by the glorious beauty of a large, golden-yellow flower in the very top of small trees along the highway. Not a leaf went with the flowers; they were decorating a bare skeleton of branches. What was the name of it? Why didn't everybody know about it?

A botanist to whom I described it suggested *Thevetia;* its description did not tally. One local name, **CARNAVAL**, seemed to fit its blooming time, before Lent. Most people shrugged their shoulders; **ROSAMARILLA** was suggested, which sounded like a good name for a charming lady, but merely means "yellow rose"; it definitely was not a rose. We continued in ignorance.

Finally, far south in Tuxtla Gutierrez, we came across the name **TECOMASUCHIL**, and the director of the Botanical Garden dug up the botanical equivalent as *Maximilianea vitifolia*. In the end, at the Boyce Thompson Southwestern Arboretum in Arizona, I was given the present scientific name *Cochlospermum vitifolium*, a synonym of *Maximilianea*. The latter is too easily confused with the name of a palm, *Maximiliana*.

The most widely used common name, Shellseed, is a direct translation of the botanical name, and for this particular one, Yellowsilk Shellseed, refers to the seeds being covered with silky hair.

So there we have it, after a 3 years' search!

Once you have a name, more details are much more easily available. Dr. Miranda in *La Vegetación de Chiapas* describes it as **POMPOSHUTI**, tells about its beauty of bloom before the leaves, adding that the bark and leaves are used in a concoction to combat jaundice, and that the flowers are good for the chest. Paul C. Standley, of course, describes it in *Trees and Shrubs of Mexico* — but uses the name **TECOMAXOCHITL** for *Swartzia* or *Solandra nitida*, which adds to the confusion (both flowers are beautiful and golden yellow).

I am telling this story in detail to illustrate the difficulty a non-botanist would have in tracing a flowering tree even as gorgeous as this Shellseed.

Examples could be multiplied manifoldly. There is, for instance, a striking, white, tube-shaped blossom on another naked tree, bound to catch the eye since it blooms even in midwinter in northern Mexico. It goes by the popular name of **PALO DEL MUERTO**, or Tree of the Dead — appropriately. That name is the clue: *Ipomoea arborescens* or Morning-glory Tree. Sure enough, close inspection indicates a morning-glory, but the amateur might have a hard time tracing it in botany books.

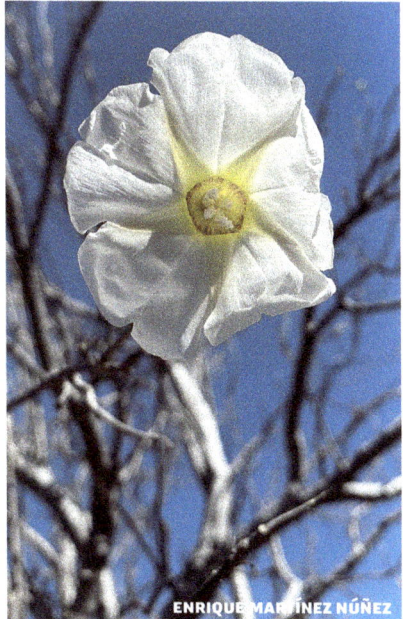

ENRIQUE MARTÍNEZ NÚÑEZ

MORNING-GLORY TREE

These experiences with highly fascinating Mexican plants made me realize that a popular guide was needed.

How could we make it usable in the hands of a tourist, who has the interest but not the botanical knowledge and technique to follow through in intricate botanical keys? The very multiplicity of Mexico's climate gives a hint. There are natural boundaries around each type of plant vegetation. Outside of these boundaries certain plants just will not grow.

Saguaro, for instance, cannot take temperatures below 17° F. It prefers rolling, hilly ground. Thus it is limited to a restricted area, beyond which you waste your time looking for it.

The southwestern boundary of **creosote bush** is a bit south of Guaymas; it is never found in the tropics.

Coconuts are restricted to low grounds and warm climates; **oaks** and **pines** prefer mountainous territory.

Thus it would be possible, in theory, to make location maps of each plant species, showing the tourist where to look for each. It would be a rather complicated task. Luckily nature provides a simplification. Certain groups of plants generally go together because they need the same conditions of growth.

In the same general neighborhood, for instance, we'll find a highly interesting tree that bears green "grapefruit" right on the branches (called **Gourd tree**), a crooked tree with clusters of reddish purple "grapes" (**Sea grape**), and a medium-sized tree with opposite evergreen leaves, long clusters of yellow flowers, and later, fleshy yellow fruit (**Pickle tree** or **NANCHE**) . A bit farther we may find a grove of **fanpalms** (**SABAL**). Knowing that, why not group these plants together in what we might call an ecological classification? Certainly the plant lover would recognize them more easily if he could find their pictures close together in a zone which we may roughly call the Mexican Savanna, even though in reality it consists of three groups, that botanists in Mexico call the **SABANA, PALMARES** and **MANGLARES**.

As a simple illustration: it might be interesting enough to trace the relationship between all the Lowells and Hydes. But if you are trying to find a certain Mr. Lowell or Mrs. Hyde, it is much easier if you know on what street they live and in which town.

In a nutshell then, this book is arranged more or less like a regional directory. It does not claim to have any genealogical value, even if it does occasionally make reference to plant families, and to how certain species are related.

The geographic regions referred to are called **vegetation zones**. Most plants in Mexico are restricted to one or two of these zones, and may thus be identified by their general location.

The outstanding exception is furnished by plant introductions and by cultivated plants. For that reason it became necessary to add two final chapters, "Introduced and Cultivated Plants" and "Ornamental Plants". These plants are found in unexpected places, along highways, in parks, in private grounds — wherever people are tempted to grow them and wherever they are willing to plant them and to care for them.

F or the plant lover Mexico furnishes unending delight. It has an estimated 23,500 to 26,500 species of vascular plants, and is the third or fourth most biodiverse country in the world. Plants vary according to climate, and Mexico has just about all climates, from Canadian cold (on high mountain tops) to tropical heat along the south coast. With the Tropic of Cancer cutting through the middle, latitudes stretch from 32° at Mexicali to 14° at the southernmost tip at Tapachula. Altitudes from Orizaba's 18,700 ft. in elevation (Mexicans call it CITLALTÉPETL), down to sea level, increase this variation due to latitude.

Rainfall figures point up another factor in the great variety of plant life. An entirely different type of vegetation results from the 77 mm. rainfall reported from Mexicali, as compared with the 3967 mm. shown by Teapa, in the State of Tabasco (Climatological Report, Mexico's Department of Agriculture, 1942). The picture becomes even more complicated if we study the seasonal periods of rainfall over the country.

The result of all these variations in altitude, latitude, and aridity is a number of fairly well-defined vegetation zones; the traveler soon begins to recognize the following zones:

1. Large **DESERT** areas, typified by cactus and yucca, or by large fields of creosote bush. Hundreds of miles are found in the northern plateau from Juarez south and in Lower California.

2. Almost as dry is the **MESQUITE GRASSLAND ZONE** through which both the Laredo and the Nogales highways enter Mexico. Mesquite is a thorny straggling shrub or small tree with crooked branches, long pods, compound leaves that consist of a couple of dozen (more or less) small leaflets, attached in pairs along a center stalk (pinnate). In early spring a wealth of greenish-white or yellow, fragrant, fuzzy flower clusters give the entire shrub a soft appearance. Long, flattened, yellowish pods (4-8 in.) follow. It is a variable shrub, with smaller or larger leaflets and thorns depending on its location. It occurs as far south as Chile. Its taproot may go down as much as 40 to 50 ft.

Yucca elata often accompanies mesquite. Ironwood and palo verde are found. Blue grama grass occupies much ground; prickly pear and thorny hackberry occur. In open spots brittlebush (*Encelia farinosa*) is common with its numerous yellow blossoms and white-felty leaves.

3. More than one-fourth of Mexico is taken up by the **PINE-OAK FOREST**. Its rainfall varies from 18 to 70 inches per year, the altitude from 4,000 or 5,000 feet to 10,000 or more, depending upon the proximity to the equator. (Timberline on the high volcanoes is around 13,000 ft.)

In general the order of growth in this Pine-Oak Forest, as it adjoins the desert range below it, is from a scrawny scrub oak stand up to a pinyon-juniper woodland zone on the more arid foothills, followed by an almost pure oak woodland, with a very large number of different kinds of oak, up through the typical Pine-Oak Forest, and still higher giving way to a dense pine forest, of different species, just below 9,500 ft. in elevation.

Few shrubs are found here. Mexican elder and Mexican hawthorn should be mentioned. At its lower edge the Charcoal shrub (*Baccharis conferta*) with its cleancut small shiny leaves, is easily recognized. Some typically Mexican flowers, like zinnia, have their home here.

These three zones, Desert, Mesquite-Grassland, and Pine-Oak forest, account for over 70 percent of Mexico's total land area. But some of the following zones steal a great deal of the interest for the traveler. The next largest zone, easily accessible, is the:

4. TROPICAL DECIDUOUS FOREST, occupying a little less than one-tenth of Mexico. It is found on the more humid foothills below the pine-oak uplands, and is sometimes called the SHORT-TREE FOREST. A number of main highways in Mexico either skirt this zone or cross it at various places, so there is no danger of missing it on a trip into the interior.

What an experience, to come from the more staid northern part of Mexico, and then, on entering this Tropical Deciduous Forest, to find yourself surrounded by colorful tree blossoms, interesting shrubs and flowers, unusual vines, thorny nightshades, interspersed by fruit trees of all descriptions.

Even the names are intriguing: here are some picked at random: Treadsoftly, Strangler fig, Springbells, Trumpet tree, Yellowsilk Shellseed, Mousekiller, Sunfruit, Rosy Cups. Some of these names are translations from the original Spanish or from the Nahuatl language; some like Sausage Tree or Stinking Toe suggest themselves naturally.

Colors of the flowers range from the brightest red to a deep purple and golden yellow. Temperate regions are more given to temperate colors. No wonder the Mexican people take to bright colors in their native dress: nature shows them the way.

5. TROPICAL EVERGREEN FOREST is the name given to a somewhat smaller zone, and one that is found most commonly in the coastline region of the Gulf of Mexico. The Pan-American highway strikes it at Tamazunchale. Other highways cross it from Puebla to Vera Cruz, from Pachuca to Tuxpan, and crossing the Isthmus of Tehuantepec. Altogether it occupies 5.5% of the land surface of Mexico.

The accepted scientific Mexican name is SELVA ALTA SIEMPRE VERDE.

This is the land of broadleaf evergreen trees like Kapok tree, Pumpwood, Cigarbox tree. It is the land of strangler fig, of palms, and ferns. On the tree trunks are rare orchids and bromeliads; between them there may be a maze of woody vines (lianas). It is like the rainforest (see below) but not quite so tall or dense.

The combination of warm climate and high moisture (36–112 in. rainfall) makes for rampant growth. Leaves of enormous size and bizarre shapes make one realize that we have really come close to the original tropical "jungle". It is the land the winter-bitten northerner yearns for in his dreams. One point of warning is in order: some of these leaves have unpleasant stinging qualities, others have thorns, still others harbor stinging ants that can make life miserable.

6. Equally inhospitable is the THORN FOREST of the more arid tropical region. It is easily accessible by the West Coast Highway; it is also found along the east coast north of Tampico, with rainfall from 16 to 34 in. annually. Thorny members of the Pea family, particularly acacias, make up much of this scrubby forest. Tall columnar cacti are found. An interesting oddity is the PALO DEL MUERTO or Tree Morning-glory, that flaunts its white trumpets before even a leaf shows.

This zone is in many ways a separation between the Tropical Deciduous Forest and the drier areas of mesquite and creosote bush domination. It occupies 3.2% of the land area of Mexico.

7. RAINFOREST. Where there is hardly a difference between the seasons, and the annual rainfall reaches from 60 to 200 inches, we encounter the presently almost inaccessible rainforest. All of the southeast portion of Yucatán is in it, and along the Gulf Coast it reaches as far west as Coatzacoalcos. It occupies 7.3% of Mexico. Some day there will be main highways through this rainforest; at present it takes a special excursion for exploration.

Here is the "forest primeval". Immense trees, growing to a height of 120 to 160 ft., occupy its "upper story": tropical hardwoods, such as mahogany, breadnut tree (*Brosimum*) and chicle or chewing-gum tree (*Achras zapote*).

In their mystical half-shade the "lower story" is formed by smaller, sparse, narrow-crowned trees. Nestled on their branches are a number of plants that live on them, but not off them: so-called epiphytes, in contrast to parasites. It is a paradise for orchid and bromeliad hunters. Slender or thick lianas abound. Animal wild life is more abundant here than in any other zone.

8. **SAVANNA** is the name given to the flat coastal plains along both coasts and to some interior marshy basins. Properly speaking, the name should be reserved for a zone, marshy at times of heavy rains, dry during the arid season, generally with poor drainage. Coarse tropical grasses dominate; a few scattered trees like Gourd tree (*Crescentia alata*) and Pickle tree (**Byrsonima crassifolia**) manage to survive not only the untoward seasonal changes but also the savanna fires that often occur during the dry period.

For the sake of simplicity we are including the **Mangrove Woodland** and the **palm groves** in this zone (called **MANCLARES** and **PALMARES** in Mexico). Coconut trees are found all along the coast; sea grapes belong here. Oaxaca palms are found in scattered groups. Occasionally we are pleasantly startled by the sight of a large, ethereal star-flower that opens wide with a shower of snow-white stamens: it is the Guiana Chestnut Tree, **PACHIRA**, sometimes irreverently called 'Shavingbrush tree', because it provides both shaving stick in bud and shavingbrush in full bloom.

9. **CHAPARRAL** is limited to Baja California and a few spots in the neighborhood of Monterrey. It is a continuation of the typical California chaparral, with oakbrush, sumac, madroña, etc.

10, 11 and 12. To complete the list of plant zones we should add the **BOREAL FOREST** in the temperate climate, confined to high volcanic peaks, and showing a similar gradation of evergreens and shrubs as found in northern regions; the **CLOUD FOREST** (or **Subtropical Rainforest**) on mountain peaks of the tropics, and finally an **ARID TROPICAL SCRUB** zone between Mexico City and Acapulco in the Rio Balsa valley. The latter has a good many characteristics of the Thorn Forest farther north.

These three zones are generally of small extent and not often seen by the average tourist. They do, again, emphasize the fact that Mexico has practically any climate and plant growth you want.

Why travel around the world to study plants when you can find them right next door in Mexico? That is becoming more and more true as new plants are brought in from the rest of the world.

Few people realize how many plants, now common in Mexico, were introductions from Europe, Asia, Africa, Australia, and of course South America. To mention just a few: all citrus fruits came from Europe and Asia; so did oleander, pomegranate, chinaberry, peach and apricot, olive and pear. Brazil furnished bougainvillea (called **BUGAMBILIA** in Mexico) and jacaranda; New Zealand and Australia, eucalyptus; Africa, the royal poinciana, African tulip tree, and gladiolus. Bananas came from India, coffee from Arabia.

Even wheat, barley, cabbage, onions, parsnips and turnips, lettuce and sugarcane were not originally growing in Mexico.

On the other hand, such common things as potatoes, tobacco, corn and tomatoes, were unknown in Europe before Columbus, not to talk about chocolate, and such standby garden flowers as dahlias, zinnias, ageratum, cosmos, tithonia, lantana and marigold.

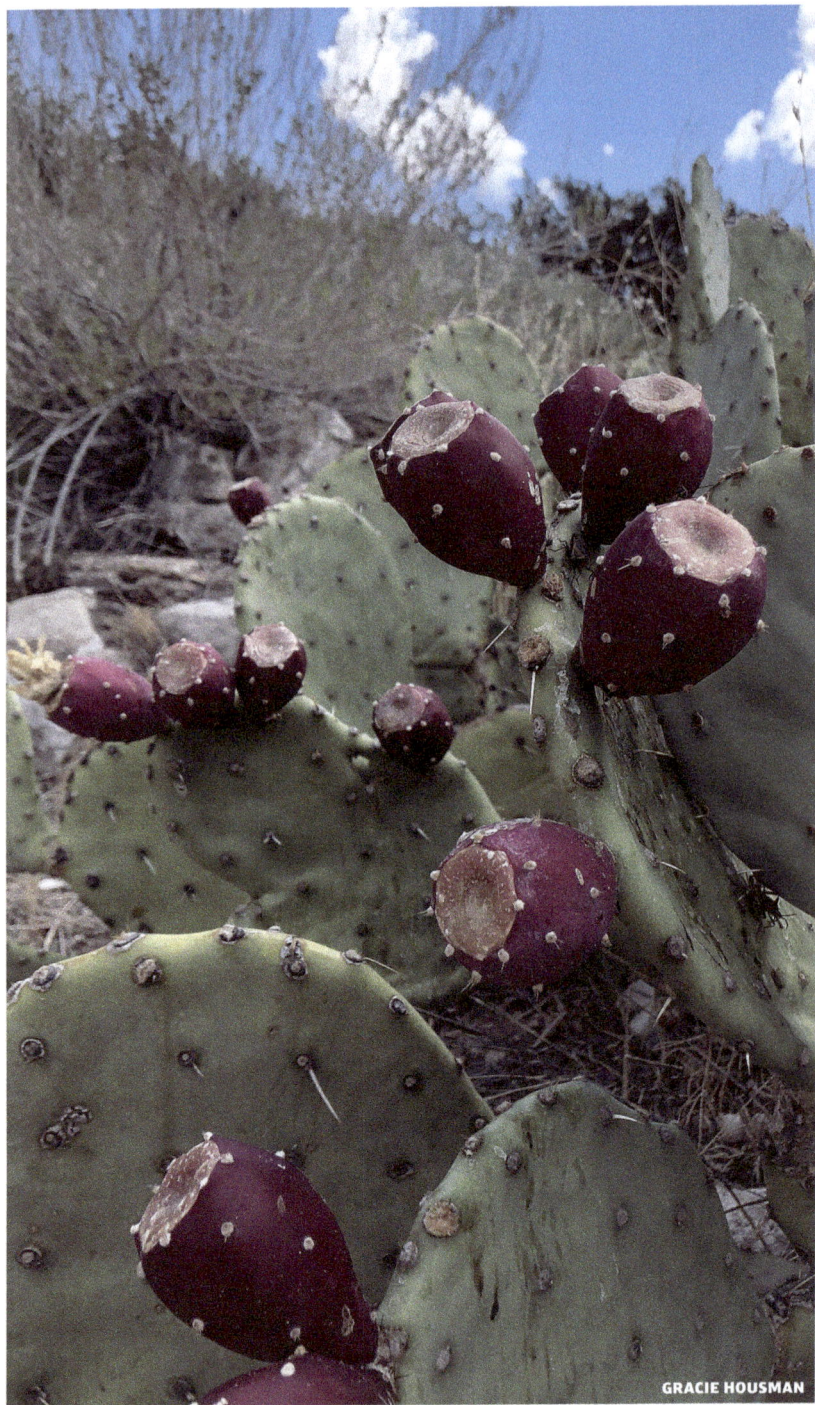

ENGELMANN PRICKLY PEAR, *Opuntia engelmannii*

Desert Vegetation Zone

The name "Desert" conjures up a variety of images to different people, many of them erroneous. Seldom in Mexico do we find the windblown desert sands without vegetation, the Sahara type. The nearest to this are the sand dunes in Chihuahua some 50 miles south of El Paso.

The desert, on the whole, is not devoid of plants. Even with as little rainfall as 5 in. per year (and some of the desert area has as much as 15 in. annually) there are three types of plants at home in the desert, and form three major kinds of Mexican deserts:

(1) the **CACTUS DESERT** with a number of almost leafless plants that have a special mechanism conserving water in a most efficient way; surfaces are rounded, showing the minimum of area, and the plants themselves are apt to be succulent.

(2) the **CREOSOTE BUSH DESERT**, consisting almost entirely of the small-leaved yellow-green **Creosote-bush** shrub (p. 35) with a glistening varnish protection; it is spaced evenly over thousands acres and has deep roots.

(3) the **ALKALI FLATS**, also called **LLANOS** or **BOLSONES**, the least interesting type, covered almost entirely with the wiry, unpalatable **Galleta grass** (*Hilaria*), that will grow in alkali spots lacking drainage; it is most common in the Chihuahuan desert.

Before long the traveler discovers two things: first, that many succulent plants are not cacti; and second, the enormous variety of real cacti. Mexico is called the homeland of the cactus: a very large number of the 1,800 species of cactus now recognized worldwide are found here. For the cactus lover this cactus desert is paradise—certainly a different kind of paradise from the Garden of Eden, but breathtaking and fascinating nevertheless.

In a way, the middle road into Mexico from the north, at El Paso and Juarez, is a proper introduction to the Cactus family. It makes one acquainted with the "flat-pad" **NOPAL**, featured in the Mexican flag. But starting with the giant **Saguaro** in southern Arizona is like having the climax of a play in the first act; after that almost every other cactus appears somewhat second-rate!

One does not have to be a cactologist to become interested in the different types of cactus. **CHOLLAS** (pronounced cho-yahs) are the spiny naked-branch type, sometimes almost tree-like, sometimes like bare winter shrubs, suddenly transformed into flower arrangements when in bloom; yellow or red or purple. One of them has such dense silvery spines that it goes under the name **Teddybear cholla** (*Cylindropuntia bigelovii*, p. 16). This is one of the "jumping chollas", not because it actually jumps at you as sometimes claimed, but because its joints break off so easily, hitch-hiking on your clothes. The **Christmas cholla** (p. 28) is also soon recognized. The lacelike canes on the market are the skeletons of **CHOLLAS**.

Prickly Pear is the accepted name for the flat-pads or **NOPALS**; the fleshy, edible fruit of many of them is called **TUNA**. They come in many sizes, these nopals; all have similar jointed stems, and all have lovely blossoms, with a large range of color.

Saguaro, growing to a height of 36 ft. or more, are generally identified in people's minds with Mexico. The fact is, however, that they are restricted to only its northwest section, following the Gulf of California south to a little beyond Guaymas. Prolonged freezing weather longer than 19 hours seems to be fatal. They prefer rolling topography. The local Indian New Year was set at the fruiting period of the Saguaro. It is also called **Giant Cactus**, although it is certainly not the only tall cactus in Mexico (see p. 57).

Most tall upright cacti extend farther south than does the saguaro. One has the picturesque name of **Trajan's Column** (*Cephalocereus columna-trajani*, p. 58). This cactus starts as a single column, and as it matures, develops a few side branches like a saguaro. It reaches 30 or even 45 feet.

Very well known in southern Mexico is the **Organpipe Cactus** (*Lophocereus marginatus*). Whether you think of it as resembling a grand organ, or merely as a natural fencing material, you'll recognize it by the upright straight stems growing close together.

A close relative has a more curved appearance of the stems coming from a common trunk (*Isolatocereus dumortieri*, p. 58). Still wider spreading is **GARAMBULLO** (*Myrtillocactus geometrizans*, p. 59), after its small fruit. It is common in the desert area north of Mexico City, along the highway connecting Pachuca with Guanajuato.

We cannot leave the Cactus family without making mention of the **Barrelcactus** (*Ferocactus*, p. 28), the largest of which reaches to about 6 ft. Most of them are "compass plants", being slanted somewhat to the southwest. It is claimed that travelers in the desert have been able to save their lives by cutting off the top portion and drinking the juice collected in the opening. Many of them are simply gorgeous in bloom.

There is no end to the interesting items about the Cactus family. But other desert plants are equally fascinating.

Only about 20 species of **Yucca or Soapweed** are of tree size, as compared with more than 500 kinds of woody cacti. Most of the Yuccas are easily recognized by their stiff narrow leaves, in a rosette either on the ground or raised up high on weirdly shaped trunks. The large flowers are produced on a stout flower stalk, generally upright, and usually of a beautiful white color. Leaves may be sharp-pointed, but have no thorny edges. In this they can be distinguished from the **Sotols** which have spiny leaves, split at the ends, and tiny flowers on a very tall stalk, up to 15 feet. The base of each Sotol leaf has a broad, curved blade, sold in curio-shops as "desert spoon".

Nearly 200 kinds of **Agaves**, often called **Century plants**, are found in Mexico. Some are cultivated for the use of fiber (**ZAPUPE** and **LECHUGUILLA**), for the production of such alcoholic drinks as **MEZCAL, TEQUILA** and **PULQUE**, and in the manufacture of soap under the name **AMOLE**. In pre-conquest days a kind of paper was made of its fiber, on which manuscripts were written. No wonder the legend originated that the Maguey (*Agave*) was given the Indians by their deity.

One more desert plant should be mentioned here: the **Ocotillo** (*Fouquieria splendens*). It is a tall spiny shrub to 10 or 20 ft. tall, generally seen without its short-lived leaves. It is not a cactus, flowers look more like a fuchsia (brilliant red); these are in dense clusters at the end of the slender, thorny branches.

Many other interesting desert plants could be added. It should be noted that many of the desert species described here are most common in northern Mexico. The southern Mexican desert and southern Baja California are home to additional, highly interesting desert plants.

JAREK TUSZYNSKI

TEDDYBEAR CACTUS

COPPER ZEPHYRLILY

DESERT MILKWEED

Copper Zephyrlily
Zephyranthes longifolia
ATZCAXOCHITL, CEBOLLA DE MAYO (MAY ONION) AMARYLLIDACEAE Daffodil Family
NATIVE RANGE Southeastern Arizona to western Texas and Mexico.

A beautiful, single, funnel-shaped flower on a long stalk, growing from a large bulb in gravelly soil of the creosote bush country. Blossoms are yellowish-white or darker on the outside, especially as they fade. They are particularly apt to bloom after a rainy period. Leaves are grasslike.

Desert Milkweed
YAMATE *Asclepias subulata*
APOCYNACEAE Dogbane Family
NATIVE RANGE Southwestern U.S.A. to northwestern Mexico.

Since both have milky sap, this **YAMATE** might be confused with Waxplant; this is possibly the reason why it is also called **CANDELILLA BRONCA** (coarse). It may grow up to man-size with straight, upright, rushlike stems, somewhat like waxplant—herbaceous on top, woody at the bottom. Its green-yellow flowers of intricate makeup are followed by typical milkweed pods, from which the fluffy seed pops out.

Mexican Coral Drops
CORALITA *Bessera elegans*
ASPARAGACEAE Asparagus Family
NATIVE RANGE Mexico.

Summer flowering bulb with few slender, narrow leaves, and numerous bright red flowers hanging from tall hollow stems. Stamens are purple and extend beyond a white cup which is inside a flower of six ridged parts with vermillion markings. This is a close relative of the white **Mexican starflower** of the Pine-Oak Forest (p. 73).

PEGANUM

Soaptree Yucca
PALMILLA

Yucca elata
ASPARAGACEAE Asparagus Family

NATIVE RANGE Arizona to western Texas and northern Mexico.

Of the numerous woody yuccas of Mexico this one can be recognized by its beautiful, tall, upright flower clusters, its narrow white-margined leaves, its erect edible seedpods, its great height (up to 20 ft.), and its location on the dry plains of Chihuahua. Some tall plants may be 200 or 300 years old, since they grow only about 1 in. per year. They may dominate the grassy landscape for miles. Production of seed depends on the mutual cooperation with Pronuba moth, which pollinates the flower and lays its eggs in the ovary.

The large roots are used for soap (**AMOLE**), the leaves for fiber; both fruit and flowers are eaten as food: the latter used raw as a salad, made into a preserve, or cooked in various ways.

DANIEL MCNAIR

BERNARD GAGNON

SOAPTREE YUCCA

OTHER YUCCA SPECIES

ASPARAGACEAE Asparagus Family

As compared with the multiplicity of cacti and agaves, yucca species are not as numerous. Even at that, more than 50 species are reported worldwide, about half of which are of tree size. See descriptions and illustrations for commonly seen yuccas.

One of these, *Yucca × schottii*, often referred to as **Mountain Yucca**, properly belongs to the Pine-Oak Forest region of Sonora and farther north; it is an attractive ornamental, with banana-like green flesh, the fruit sometimes reaching 4 in.

Many tourists, returning from Mexico, report having seen **Joshua trees**. This species, *Yucca brevifolia*, the characteristic tree on desert plains in the Mohave desert, is found from southwestern Utah to southeastern California, and into northwestern Mexico.

How to identify the different kinds of yucca? Local names are small help: **PALMA, PALMITA, IZOTE, SOYATE, ITABO**, and even **PALMA DE DATILES** and **PALMA LOCA** are used more or less indiscriminately.

Botanists generally begin by examining the fruit: erect pods, opening up on ripening, as in *Yucca elata, Y. luminosa, Y. rostrata, Y. rupicola* and *Y. thompsoniana*, but fleshy, pendent, often edible and dropping off in the other species.

The ultimate height helps to recognize such tall yuccas as *Yucca decipiens*, 35–40 ft.; *Y. filifera*, 40 ft. or more; *Y. gigantea*, 35–40 ft. and compact; *Y. × schottii*, 5–15 ft. Next in height come *Y. schidigera*, 12–15 ft. or less; *Y. treculiana*, 10–15 ft.; *Y. valida*, 50–60 ft. and *Y. periculosa* of southern Mexico, sometimes 20 ft. tall, but with few branches.

One interesting characteristic of *Yucca filifera,* is that its terminal flower cluster is erect to begin with, but droops after blooming.

Hesperoyucca whipplei

SYNONYM *Yucca whipplei*
NATIVE RANGE South-central and southern California to Mexico (Baja California).

Chaparral Yucca, Quijote plant; practically stemless, but with a 6–15 ft. flower stalk, having numerous, white, large, fragrant, hanging flowers; stiff, thick, bluish, long leaves with fine but sharp teeth and sharp points. Fruit splits open on maturity.

CHAPARRAL YUCCA

YUCCA FILIFERA

YUCCA GIGANTEA

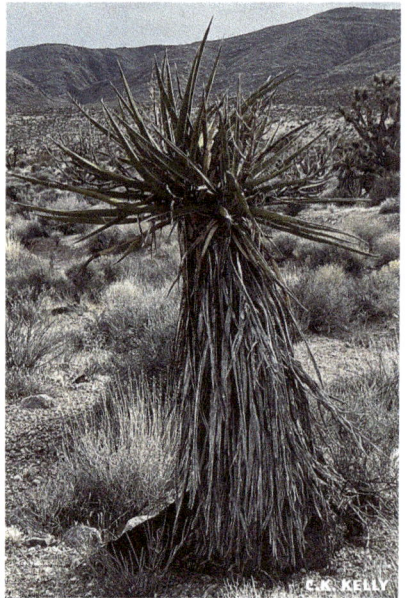
YUCCA SCHIDIGERA

Yucca filifera
SYNONYM *Yucca australis*
NATIVE RANGE Mexico.
   IZOTE; tall, much-branched; leaves to 1 in. wide, 12–18 in. long; flowers cream-colored, cluster drooping after bloom; hollow trunks used as beehives; its spongy interior is prepared for pads (SUDADEROS) for pack animals.

Yucca gigantea
SYNONYM *Yucca elephantipes*
NATIVE RANGE Central Mexico to Central America.
   DATILES; 20–30 ft., often with swollen base; Veracruz, Oaxaca, Morales; cultivated as hedge plant in Central America.

Yucca schidigera
SYNONYM *Yucca mohavensis*
NATIVE RANGE Southern Nevada to Mexico (Baja California).
   Mojave Yucca, 12–15 ft., simple; flowers white and purple; fruit turns purple or black. Baja California where dry.

Yucca × schottii
NATIVE RANGE Southern Arizona to New Mexico.
   Mountain Yucca; usually two or three branches from base, often leaning; leaves nu-

YUCCA × SCHOTTII

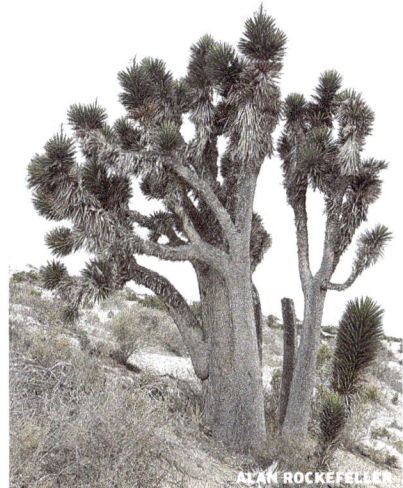

YUCCA TRECULIANA

merous, long and narrow, bluish-green with reddish edges, with very short, sharp spine; blooms April–August; fruit edible; attractive, ornamental. A hybrid between Y. *baccata* x Y. *madrensis*.

Yucca thompsoniana
NATIVE RANGE Southwestern Texas to northeastern Mexico.

Neat and small tree; trunk 3 ft. high; leaves flat, rigid, bluish, pungent, 12–15 in. long.

Yucca treculiana
SYNONYMS *Yucca macrocarpa, Yucca torreyi*
NATIVE RANGE South-central U.S.A. to Mexico.

PALMA CRIOLLA; trunk up to 15 ft. tall, up to 2 ft. in diameter, usually simple; used for landscaping highways; flowers bell-shaped, up to 4 in. March–April.

Yucca valida
NATIVE RANGE Mexico (Baja California).

An unusual tree yucca of southern Baja California, simply branched with trunks to 2 ft. in diameter, and with leaves distributed evenly along the stem, 6–10 in. long; total tree 15–18 ft. tall. Often forming large groves.

YUCCA VALIDA

YUCCA LOOK-ALIKES

Once we have become acquainted with a certain plant name, most of us are inclined to apply it to any group of plants that reminds us of it. This accounts, as an example, for the unfortunate tendency to call every succulent (fleshy) plant a cactus, simply because cacti are succulents.

Thus with yuccas: after we have fallen in love with their beautiful clusters of cup-shaped or bell-shaped flowers arising out of a rosette of narrow stiff leaves, we find it difficult to realize that there are more plant species resembling them, also in the Asparagus family, but not really yuccas.

Of these a couple of agaves, *Agave lechuguilla* and *Agave attenuata* (pp. 150 and 41) are yucca-like in appearance. *Furcraea*, also of the Asparagaceae, somewhat resembles a yucca, and, like it, grows in arid regions; it is most common in southern Mexico and Guatamala, with flowering stems of 15 to 30 ft. in height.

Yucca, Beaucarnea, Dasylirion, and *Nolina* can be told apart by:

YUCCAS can generally be distinguished by their dagger-like, rigid leaves having fibers protruding from the edge (no thorny teeth). In many other aspects they differ considerably from each other.

BEAUCARNEA often in the past was lumped together with Nolina. It is even taller, some growing up well over 35 ft., and openly branched. Trunk often swollen at the base. More common in arid parts of southern Mexico (see p. 40).

DASYLIRION (*Sotol*) has small whitish flowers, arranged along tall, tight, slender stalks, and prickly leaves, much enlarged at the base (desert "spoons"). They prefer rocky or gravelly desert regions (see below).

NOLINA, on the other hand, has flexible, drooping and grass-like leaves (called Beargrass), and a more ample flower panicle. It is generally tree-like, 4–16 feet tall, with massive, unbranched trunk, and a tall, upright flower stalk.

For the sake of completeness we should mention *Hesperaloe parviflora,* found in southwestern Texas and northeastern Mexico; plants have tall flower clusters with rosy-red or salmon-colored flowers, 1¼ in. long.

Lechuguilla
Agave lechuguilla
LECHUGUILLA
ASPARAGACEAE Asparagus Family
NATIVE RANGE Southern New Mexico to central Mexico.

This is the dominant plant over thousands of square miles of the Chihuahuan desert; in many places the cover is so thick that you can hardly walk through it. Flower stalks are 8 to 25 ft. tall; flowers (in April) are greenish-white to lavender-brown. Leaves are few, thin, straight, bluish-green, their upper face often with a paler stripe; they have a detachable horny border and downward-pointing spines. Their fiber, called IXTLE, is used for ropes, brushes, and bags, being woven into a coarse fabric.

Lechuguilla is representative of the many species of Agave with flowers in a spikelike cluster. (See also **Agave** on p. 148).

Desert Spoon
Dasylirion wheeleri (and others)
SOTOL
ASPARAGACEAE Asparagus Family
NATIVE RANGE Southern Arizona to western Texas, Mexico (Sonora, Chihuahua).

Sometimes quite abundant and conspicuous on dry rocky hillsides of the upper desert are tall, dense, upright flower clusters (5 to 15 ft. high) of numerous small, creamy-white blossoms. Stems arise from a thick, cabbage-like base, to which the 3-ft. long spiny-

LECHUGUILLA

DESERT SPOON

toothed leaves are attached with a spoon-like (called "desert spoon") enlargement. Leaves are split at the tip. They are used for thatching, baskets, rough hats, mats, and fiber.

SOTOL is the name for the plant and also for the potent drink of penetrating odor and peculiar taste, distilled from the fermented roasted trunks, which are high in sugar.

The similar **Beargrass (NOLINA)** has tiny blossoms on plume-like and often drooping flower stalks, which frequently retain their papery, dry-winged fruits until fall.

Bigelow Nolina
ZACATE

Nolina bigelovii
ASPARAGACEAE Asparagus Family

NATIVE RANGE Southern Nevada to northwestern Mexico.

A conspicuous yucca-like tree, 4–16 ft. tall, that grows on dry, rocky hillsides. Its massive, unbranched trunk may be 2 to 3 ft. in diameter, mostly covered with old dead leaves. On top are the large tufts of numerous, very long and narrow leaves, ⅜–¾ in. wide and 2 to 4½ ft. long; they are grass-like, stiff and leathery, with slightly rough edges, which shred with brown, long fibers.

Flowerstalks upright, 3–8 ft. tall, the upper part much-branched, bearing small greenish-white flowers (⅛ in. long) in June and July. Seed capsules ½ in. in diameter, with three thin, membranous wings. Found on hillsides and in desert canyons at 500–3,500 ft. in Baja California and Sonora.

DESERT MARIGOLD

WILLOW-GROUNDSEL

Desert Marigold
FLOR DE PAPEL

Baileya multiradiata
ASTERACEAE Aster Family

NATIVE RANGE Southwestern and south-central U.S.A. to Mexico.

There aren't a great many annual flowers in the desert, but this densely woolly Paper Daisy is so showy with its golden composite flowers that it actually dominates the northern Mexico desert landscape from early spring to late-fall.

The flower heads are usually over an inch across and bloom in great quantities; they grow on a long, solitary stem which has a few small leaves at the lower end. At the base of the plant the leaves are irregularly lobed.

As the flowers age, their rays become pale and papery, hence the name **Paper Flower** in some regions. It appears to be poisonous to sheep but not to horses.

Willow-groundsel
JARILLA

Barkleyanthus salicifolius
ASTERACEAE Aster Family

SYNONYM *Senecio salignus*
NATIVE RANGE Arizona to Texas and Honduras.

This cheerful, golden yellow-blossomed medium-sized shrub, blooming in early spring, keeps appearing where desert and oak forest meet. After some careful observing one gets to recognize it by its droopy, willow-like leaves, and its association with both desert and oak-scrub vegetation. It grows to a height of 2–4 ft., and has ill-scented blossoms.

Tarbush
HOJASÉN

Flourensia cernua
ASTERACEAE Aster Family

NATIVE RANGE Arizona to Texas and Mexico.

As typical of the Chihuahuan Desert as the Creosote-bush is this Tarbush, also called **Blackbrush** or **Varnishbush**. It is apt to be found together with it and with the **Allthorn** (*Koeberlinia*), see p. 36. It is resinous and is said to smell of hops and to have a bitter taste. Both leaves and dried flower heads are sold in drug markets as **HOJASÉN** for indigestion.

A much-branched shrub, less than 3 ft. tall, with roundish, nodding, yellow flower heads from July onward.

TARBUSH

BOB NIEMAN

TARBUSH

Desert Willow
MIMBRE

Chilopsis linearis
BIGNONIACEAE Trumpet-Creeper Family

NATIVE RANGE Southwestern and south-central U.S.A. to northern Mexico.

We came to call it "grass-tree", this interesting shrub or small tree (6–24 ft. tall) — not noticing the showy, white-and-purple flowers like a catalpa, its relative. It grows in dry, well-drained, sandy soils along washes all over the northern part of Mexico and is sometimes planted for ornament along roadsides and for erosion control. Slender pods, up to a foot long, with numerous, papery brown, winged seeds, are also like a catalpa; they are persistent, dangling from the branches, helping identification.

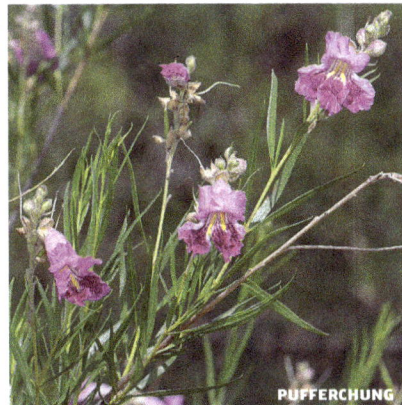

PUFFERCHUNG

DESERT WILLOW

Elephant Tree
TOROTE, COPAL

Bursera microphylla
BURSERACEAE Frankincense Family

NATIVE RANGE Southern California, Arizona, northern Mexico.

It's an odd-looking tree, up to more than 25 ft. in Mexico, due to its overgrown, papery-white trunk, sharply tapering into reddish-brown twigs, said to resemble an elephant's trunk. Found on rocky slopes of the arid desert mountains, 1,000 to 2,500 ft.

ALEXIS LÓPEZ HERNÁNDEZ

ELEPHANT TREE

elevation, together with ocotillo, ironwood, tarbush, crucifixion trees and saguaro. Its aromatic leaves are compound with 10 to 35 pairs of tiny leaflets and a winged axis. They yield **COPAL**, burned as incense in religious ceremonies of the Indians. (It belongs to the same family as the frankincense tree [*Boswellia*] of East India). The bark is used in Mexico for tanning and dyeing. Most of the commercial copal of today comes from Zanzibar, East India, or South America.

CRICKET RASPET

Saguaro, Giant Cactus
SAGUARO

Carnegiea gigantea
CACTACEAE Cactus Family

NATIVE RANGE Southeastern California to southern Arizona and Mexico (Baja California Norte, Sonora, Chihuahua).

Seeing Saguaro for the first time is an exciting experience. With its arms extended it oddly resembles a human giant. Saguaro National Park, 17 miles west of Tucson, has been set aside to preserve this desert type of plant life. Arizona adopted the saguaro as its state flower.

Its tallest representative, claimed by the Park, is 52 feet in height, has 52 arms, an age of perhaps 235 years, and an estimated weight of 10 tons. Ages of 150 to 200 years are not unusual. Growing from a tiny seedling, at a rate of an inch per year, the average annual increase later is about 3 in.

Saguaro has no leaves. Its showy, waxy-white flowers open up at night in May and June, to a diameter of 4 in.; they have a melon-like odor. Red sweet fruits follow in June: they are egg-shaped, 2–3½ inches long, later splitting open like a flower. The glistening black seeds then show against the bright red pulp.

KATJA SCHULZ

SAGUARO, GIANT CACTUS

Northwestern Mexico is the proper home of *Carnegiea*; it prefers rolling or hilly ground, with coarse, rocky soil, and can take months of rainless heat. Temperatures below 17° F. are fatal, nor can it take continuous freezing for longer than 19 hours. Groups of saguaro follow the Gulf of Mexico a little beyond Guaymas, including Hermosillo and Magdalena, but not Nogales, which is too high.

Other giant cacti, somewhat resembling saguaro, occur farther south in Mexico. See, for instance, *Pachycereus pringlei* and *Pachycereus pecten-aboriginum* on p. 57, and a number of others on pp. 58–59.

Walkingstick Cholla
XOCONOSTLI

Cylindropuntia imbricata
Cactaceae Cactus Family

SYNONYM *Opuntia imbricata*
NATIVE RANGE Southeastern Arizona to southwestern Kansas and Mexico.

"Cholla" is the Mexican name for a cactus with plump, cylindrical joints, specially common in northern deserts. This Walkingstick cholla is abundant and characteristic on the central table land, extending north into New Mexico and Colorado. It is a treelike cane cactus, up to 10 ft. in height, with well-defined rounded swellings on the younger branches. Imbricata means overlapping as shingles on a roof, referring to these "bumps". Flowers are good-sized, sometimes over 3 in. broad, purple (to pink) at the end of the branches. Fruit dry and yellow; it may look like flowers from a distance. The ornamental dry network of old woody stems is often made into canes, or used for ornate objects. Bundles of spiny stems were bound on the naked backs of **PETENTES** during Holy Week processions.

WALKINGSTICK CHOLLA

C.K. KELLY

ELEANOR PATE

PIPESTEM CACTUS

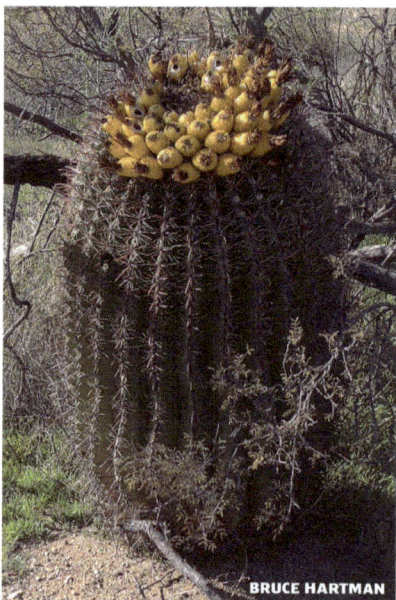

BRUCE HARTMAN

BARRELCACTUS

Pipestem Cactus
Cylindropuntia leptocaulis
TESAJO
CACTACEAE Cactus Family
SYNONYM *Opuntia leptocaulis*
NATIVE RANGE Oklahoma to Mexico.

Sometimes called **Christmas cholla** because the conspicuous scarlet fruit is so striking in mid-winter. It has slender stems (pipestems) and grows seldom over 3 or 4 ft. in height, branching from near the ground. The greenish-yellow flowers are 1/3 to 1/2 in. wide, its ovary has numerous small leaves. Tufts of reddish-brown, long bristles are on the fruit. These cactus often form dense thickets in many parts of northern Mexico.

Barrelcactus
BIZNAGA

Ferocactus wislizeni
CACTACEAE Cactus Family

NATIVE RANGE Arizona to western Texas and northern Mexico.

One of the largest barrel cactuses grows commonly in northern Mexico as well as in Texas, Arizona, and New Mexico. It reaches 6 ft. or more in height, and is known as a "compass plant," slanting Southwestern, and as a "water reservoir" for thirsty desert travelers. Flowers are mainly yellow, but with a reddish center stripe, or reddish altogether; over 2 in. long. They form a wreath on the apex of the barrel.

There are a number of other barrel cactuses; almost all are restricted to the northern Mexican desert.

Flat-Pad Cactuses
Opuntia species
NOPAL, TUNA
CACTACEAE Cactus Family
SYNONYM *Platyopuntia* species

Some tourists in Mexico use the word "cactus" loosely — and incorrectly — for any kind of succulent that is a fleshy, juicy plant, such as century plants, sedums, and the true cactuses.

They are also at sea about the names **TUNA**, the fruit, and **NOPAL** which is the Mexican term for the cactus with flat, usually oval joints. **NOPAL** can be translated as flat-pad or *Platyopuntia*, a name for a sub-genus of *Opuntia*. Other cacti may have cylindrical joints, or may be barrel-shaped or cushion-like.

The Mexican national banner shows an eagle perched upon a **NOPAL**. Legend has it that it is a god-given emblem. Flat-pad cacti are of great diversity; a number of them produce **TUNA** fruit.

Well-known in cultivation, in almost all of Mexico, is the **Indian-fig cactus** (*Opuntia ficus-indica*). It is now not found in the native state, has excellent fruit, few spines, and grows up to 15 feet tall. In Oaxaca it is used for the production of cochineal-dye insects, as well as for the growing of tunas.

All the early writers about Mexico mention **TUNAS** as the edible fruit of **NOPAL**, used as the principal food during its season. All markets show this dark reddish-purple, pear-shaped fruit. Its seeds are ground and used to prepare a kind of **ATOLE**. Tender young joints are cooked as a vegetable. **QUESO DE TUNA** consists of the dried fruit pressed into large cakes. **MIEL DE TUNA** is a syrup prepared from the fruit. Beverages are made from **TUNA** juice. Stock relish cacti in arid regions, especially in times of drought.

Tuna Prickly Pear
Opuntia tuna
TUNA
CACTACEAE Cactus Family
NATIVE RANGE Mexico, Jamaica.

Tuna Prickly Pear is described as a fast grower up to 10 or 12 feet tall, erect and wide-spreading. "Joints are deep green, mostly elliptical, 10–14 in. long, and 6–10 in. wide; spines 4–6, rigid, stout, yellow, spreading, unequal in length, 1–2 in. long; flowers 3–4 in. wide, yellow fading to red; fruit pear-shaped or rounder, 1–1½ in. diam., sweet, edible, dark reddish purple." "Probably the most extensively cultivated of all *Opuntias*, both for the tunas and as a hedge plant. Escaped from cultivation and in some places has become a troublesome weed" (Bailey's *Cyclopaedia of Horticulture*). Among the tall species are **Opuntia megacantha** (from which the best edible **TUNAS** are obtained), *Opuntia fuliginosa*, *Opuntia pilifera*, *Opuntia tomentosa* (escaped in Australia), *Opuntia velutina*.

Engelmann Prickly Pear
Opuntia engelmannii
NOPAL
CACTACEAE Cactus Family
NATIVE RANGE Southwestern and south-central U.S.A. to Mexico.

Here is a "cactus at its best", a lusty grower, with clumps up to 5 ft. tall and 10 ft. in diameter. Its stout pads are up to 11. in. long and almost as broad, smooth and pale bluish-green. The downward stiff spines, up to 2 in. long, with reddish base, occur in

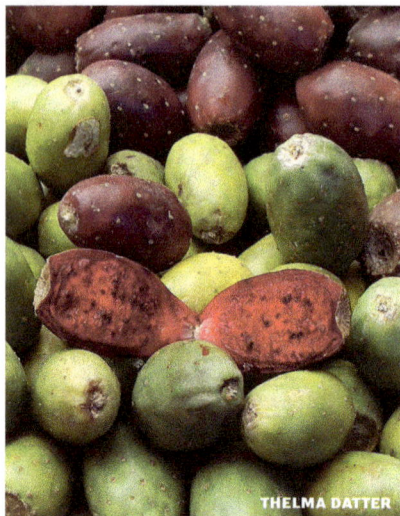

THELMA DATTER

TUNA PRICKLY PEAR *fruit*

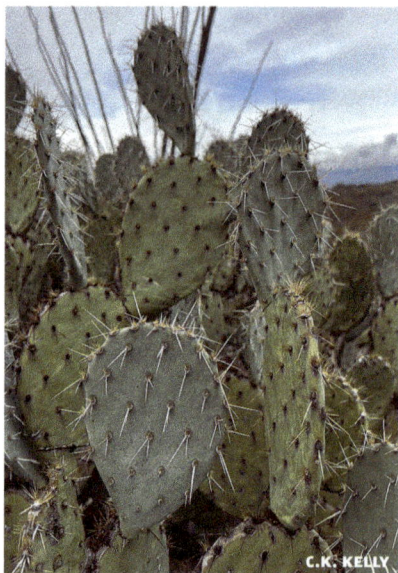

C.K. KELLY

ENGELMANN PRICKLY PEAR

threes normally, the larger one flattened. Flowers 3 in. wide, their yellow turning orange toward evening, closing in late afternoon. Fruits juicy, red to purple, 1½ in. long, quite edible but bearing clusters of barbed hairs. The color effect of fruit and flowers is heightened by the green stigmas of the latter — altogether a striking sight. Engelmann Prickly Pear is the most abundant flat-pad in Arizona, Durango to Chihuahua and Sonora deserts. Among the common nopals in the Valley of Mexico are *Opuntia tomentosa, Opuntia hyptiacantha* and *Opuntia streptacantha*, all reaching 15 ft. and with edible fruit.

Waxplant
Euphorbia antisyphilitica

CANDELILLA
EUPHORBIACEAE Spurge Family

NATIVE RANGE South-central U.S.A. to northeastern and central Mexico.

This almost leafless plant, growing up to 3 ft. tall, produces a wax, has been used for church candles, phonograph records, shoe polish and floor wax. It has given rise to a simple but extensive industry based on the collection and extraction of this valuable wax.

The botanical name indicates its ancient Mexican medical use.

Like all spurges (*Euphorbia*), such as poinsettia, crown-of-thorns, snow-in-the-mountains, cypress spurge and castor-bean plant, it has milky sap, helpful in its recognition.

Fairy Duster
Calliandra eriophylla

CABELLO DE ANGEL
FABACEAE Pea Family

NATIVE RANGE Southern California to Texas and Mexico.

Sometimes an analysis of the names of a plant tells much of its nature. Both "fairy duster" and "angel's hair" (**CABELLO DE ANGEL**) describe the ethereal loveliness of the blossoms. *Calliandra* is a combination of the Greek word for beauty with the word for stamen; it refers to the numerous lavender or white stamens with pink tips. *Eriophylla* means woolly-leaved, referring to the dainty, woolly compound leaves.

All we need to do in addition is to tell about the height of this striking desert plant

WAXPLANT

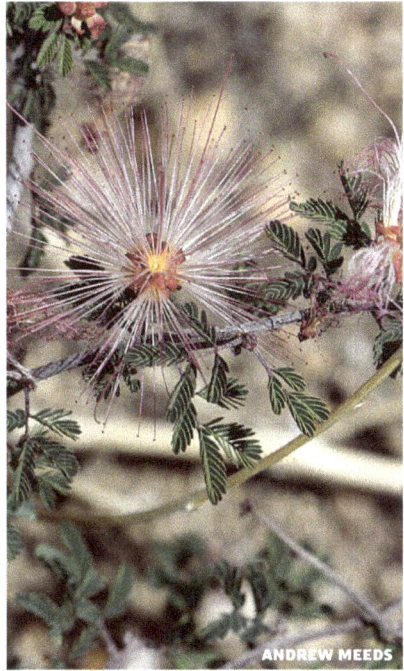

FAIRY DUSTER

(around 1 to more commonly 3 ft.), its location on slopes and mesas of an elevation of 2,000 to 5,000 ft., and its pods (velvety-hairy like the rest of the plant, and with cord-like margins, 1½ to 3 in. long).

Cat-claw Acacia
UÑA DE GATO

Senegalia greggii
FABACEAE Pea Family

SYNONYM *Acacia greggii*
NATIVE RANGE Southwestern and south-central U.S.A. to northern Mexico.

Torn clothes and scratched skin make one remember intimate contact with this very widespread acacia and its numerous hooked, rose-like prickles. It grows in even the driest and poorest soils, often forming thickets along streams and washes.

Pale yellow fuzzy flower clusters like "pussy-willows" appear in April; they are quite decorative, and attract numerous insects. In August the curved and twisted seedpods turn reddish; they stay on the tree all winter: a good way of identification.

Even if some shrubs grow into trees, rarely up to 30 ft., the trunk is short and the crown irregular.

WENDY AVILES
BOOJUM TREE

KEN LUND
OCOTILLO

Boojum Tree
CIRIO

Fouquieria columnaris
FOUQUIERIACEAE Ocotillo Family

SYNONYM *Idria columnaris*
NATIVE RANGE Mexico (central Baja California, northwestern Sonora).

Here is a "storybook tree", that must be seen to be believed—well named boojum tree. But in Baja California — in a stony, sterile country with very limited rainfall — here it is, stark, unbelievable, like a huge, inverted parsnip, and only very small branches, growing to 50 or 60 ft. tall. Nature has reduced evaporation for this succulent tree to a minimum.

Strangely enough, it belongs in the same family as the **Ocotillo**. If you can't get to Baja California, there are a few plants in Sonora, and the Desert Museum near Tucson, and the Boyce Thompson Arboretum, near Superior, Arizona, have some growing in cultivation.

Ocotillo
OCOTILLO, ALBARDA

Fouquieria splendens
FOUQUIERIACEAE Ocotillo Family

NATIVE RANGE Southern California to southwestern Texas and north and west Mexico.

Tall, unbranched, green stems, 5 to 15 ft. in height, with numerous thorns, form spectacular clumps in northern Mexican deserts. They are, in early spring, tipped with bright red dense clusters of bell-shaped flowers. Only after a rain do small leaves suddenly appear all along the stems, soon to turn brown and fall during dry spells.

It occurs on rocky or sandy exposed places from sea level to 5,000 ft. in elevation.

A most distinctive and useful desert shrub, since it can be used for fencing, thatching, food and wax.

AGUJACERATOPS

HOPSEEDBUSH, VARNISHLEAF

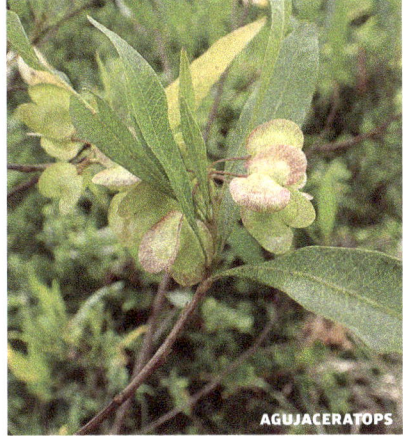

CHET BURRIER

LOTEBUSH

Lotebush
CRUCILLO

Sarcomphalus obtusifolius
RHAMNACEAE Buckthorn Family

SYNONYM *Condalia lycioides*
NATIVE RANGE Arizona to Oklahoma and northern and eastern Mexico.

A scraggly tall shrub, up to 10 ft. in height, with long, spiny branches at right angles to the larger stems. Essentially a plant of the Chihuahuan desert, but also reaches to Guaymas and Hermosillo.

Flowers are white and inconspicuous, berries blue-black with a bloom, only ¼ in. long. Leaves relatively thin, with prominent veins. Also called **Gray thorn**.

A number of other related plants (in the *Condalia* genus) are common on dry hillsides in Mexico, such as *Condalia spathulata, Condalia mexicana, Condalia hookeri* — all of similar appearance but with different-sized leaves (the latter's up to 1½ in. long).

Hopseedbush, Varnishleaf
CHAPULIZTLE

Dodonaea viscosa
SAPINDACEAE Soapberry Family

NATIVE RANGE Worldwide in tropical and subtropical regions.

An interesting desert shrub, 3–9 ft. tall, with sticky leaves, yellowish flowers, and easily recognized, winged, dry fruit, over ½ in. in diameter; these are only on the female plants.

Yes, the hop-like fruits have been successfully used in the making of yeast and beer. Leaves and bark have been used medicinally, containing poisonous saponins, and like the soapberry, its close relative, the plant is used as a fish poison.

An ornamental shrub, native in the higher arid regions, mostly in canyons and on rocky, gravelly slopes.

DANIEL MCNAIR

CHITTAMWOOD

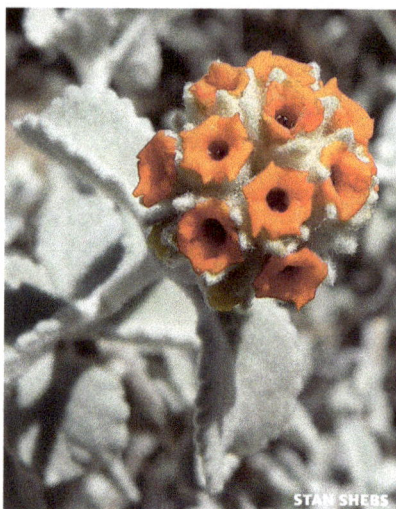

STAN SHEBS

WOOLLY BUTTERFLYBUSH

Chittamwood
MULCE
Sideroxylon lanuginosum
SAPOTACEAE Sapodilla Family
SYNONYM *Bumelia lanuginosa*
NATIVE RANGE Central and southern U.S.A. to Mexico.

In the upper regions of the desert (3,000 to 5,000 ft. elev.) and reaching into oak woodland we may find a small tree, up to 12 ft. in height, that prefers watercourses and washes. It has smallish leatherly leaves, hairy below, and milky sap (from which exudes a gum chewed by children) — being a relative of the **Chicle tree** in the rainforest (see p. 139). Fleshy oval fruits of a purplish cast are more conspicuous than the tiny green flowers.

Woolly Butterflybush
AZAFRÁN DEL CAMPO
Buddleja marrubiifolia
SCROPHULARIACEAE Figwort Family
NATIVE RANGE Texas to northeastern Mexico (to Jalisco).

A velvety hairy shrub of arid areas, 3 ft. tall, the leaves of which look like those of **hoarhound** (*Marrubium*).

The yellow small flowers are of four parts; they occur at the ends of branches in tight balls and are used for coloring butter and cheese, or vermicelli (**AZAFRÁN** means saffron). The name **AZAFRÁN** is used for other plants as well.

Greenbrier (not illustrated)
COCOLMECA
Smilax bona-nox
SMILACACEAE Greenbrier Family
NATIVE RANGE Central and eastern U.S.A. to Mexico, Bermuda.

Occasionally, in this zone, our attention may be drawn to a tree that appears partly bare, partly covered lusciously with shiny, leathery, roundish leaves which form a dense foliage. On closer investigation this may prove to be a woody climber, with a thorn opposite to each leaf. There may be some small black fruit among the leaves.

Following the plant down to earth we find a thick, heavy root of reddish color, often with large tubers sold in markets for 'dropsy' (edema).

A number of closely related greenbriars occur in other parts of Mexico, with various shapes of leaves.

CREOSOTE-BUSH
ERIC IN SF

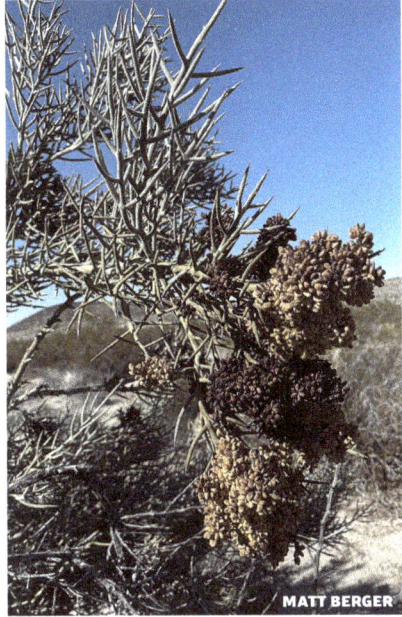
CASTELA EMORYI
MATT BERGER

Creosote-bush
Larrea tridentata
GOBERNADORA
ZYGOPHYLLACEAE Creosote-bush Family
NATIVE RANGE Southwestern and south-central U.S.A. to Mexico.

Many thousands of square miles in the Lower Sonoran desert are covered with pure stands of creosote bush, or mixed with bur-sage and other plants. It may well be called the most successful and conspicuous dry land plant of the region (San Luis Potosi, Coahuila, Durango, Chihuahua, Zacatecas, Sonora, Baja California and north).

Often it is evenly spaced to utilize the moisture efficiency and accommodate its deep roots. Once you have spotted it, you'll easily recognize it again by its varnished, twin leaflets, yellowish green in color on man sized, much-branched shrubs. Especially after a rain a resinous odor is given off, which has given rise to the name "creosote bush" and to "**HEDIONDILLA**" which may be translated as "little stinker".

Early spring rains cause a burst of bright yellow flowers to adorn the bush with twisted five-petaled bloom; they are followed by fuzzy white seedballs, equally conspicuous. Excretions of the lac scale, found on the branches in quantity, are used by the Indians for mending pottery, making mosaics, fixing arrowpoints, and for waterproofing baskets. A "cure-all" for many ills, but some people are allergic to it.

CRUCIFIXION THORNS
CORONA-DE-CRISTO

This name is given to many shrubs that are bare of leaves and flowers during most of the year, showing instead a bare mass of spines (see also **Lotebush**, p. 33, **Randia** p. 66).

KOEBERLINIA SPINOSA

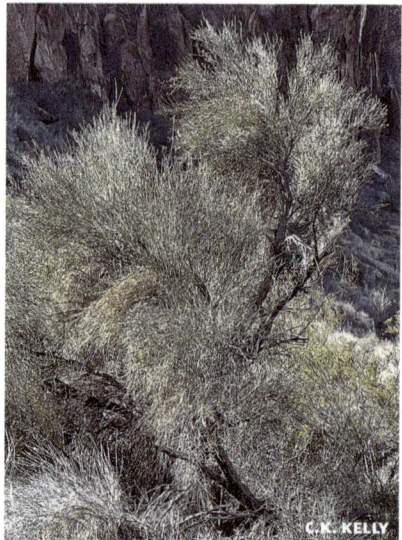

CANOTIA HOLACANTHA

Castela emoryi

SIMAROUBACEAE Quassia-Wood Family
SYNONYM *Holacantha emoryi*
NATIVE RANGE Arid regions of southeastern
California to Arizona and northern Mexico.

This shrub carries masses of brown to
black fruits of interesting shape, for years
and years, often mistaken for a parasite.
Young branches, yellow-green, densely
hairy at first.

Koeberlinia spinosa

KOEBERLINIACEAE Crown-of-Thorns Family
NATIVE RANGE Texas to eastern and central
Mexico.

This shrub, over 3 ft. tall, and often
called **Allthorn**, is intricately thorny: its
inch-long, stout, green spines are at right
angles to the main branches. It grows with
creosote bush and tarbush, sometimes

PSOROTHAMNUS SPINOSUS

forming a small bushy tree. The minute scale-like leaves are dropped shortly as are the
small greenish flowers (March–June). Fruit is a small shiny black berry tipped with the
remnant of the style; flesh is thin and juicy.

Canotia holacantha

CELASTRACEAE Bittersweet Family

NATIVE RANGE Southern Utah, Arizona, Mexico (Baja California Norte, Sonora).

While called **Crucifixion Thorn**, this shrub or small tree might well be taken for a **palo
verde** (see p. 48) on account of its yellow-green, upright, rushlike branches, which appear
broom-like. The bark is yellow green and quite flammable: do not start a fire underneath!
It may reach 18 ft. in height; called **Mojave-thorn** in much of north Sonora.

Psorothamnus spinosus   FABACEAE Pea Family
SYNONYM *Dalea spinosa*
NATIVE RANGE Southwestern U.S.A. to northwestern Mexico.

This shrub or small tree is often called **Smoke-tree** on account of its gray-green, plume-like growth. In May or June it is highly attractive with its blue-violet pea-like blossoms. Its small simple leaves occur only for a few weeks before blossoming. Found in both Sonora and Baja California; it may grow into a small upright tree to 25 ft. or more.

CREOSOTE-BUSH

Mesquite and Grassland Vegetation Zone

Over one-fifth of Mexico is occupied by this type of vegetation. While not quite as arid as the Desert Zone, it has a rainfall of only 9 to 36 in. per year. Much of the ground is covered by **Blue grama grass** (*Bouteloua gracilis*), a grayish short grass, common on the extensive short-grass prairie of the Great Plains. Some of it has been changed into highly productive farmland; some to brushland, due to overgrazing.

At least four different types of this zone can be distinguished:

The **SHORT-GRASS PLAINS** of the north central states: Chihuahua, Durango, and Zacatecas (from Alberta, Canada, into South America), with the ubiquitous blue grama grass. The middle highway from Juarez runs through it and desert.

MESQUITE SCRUB type, most common in northeast Mexico. With it we may find a number of acacias, an interesting white-flowered shrub with leaves gray-white below, called **ANACAHUITL** (p. 44); a compact yucca with 10 ft. trunk and thick, firm leaves (*Yucca treculeana*, p. 41); **Mexican buckeye**, occupying mountain canyons and limestone hills (p. 53). In northwest Mexico, Mesquite is found with **Ironwood** (*Olneya tesota*), a tallish tree with purplish pea-like blossoms (p. 48), and with **Yellow palo verde** (*Parkinsonia microphylla*) p. 49; **Brittlebush** (*Encelia farinosa*) with masses of yellow flowers in spring, covers rocky slopes in southern Sonora (p. 43).

ERIC LAMB

BLUE GRAMA

CACTUS-ACACIA GRASSLAND, together with Mesquite, *Neltuma laevigata*, and *Vachellia constricta*, has a thorny hackberry (p. 46), prickly pear, and yuccas.

GULF-COAST BLUESTEM PRAIRIE, originally occupied by tall bunchgrasses, is now largely occupied by brush through overgrazing.

How do we distingish this zone from the **Desert Zone**, and where do we find it?

Naturally, there is no definite line we can draw on a map and say: on this side is Desert, on the other side is the Mesquite and Grassland zone. Nature does not operate that way. But in a general way we can say this zone is between the desert on one side — the lower and drier side — and the Pine-Oak Forest on the other, that is, almost invariably the higher and more humid side.

As a natural consequence, the desert vegetation, such as creosote bush and **PALMILLA** (*Yucca elata*) will come into it on the gravelly, sand-covered plains, and, on the other hand, the lower range of Pine-Oak Forest, such as junipers, scrub oak, and certain agaves, penetrates it from above.

It is not at all uncommon, then, for a highway to show this natural graduation from true desert plants (as cactus, Sotol, creosote bush, ocotillo and palmilla) passing into mesquite, acacia and palo verde, then, as the highway climbs into higher elevations, coming into junipers, oakbrush, and agaves until the real pine-oak forest is reached.

In a few places Mesquite and grassland borders the tropical deciduous forest and the thornforest, as in the neighborhood of Ciudad Obregon and Ciudad Victoria. That, however, is less common. Noticing this transition is a unique experience. It is also one that gives us an illustration of nature's gradual processes: while there are definite plant zones, their outlines are marked by an intermingling of plants from adjoining zones.

Mesquite and grassland thus shows itself as a sort of buffer zone between desert and woodland.

HUMMINGBIRD BUSH
MICHAEL TIDWELL

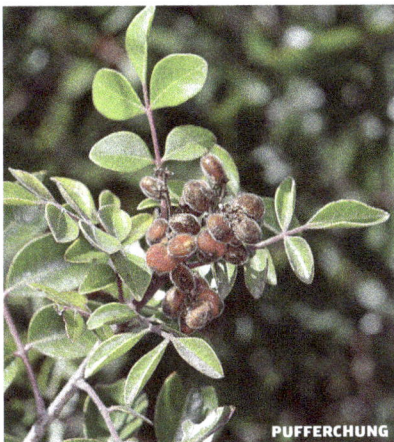
PUFFERCHUNG
EVERGREEN SUMAC

Hummingbird Bush

Justicia californica

CHUPAROSA, BELOPERONE

ACANTHACEAE Acanthus Family

SYNONYM *Beloperone californica*
NATIVE RANGE California to northwestern Mexico.

On moist sandy soils in the northwest desert region, as far south as Sinaloa, you are apt to be attracted by a brilliant red, two-lipped flower on a dense bushy shrub, 3–6 ft. tall. Or a hovering hummingbird may draw your attention to it. Flowers are about 1 in. long, with a distinctive lower lip. The name **BELOPERONE** refers to the arrow-shaped tip of the stamens. Leaves are hairy, opposite, and as long as the flowers.

Another **BELOPERONE** is called **Shrimp plant** (*Justicia brandegeeana*, synonym *Beloperone guttata*) on account of its showy reddish-brown spikes tipped by white flowers: a tropical Mexican herb.

Belonging to the same Acanthus family are *Thunbergia* vines, and the Greek *Acanthus*, the basis of the foliage design on Corinthian columns.

Evergreen Sumac

Rhus virens

ZUMAQUE

ANACARDIACEAE Sumac Family

SYNONYM *Rhus sempervirens*
NATIVE RANGE South-central U.S.A. to Mexico.

In the northern part of Mexico this good-looking shrub is apt to draw attention by its glossy, evergreen leaves of five leaflets and reddish leaf-stems. It is common on dry rocky slopes. Fruits in red pyramidal trusses, slightly acid. Also called **LAMBRISCO** and other variants of **LENTISCO**, or **ARUMI**.

CALIFORNIA FANPALM

SOYATE

California Fanpalm
Washingtonia filifera
PALMA DE CASTILLA
ARECACEAE Palm Family

NATIVE RANGE Southern California to southwestern Arizona and Mexico (Baja California, western Sonora).

While found wild in northern Mexico (in moist soils along streams or in desert mountains), this 60 ft. fan palm is more commonly found where planted as an ornamental.

It may be recognized by the spiny leaf blade and the deeply split fan leaf with fibers fraying from the edges. Its stout trunk is unbranched and enlarged at the base. Old leaves commonly provide a rather unsightly "skirt" above the lower smooth stem.

The Mexican type of *Washingtonia* is distinguished by more slender and taller trunks, otherwise similar to the northern type.

Soyate
Beaucarnea recurvata
ZOYATE, COYOLITO
ASPARAGACEAE Asparagus Family

SYNONYM *Beaucarnea inermis*
NATIVE RANGE Mexico (Oaxaca, Puebla, San Luis Potosí, Tamaulipas, Veracruz).

If it looks like a tall yucca tree, but has drooping, slender leaves, small flowers in creamy trusses, and a tendency toward a swollen base, chances are it is *Beaucarnea*. Like yucca, beargrass (*Nolina*) and sotol (*Dasylirion*) it belongs to the Asparagus family.

Beaucarnea recurvata is a tree up to 40 ft. tall, openly branched, with a trunk 6 ft. in diameter and a black, hard, scaly bark. It is particularly handsome when in full bloom. Leaves are somewhat ribbed, ½ in. wide, and lack prickly edges.

They are used for thatching, coarse hats, mats, etc. The soft spongy wood is used for corks.

CABBAGE AGAVE

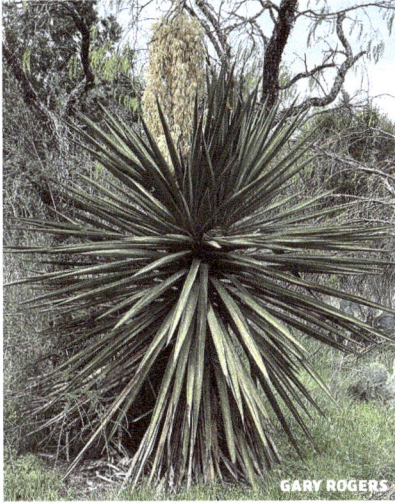

SPANISH BAYONET

Spanish Bayonet
Yucca treculiana
PALMA DE DATILES
ASPARAGACEAE Asparagus Family

NATIVE RANGE South-central U.S.A. to northeastern Mexico.

A fleshy-fruited small tree of the north and northeast part of Mexico, with pungent, thick, firm, channeled leaves, 3 ft. long, 1–2 in. wide, brown-margined. When young they are slightly toothed. Trunk usually less than 16 ft. tall. Flowers are in compact trusses with a large bract below; they are sometimes tinged with purple. Fruit with a peppery core, the pulp greenish or whitish. Other names are **PALMA PITA** and **PALMA LOCA**. Many yuccas are called **IZOTE** in common parlance; **SOYATE** is used in some locations for both yuccas and some palms. See also *Yucca elata* on p. 18, and other yuccas on pp. 19–21.

Cabbage Agave
Agave parryi
MESCAL
ASPARAGACEAE Asparagus Family

NATIVE RANGE Southeastern Arizona to Texas and northern and western Mexico.

It is not easy to tell the numerous species of agaves apart. The Cabbage agave in the northern mountains of Chihuahua (4,500 to 8,000 ft. elev.) is an exception; its neat, round, cabbage-like plants, 3 ft. in diameter, with bluish-green, crowded, spiny leaves, grow in conspicuous colonies. They spread by underground sprouts.

In June and July the 10–15 ft. high stout flower stem draws attention to itself with its red flower-buds and crowded blossoms, greenish-yellow with a tinge of red.

According to Benson and Darrow they can survive when covered by snow in winter and where temperatures can sometimes drop to zero for short periods.

Drooping Agave
Agave attenuata
COLA DE LEÓN
ASPARAGACEAE Asparagus Family

NATIVE RANGE Mexico (Mexico State, Central Jalisco, Michoacán).

When in bloom the Drooping Agave is easily told by its tall flowering stalk (from 5 to 10 ft.), appropriately described by its Spanish name **COLA DE LEON** ('lion's tail'), showing sections of thickly crowded, greenish-yellow flowers in pairs, each flask-shaped, ¾ to 1 in. long, and with six slender stamens.

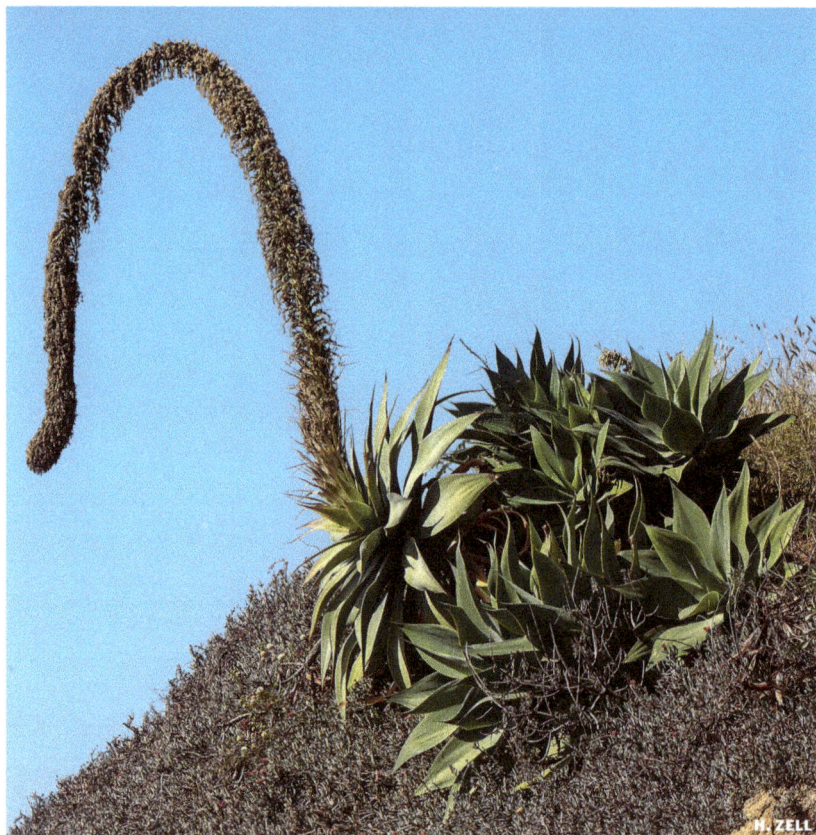

DROOPING AGAVE

After blooming, bulbils may be produced among the seed capsules; they drop to the ground developing new plants. The same flower stalk is sure to show separate sections of buds, at the tip, flowers in the middle, and seed in the older section.

Unlike the **Cabbage agave** and the **Maguey** (pp. 41 and 149), both of which have candelabra-like flower stalks, this species belongs to the spike-bloomers as does **LECHUGUILLA** (see pp. 22).

Its leaves are smooth, glaucous, thin, entirely without spines, 25 to 30 in. long, with recurved tip. Trunk may reach 3 to 4 ft., sometimes prostrate. This agave occurs in warm, dry **BARRANCAS** (gullies); it is cultivated in gardens in a number of varieties, all striking.

Seep Willow
Baccharis douglasii
BATAMOTE, CHILCA, HIERBA DEL PASMO (SPASM HERB)   ASTERACEAE Aster Family
SYNONYM *Baccharis glutinosa*
NATIVE RANGE Oregon, California, to Mexico (Baja California).

Along water courses in semi-arid regions we are apt to find dense thickets of medium-sized to tall wandlike shrubs with willow-like leaves and flat-topped clusters of flower heads, some of which develop spectacular white seed brushes (the female shrubs only). The strongly angled resinous branches are used for crude brooms and for supporting mud roofs. Other names are **Watermote, Waterwally,** and **Rosinbush.**

CRICKET RASPET

SEEP WILLOW

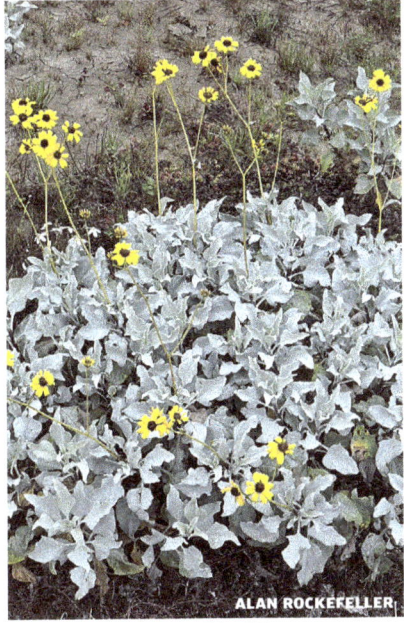

ALAN ROCKEFELLER

BRITLEBUSH

Not to be confused with **Charcoal shrub** (*Baccharis conferta*), found in the Pine-Oak Forest zone (p. 73).

Brittlebush
INCIENSO

Encelia farinosa
ASTERACEAE Aster Family

NATIVE RANGE Southwestern U.S.A. to northern Mexico.

Highly spectacular and colorful in winter and early spring is this free-flowering yellow relative of the sunflower, a compact woody plant, up to 3 ft. tall. Its gray-green leaves, densely covered with short crooked hairs, are conspicuous in themselves. Abundant on rocky or gravelly slopes and desert mesas where the golden-yellow blossoms literally cover the ground during blooming season. Its brittle wood exudes a fragrant clear resin, sometimes used as incense in churches, and as chewing gum.

Texas Algerita
PALO AMARILLO

Berberis trifoliolata
BERBERIDACEAE Barberry Family

SYNONYM *Mahonia trifoliolata*
NATIVE RANGE Southeastern Arizona to Texas and northern Mexico (to Jalisco).

Highly decorative, blue-leaved shrub, extending into Mexico from the Texas desert. In early spring the red buds add to its beauty: the small flowers are fragrant and yellow. Leaves are like very thorny holly leaves. The small berries are red and quite tasty; they make excellent jelly. Indians get a brilliant yellow dye from the stems and use the roots as a tonic.

PUFFERCHUNG

LAUREN MCLAURIN

ANACAHUITA

RAFAEL CANO

BURSERA

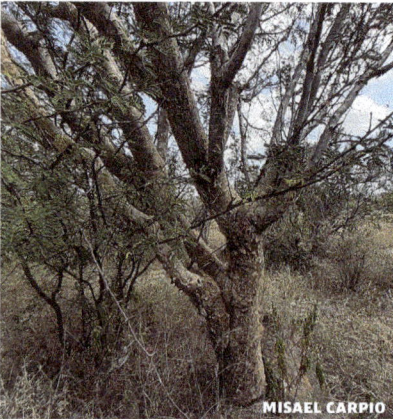

MISAEL CARPIO

BURSERA

Anacahuita

Cordia boissieri

ANACAHUITL, TROMPILLO (LITTLE TRUMPET)   BORAGINACEAE Borage Family

NATIVE RANGE Southern Texas to eastern Mexico.

Entering Mexico from Texas in winter, one of the first flowering shrubs to draw attention has white, funnel-shaped, five-pointed stars, in clusters at the ends of stout twigs; leaves are simple, oval and densely white-felty underneath.

It is an aromatic shrub or small tree. Soon after flowering the interesting hard, ball-shaped fruit appears, light green first, then bright reddish-brown, partly enclosed by the thin brown calyx. It is almost 1 in. long; flesh thin, sweet and pulpy; stone hard and bony. Surprisingly enough, **ANACAHUITL** belongs to the Borage family, together with heliotrope and forget-me-not. In tropical regions there are other *Cordias*, also mostly with attractive white blossoms. (See also **Starbell** under Tropical Deciduous, p. 94). Many are called **PAJARITO** (little bird) for the variegated wood.

Bursera

Bursera fagaroides

TOROTE   BURSERACEAE Frankincense Family

SYNONYM *Bursera schaffneri*

NATIVE RANGE Arizona, Florida, Mexico.

ORGANPIPE CACTUS

FRANK VINCENTZ

This much-branched shrub is not easy to recognize: leaves are compound with three to seven leaflets, smooth and rounded; flowers small in clusters, followed by red, somewhat angular berries, each with one seed.

Luckily the strong aroma of the plant helps identification. It is due to a form of **COPAL** (the Nahuatl name), which is also derived from *Hymenaea courbaril* (see page 98). This resin is used for cement and varnish, as well as medicinally.

Related species are ***Bursera simaruba*** of the Rainforest, p. 133), locally called **Naked Indian** for its coppery-red smooth bark, and which yields a sweet aromatic balsam known as **CACHISOU** resin or **GOMANT** resin (also named **GUMBO LIMBO**) — and *Bursera microphylla* of the Desert (p. 25) called **Elephant tree** due to its oddly shaped trunk and branches.

Quite a number of closely related species are found in Short-tree forest and Thorn forest. ***Bursera penicillata*** may dominate some places in the Short-tree forest (Tropical deciduous forest). Other species of *Bursera* are common in southern Mexico (Chiapas), often under the name of **COPAL** or **COPALILLO**.

Organpipe Cactus
ÓRGANO, JARRITOS
Lophocereus marginatus
CACTACEAE Cactus Family

SYNONYMS *Cereus marginatus, Marginatocereus marginatus*
NATIVE RANGE Mexico.

The name Organpipe has been given to a number of tall, upright cacti of the *Cereus* cactus tribe. The Organpipe cactus of the U.S.A. national mounment of that name is ***Stenocereus thurberi***. More typically, particularly in Mexico, the name belongs to *Lophocereus marginatus*, which is cultivated in almost all of Mexico, and consists of simple,

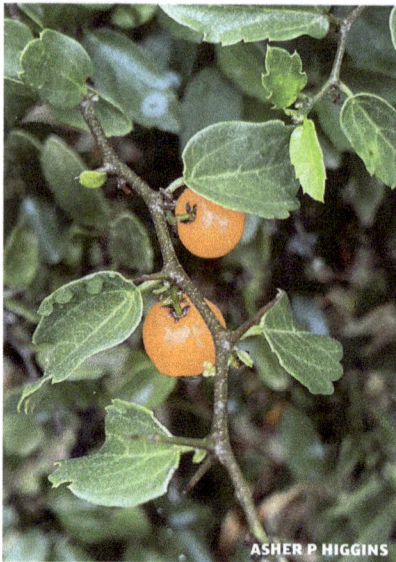

ASHER P HIGGINS
DESERT HACKBERRY

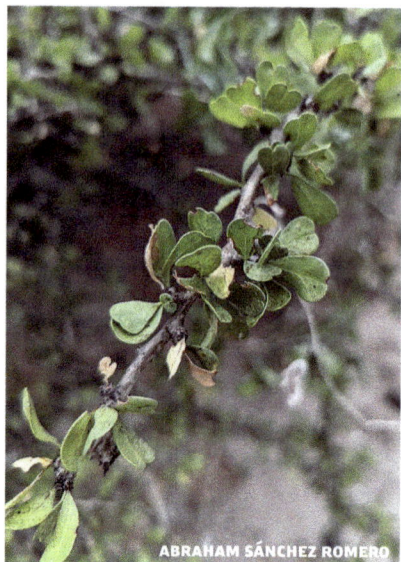

ABRAHAM SÁNCHEZ ROMERO
LEATHERPLANT

green, columnar stems of rapid growth, reaching 10 to 20 feet in height. Another common name is **Mexican Fence-post Cactus.**

The stems have five to seven ribs and are not very bristly. They are quite often used for fences, hence the name marginatus. In the native state they may branch at ground-level or form a candelabra-like tree. Flowers, in pairs, pink varying to greenish mahogany, over an inch tall. Fruits 1½ in., round, yellowish to reddish, spiny, not very fleshy, yellowish-red within; seeds numerous, black.

See also *Pachycereus pecten-aboriginum* and *Pachycereus pringlei* in the Thorn Forest Zone (p. 57, and other tall cylindrical cacti on pp. 58–59).

Desert Hackberry
Celtis pallida
GRANJENO, HUASTECO
CANNABACEAE Hemp Family
NATIVE RANGE Southern U.S.A. to Mexico, Caribbean, Brazil to northern Argentina.

An attractive evergreen shrub, not too difficult to tell as a hackberry by its fruit and leaves, but confusing to many people because of its pronounced thorns. Even more confusing is the fact that leaves grow on these thorns. Leaves are pale underneath. Common on gravelly and well-drained sandy soils of both desert and desert grassland.

Leatherplant
Jatropha cuneata
SANGRE DE DRAGO
EUPHORBIACEAE Spurge Family
NATIVE RANGE Southern Arizona to northwestern Mexico.

This "poor relative" of the poinsettia and castor bean has adapted itself to desert conditions by its clusters of small fleshy leaves and its grotesquely thick stem and branches. These branches are quite pliable (sometimes the shrub is called **Limber bush**); the bark is reddish black; a clear sap oozes out freely if the bark is damaged.

The name dragonblood is derived from the reddish sap of the roots. It is often scrambled to sound like **SANGREGADO**. Height is about 3 ft., with sparse branching. Male and female flowers grow on different plants. There are other species in similar locations, some with heart-shaped leaves and reddish sap.

HONEY MESQUITE

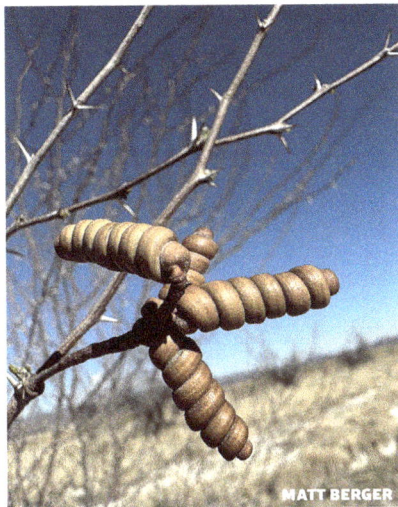

SCREWBEAN MESQUITE

A near relative is one of the two Mexican jumping beans, *Pleradenophora bilocularis* (synonym *Sapium biloculare*), a small tree with willow-like leaves, found in Sonora. The jumping is caused by the larva of a moth, *Cydia saltitans*, which by its violent movements inside makes the seed move. The other Mexican jumping bean is *Sebastiania pavoniana*, of the same family, in Sonora, Nayarít, and San Luis Potosi.

Honey Mesquite
MEZQUITE

Neltuma juliflora (and others)
FABACEAE Pea Family

SYNONYM *Prosopis juliflora*
NATIVE RANGE Mexico to Venezuela, Peru, Caribbean.

"I know it's mesquite, because it looks like mesquite". But that doesn't help the new-comer, who finds himself bewildered by the number of similar compound-leaf shrubs or trees in dry regions: are they mesquite, acacia, mimosa, ironwood, locust, lysiloma, Eysenhardtia (kidneywood)?

To begin with, mesquite blooms with large numbers of fragrant, catkin-like clusters of greenish-yellow, tiny flowers, each flower with io stamens. Each leaf consists of an assembly of two (or four) feathery units. At its base is a pair of rigid straight spines, ½ to 2 in. long (compare them with the curved hooks of **Cat's claw**, p. 31). Pods look like gnarly, knobby stringbeans, 4–9 in. long; unlike most legumes they do not open.

The shrub is of straggling, crooked growth, reaching up to 15 or even 30 feet in height. It dominates much dry land all over Mexico, often following washes. Occurring as far south as Chile, it has been introduced in many countries for its valuable wood. Its roots are said to extend to 60 ft. underground.

In desert regions it has great importance as firewood and for fence posts and other construction. **PINOLE** is a meal made from the sweet pods; gum, exuding through the bark, was eaten as candy, used as a pottery-mending cement, and as a black dye.

Screwbean Mesquite
TORNILLO

Strombocarpa pubescens
FABACEAE Pea Family

SYNONYM *Prosopis pubescens*
NATIVE RANGE Southwestern and south-central U.S.A. to northern Mexico.

Screwbeans grow with Honey mesquites at altithdes below 4,000 ft. In winter the scrubby tree can be distinguished from the brownish-barked honey mesquite by its gray-barked twigs. Spines are up to half an inch long. The curiously twisted pods are a sure "give-away", looking like a pale yellow-colored tight spiral with 10 to 12 turns. It occurs all along the northern boundary of Mexico, in Baja California, Chihuahua, Sonora, Coahuila.

Ironwood
Olneya tesota
PALO DE HIERRO (TESOTA)
FABACEAE Pea Family

NATIVE RANGE Southern California to Arizona and northwestern Mexico.

Ironwood's purple pea-blossoms in May or June are an easy identification. At other times its dense blue-green foliage of compound persistent leaves on a picturesque, small, (up to 30 ft.) tree in desert washes, may draw attention to it. Its bark is brownish-gray, not blue-green as the (likewise thorny) **bluestem palo verde**; it is thin and scaly, peeling off in long strips. Attacked by mistletoe.

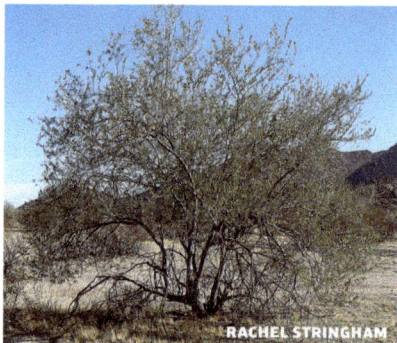
RACHEL STRINGHAM

It is restricted to a strip of land generally following the Gulf of California, in hot regions from Arizona south to Sinaloa. Where ironwood grows naturally, citrus fruits can be cultivated profitably, they say.

Its wood was used for arrow points by the Indians, being hard enough to dull a saw.

PALO VERDES
Cercidium, Parkinsonia

Even if the blossoming forth of a palo verde were a common spring affair of, for instance, a cultivated ornamental tree, it would be exciting. The tree becomes literally covered with a golden rain of thousands of individual blossoms in masses, each one delicate in shape and hue. The suddenness of this transformation is star-

BOB MILLER
IRONWOOD

tling. It is enough to evoke the phrase "the desert blooms". But palo verde is not a common ornamental tree, even if some species, at least, are beginning to be cultivated more and more.

Palo means more than just tree, it can be translated as stick. *Verde* being green, we get "green stick"; a bunch of sticks would be more apropos. For palo verdes have no leaves normally, only for a very short period do they emerge. Soon after, they dry up and disappear, leaving the tree bare but with bright green branches, sure to draw attention. The shade of green is indicative of its species, as shown by the designation "blue-stem" for one. These green branches are able to carry on the business of food production even without leaves.

FOOTHILL PALO VERDE

SULA VANDERPLANK

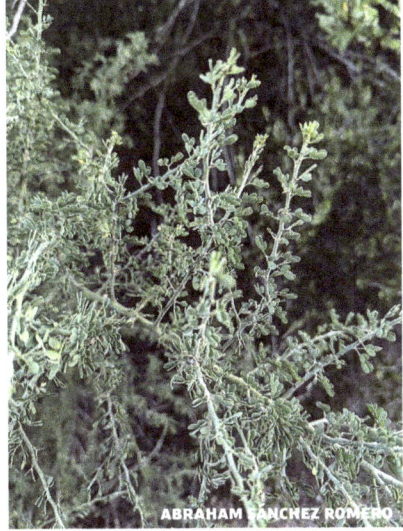

BLUESTEM PALO VERDE

ABRAHAM SANCHEZ ROMERO

Since the palo verdes belong to the Pea family (Fabaceae), they each have their individual type of beans hanging down from the branches and furnishing a means of propagation.

Northern Mexico has about half a dozen native palo verdes, all with yellow blossoms, all with spines, and normally leafless.

Three of the most familiar are described below.

Foothill Palo Verde
Parkinsonia microphylla
PALO VERDE
FABACEAE Pea Family

SYNONYM *Cercidium microphyllum*
NATIVE RANGE Southeastern California to Arizona and northwestern Mexico.

Commonly associated with ironwood, saguaro, and ocotillo, it inhabits the hill slopes rather than the washes; it shows a greenish yellow cast. Normally without leaves (tiny compound leaves for a short time only), it must be recognized by its short, stiff, lateral twigs ending in a stout spine, and possibly by its long pods with many separate bulges and with a long beak (total length 2 to 3 in). Flowers numerous and covering the tree in April and May, pale yellow, about ½ in. in diameter, the upper petal white or cream. At its northern limit it is replaced by one of the **Crucifixion thorns**, *Canotia*. (see p. 36).

Bluestem Palo Verde
Cercidium floridum
PALO VERDE
FABACEAE Pea Family

NATIVE RANGE Southeastern California to Arizona and northern Mexico.

Bluestem palo verde grows in washes and depressions with underground water, often not too far from its hillside relative, the foothill palo verde with a greenish-yellow cast. It blooms somewhat earlier, late March or April; branches are not spine-tipped, but carry thorns at regular intervals. Its bright yellow flowers have some red spots at the base of the upper petal. Pods are flattened, up to 3 in. long. Leaves doubly compound, temporary; there may be a second crop during the rainy season of July and August.

SONNIA HILL

BJOERTVEDT

JERUSALEM THORN **YELLOW PRICKLEPOPPY**

Jerusalem Thorn
PALO VERDE

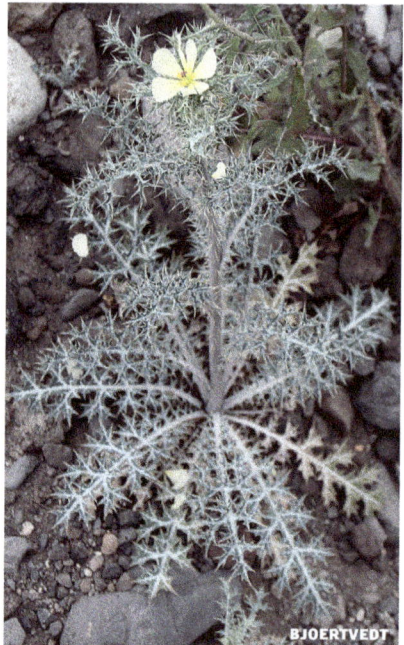

Parkinsonia aculeata
FABACEAE Pea Family

NATIVE RANGE Mexico to northern Argentina, Caribbean.

This palo verde is both native and widely cultivated (see also *Cercidium* on p. 48). Its drooping yellow-green zigzag twigs have 10-inch "streamers" coming from a short spiny stub, and, for a very short time, carrying 25 to 30 tiny leaflets. The attractive golden yellow flowers (in loose clusters) have one special upper red-spotted petal which turns red with age (unlike *Cercidium*). Particularly picturesque is the **BIGOTE** (mustache) phase, referring to the bunches of dry leaves hanging on until the rain brings out the new crop of tiny small green leaves. The name Jerusalem Thorn is a corruption of **GIRASOL**, meaning "turning to the sun". Other names are Horsebean and **RETAMA**.

Yellow Pricklepoppy
CHICALOTE, CARDO SANTO

Argemone ochroleuca
PAPAVERACEAE Poppy Family

NATIVE RANGE Mexico.

To some uninitiated people it's a distinct shock to find the ethereal delicacy of this large poppy combined with thistle-like foliage and sharp, yellow spines. We soon realize that those protective devices are quite effective in desert regions. Then we begin to associate pricklepoppies with warm, dry, sunny weather. *Argemone ochroleuca* is yellow, others are white, some with a rose-colored tinge (**Argemone platyceras**). All have yellow or orange-colored sap and a very prickly seed pod; they are perennial herbs up to 2–3 ft. Pricklepoppies are abundant in the Valley of Mexico and in waste places all over the country. Used as a remedy for cough and convulsions; it has a soothing effect but does not contain morphine.

HUMMINGBIRD FLOWER

COYOTILLO

Hummingbird Flower
ESPINOSILLA

Loeselia mexicana
POLEMONIACEAE Phlox Family

NATIVE RANGE Mexico.

Bright-red tubular flowers with protruding stamens, on slender stems with numerous spiny, glandular, gray leaves. Fairly common, shrubby, winter bloomer in this Mesquite and grassland zone. Plant contains a natural fragrant preservative, as I discovered when it was left soaking in water for weeks. Up to 3 ft. in height, and found in many places.

Coyotillo
TULLIDORA, PIMIENTILLO, NEGRITO

Karwinskia humboldtiana
RHAMNACEAE Buckthorn Family

NATIVE RANGE Texas to Mexico, northwestern Venezuela.

This is a fairly common woody plant, 3–20 ft. high, in arid warm regions, that should be known if for no other reason than to be avoided. Swallowing its seeds is said to result in paralysis and spasms, hence the name **TULLIDORA**, from **TULLIR**, meaning to be crippled. Depending on the dose, results show up in two days or more.

The fruit itself, strangely enough, seems to be harmless without the seeds; it is a black berry, generally in the axils of the opposite leaves. The roots are said to yield an extract acting as an antidote, when administered immediately upon the paralysis.

Leaves are dark green with prominent veins. Baja California to Tamaulipas, Vera Cruz and Oaxaca, also Nayarít, Jalisco, Colima, Sinaloa and Durango, under different local names.

False Rosewood
VAUQUELINIA

Vauquelinia corymbosa
ROSACEAE Rose Family

SYNONYM *Vauquelinia karwinskyi*
NATIVE RANGE Eastern Mexico.

To paraphrase Lincoln: "God must have loved these common-leaved plants — he made

BARETTA

FALSE ROSEWOOD

so many of them!" There is really little to distinguish this shrub or small tree: evergreen leaves, narrow but not too narrow; small white five-petaled flowers in bunches; small woody fruits that stay on the branches a long time; dark brown, crooked branches. Even the Indians seem to have overlooked any possible properties of "what it is good for".

Barreta
BARETA

Helietta parvifolia
RUTACEAE Rue Family

NATIVE RANGE EAstern and central Mexico.

Occasionally, as in this case, an easy way of identification of a plant is its strong odor. In the orange country of northern Mexico, south of Monterrey, this leathery-leafed shrub, with three leaflets, will be recognized immediately by its smelly wood (break a twig to test it). It reminds one of the smell of the hops used in beer-making.

Western Soapberry
JABONCILLO

Sapindus drummondii
SAPINDACEAE Soapberry Family

NATIVE RANGE Kansas and southwestern Missouri, south to Arizona, Louisiana, Mexico (Sonora, Chihuahua, Coahuila).

Its marble-size, translucent, yellow, berry-like fruit hangs on this small, interesting-looking tree (30 ft. or over) until spring — an easy way of recognizing it. They are poisonous, can be used for stupefying fish, and for soap-making. Leaves are compound, leathery, pale yellow-green to dark green, deciduous. Small white flowers, many-flowered branched clusters, 6–9 in. long. Found in valleys from upper desert to woodland zone. Sometimes cultivated.

WESTERN SOAPBERRY

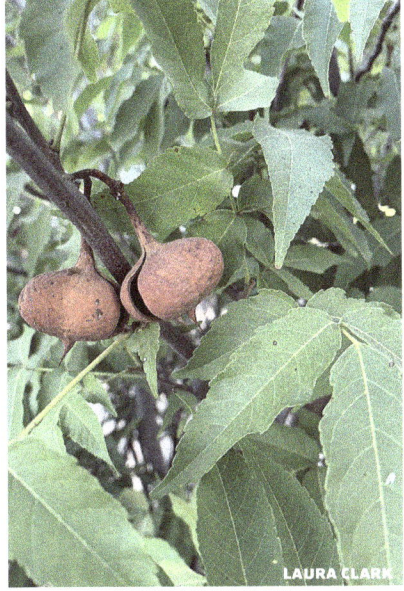

MEXICAN BUCKEYE

Mexican Buckeye
MONILLO

Ungnadia speciosa
SAPINDACEAE Soapberry Family

NATIVE RANGE Southern New Mexico to Texas and northern and eastern Mexico.

Speciosa means beautiful. The designation is properly applied to the clusters of purplish-pink, fragrant blossoms, which appear just before or with the leaves of this tall shrub. It may, rarely, grow into a small tree 25–30 ft. high and 6–8 in. in diameter, with numerous, small, upright branches. Leaves are leathery, dark, glossy-green above, pale below.

The nuts are 2 in. wide; their empty pods hang on even after the shiny black nuts have dropped. As a point of information, it is reported that one can eat one or two of these nuts with impunity, three or four with discomfort and giddiness, and a larger number with possible fatality. Let the curious beware!

Growing in mountain canyons, on limestone hillsides, and along streams, but restricted to the region on both sides of the Rio Grande (**RIO BRAVO** in Mexico).

Butterfly Bush
MISPATLE

Buddleja sessiliflora
SCROPHULARIACEAE Figwort Family

NATIVE RANGE Southern Arizona, southern Texas to Mexico.

A very sweet fragrance, very white rough leaves in pairs, and tight clusters of four-lobed greenish-yellow or purplish florets — these characteristics are generally enough to identify this tall shrub or tree (15 ft. or more). It grows on hillsides in the upper part of the desert. Other butterfly bushes are common in various dry parts of Mexico; most of them have the same sweet fragrance. (See *Buddleja marrubiifolia,* p. 34).

Barometerbush, Silverleaf
CENIZO
Leucophyllum frutescens
SCROPHULARIACEAE Figwort Family
NATIVE RANGE Southwestern Texas to Mexico.

Very suddenly, after a big rain in September, this silver-leafed shrub may change into a ball of violet flower. Some people think it predicts the rain, as a barometer. Flowers, an inch across, somewhat resemble a snapdragon (same family); they are quite hairy in the throat and on lower lobe.

CENIZO (ashy) refers to the silvery-gray leaf, striking even before the shrub blooms. No wonder landscapers use this 3 ft. shrub in native plantings. It prefers limestone soils.

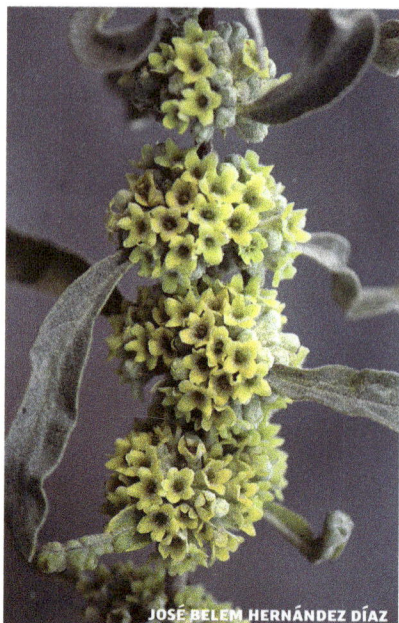

JOSÉ BELEM HERNÁNDEZ DÍAZ

BUTTERFLY BUSH

MOKKIE

BAROMETERBUSH, SILVERLEAF

THORN FOREST

There is a strip of land some 50 miles wide along the east shore of the Gulf of California where the annual rainfall varies from 16 to 34 in. and where the vegetation consists of a dense but scrubby forest, dominated by thorny representatives of the Pea Family. It is generally called Thorn Forest, or Subtropical Mimosae-Cacti and Semi-arid Scrub. To a degree it follows this west coast as far as Acapulco, interrupted by patches of Savanna (which see, p. 110).

Another strip of Thorn Forest, along the east coast of Mexico, follows in general the Gulf of Mexico north of Vera Cruz.

It is an interesting growth, if not particularly hospitable: many of these shrubs have formidable spines. The most common representatives are **Longspine Acacia** (*Vachellia macracantha*, synonym *Acacia macracantha*) and other acacias. It is described as a small tree with tortuous branches and pairs of spines over 2 in. long, with yellow, fluffy flower balls, and long narrow seed pods. Leaves are ferny, consisting of numerous small narrow leaflets arranged in double-compound fashion, like many other acacias.

Fishfuddletree (*Piscidia*) is used for poisoning fish in their watery home; it is without thorns and has pink to purplish pea flowers and locust-like leaves. Its pods are long and thick and provided with flanges..

Very spiny are Graythorn, Bluewood and Lote Bush, all species of *Condalia*, all with tiny blossoms and leaves, and with berry-like fruit. They are all common in this zone. Typical as well are Mimosas, Cassias, and Caesalpinias, all with tiny or temporary leaflets. Of all these, mimosas have fuzzy flower balls or brushes, the other two, good-looking blossoms.

Lysiloma likewise has small leaflets, of short duration; it can be recognized by its broad, long pods (4–8 in.), that have cord-like ridges along the margins. It differs from acacia in being thornless.

Then there are different types of cactus. Saguaro is gone; in its stead we find an interesting tall, ribbed, tree cactus, the **Hairbrush Cactus** (*Pachycereus pecten-aboriginum*). It has large, burry fruits, sometimes used by Indians of Sonora for hairbrushes, hence its name. You may find it in the markets for sale.

Sure to be noticed in winter is a small tree, apparently with dead whitish branches but carrying a number of white morning-glory trumpets in its top. No leaves show up until later in spring. It appears again and again among the thorny shrubs. The Mexicans call it **PALO DEL MUERTO** (Tree of the Dead, *Ipomoea arborescens*), or in English, **Morning-glory tree**.

Palo verde with many beautiful yellow blossoms draws attention to itself somewhat later (*Parkinsonia* species).

Similar to the Thorn Forest Zone, but sometimes distinguished from it is an area stretching east-west between Acapulco and Cuernavaca, along the Rio Balsas valley. One of the Organ Cacti, *Cephalocereus mezcalaensis*, is much in evidence here. Other plants of this **ARID TROPICAL SCRUB** zone, as sometimes called, can survive in the low annual rainfall (12 to 18 in.) combined with tropical heat. Thus we find some bullhorn acacias, flat-pad cacti, and other desert plants. Even Fan Palms can withstand these conditions.

In places, while driving along the highway, one is struck by a smallish tree that has spreading branches tightly clothed with dark green leaves; we came to call it the "tight-foliage tree". On closer examination we found thorny branches with peculiar leaves that consist of a double pair of leaflets. Flowers are fluffy whitish balls, followed by most intriguing curved seedpods. Even the botanist who first called this tree **Pithecellobium dulce,** realized in that name that they were fit earrings for a monkey. The common name follows the translation: **Apes-earring.** The rings finally turn red. Then the name is doubly appropriate. At any stage it is a highly interesting tree.

A tree, literally covered with blue flowers in early spring, will arrest the traveler's attention. It is **Lignum vitae,** (*Guaiacum coulteri*), which the natives call **PALO SANTO,** "Holy wood". This may convey the same idea as the "wood of life" (*Lignum vitae*) and may have reference to the extremely hard and durable wood, difficult to work but taking a beautiful polish. Flowers have a peculiar twist to their petals. An interesting box-like fruit follows the flower.

LIGNUM VITAE

Much might be said of the different types of acacias and their variety of spines, ranging from bullhorns to three-cornered hats and little canoes in shape, some of an ebony black color.

Finally, a word about the **Fan Palms.** Many people associate palms with lush tropical forests. A number of fan palms, however, are dry-land plants, occurring in almost pure stands. Three kinds are reported from this zone, even extending into the Mesquite-Grassland Zone: *Sabal, Brahea,* and *Washingtonia.* They are eminently useful, for food, drink and shelter; even oil is made from the seeds. (See Savanna, p. 113 for *Sabal*).

SHORT-TREE FOREST

Between the Thorn Forest and the Pine-Oak Forest we often find this zone of non-thorny, taller trees, especially in the canyons. Here is *Lysiloma divaricatum* as the most abundant tree (p. 99). Also common are *Jatropha cordata* and *Jatropha malacophylla* (Nettlespurge). **Hairbrush Cactus** (*Pachycereus pecten-aboriginum*) thrives especially on moist slopes.

Dr. Howard Scott Gentry, in his study of the Rio Mayo Plants, points out three layers of foliage in this forest: the top level (at 60 ft.) of *Conzattia sericea,* a yellow-flowered tree of the Pea family, with double-compound leaves, with *Ceiba aesculifolia* (**Kapok tree**), *Lysiloma watsonii* (pp. 61, 99) and *Cochlospermum* (p. 94) at 40 to 50 ft. *Handroanthus impetiginosus* (p. 92) and *Bursea* species at a level below 40 ft.

The third level is below 15 ft. In the bottoms we find such trees as **Apes-earring** (p. 62), **Dwarf poinciana** (p. 156), **Honey mesquite** (p. 47), **Strangler fig** (p. 103), and some others which we have placed in other zones.

We might conceive of these plants as a group of immigrants from other zones, who find in these canyons, about 1000 to 3500 ft. above sea level, a congenial home.

GIANT CACTUS

AMANTE DARMANIN

SERGIO NIEBLA

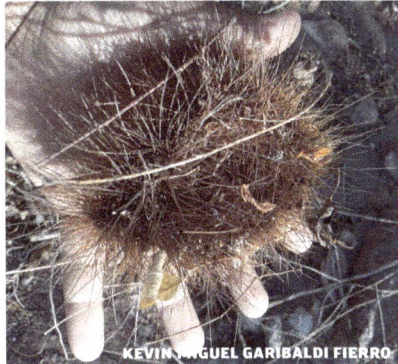

KEVIN MIGUEL GARIBALDI FIERRO

HAIRBRUSH CACTUS

Giant Cactus
CARDÓN
Pachycereus pringlei
CACTACEAE Cactus Family

NATIVE RANGE Northwestern Mexico (to Durango).

Adapted to a tropical desert climate in the ocean's proximity is the Giant Cactus. It may reach 40 ft. (or even 60 ft.) in height, its trunk 6 ft. high and 3 ft. in diameter. Generally quite spiny with good-sized spines, white with brown or sometimes black points. The branches have 11–15 ribs, sometimes 17.

Its white flowers, 2–3 in. high, occur from the top of the branches down; their lower, scaly part is hidden in a mass of brown hair. Dry globular fruit, covered with felt and brown bristles.

Hairbrush Cactus
CARDÓN ESPINOSO
Pachycereus pecten-aboriginum
CACTACEAE Cactus Family

NATIVE RANGE Mexico.

There is quite a resemblance between the kinds of tall tree cactuses. The first conquistadors designated all columnar cacti with the word CIRIO, a thick and long wax-candle, and let it go at that. Botanists now separate them into a number of groups, of which *Pachycereus* (meaning thick wax candle) is an important one.

The hairbrush cactus is the common tree cactus of Sonora and Chihuahua, both in the **Thorn Forest** and the **Tropical Deciduous Forest**. It reaches 15 to 40 ft. in height, with numerous branches. Blooming begins in January, continuing through spring; flowers are over 2 in. long; petals are purple on the outside, white inside. The interesting "hairbrush" fruit, 2–3 in. in diameter, is actually so used by the native Indians; it ripens in June.

One distinction between tree cactuses is in the number of ribs of the branches or stems: as an example, **Organ pipe cactus** (p. 45) has 5–7 ribs, **Hairbrush cactus** 10–11, **Giant cactus** 11–15, **Saguaro** 12–24.

Additional tall, upright, ribbed tree cacti are:

Cephalocereus columna-trajani (Puebla, Oaxaca), 26–33 ft.; curved columnar, pointed toward top; 20 or more slight ribs.

Cephalocereus macrocephalus (Puebla, Oaxaca), 52 ft., about 24–26 ribs, little prominent; few branches; upright, often on steep mountainsides.

Cephalocereus senilis (**Old man cactus**, northeastern Mexico [to Veracruz]), very abundant in Hidalgo and Guanajuato, 48 ft., single columns, 20–23 shallow ribs.

Cephalocereus tetetzo (Puebla, Oaxaca), 32–48 ft., few-branched, upright, 13–17 rounded, little-prominent ribs.

Escontria chiotilla, JIOTILLA, 23 ft., central and southwestern Mexico, short trunk, numerous branches, 7–8 sharp ribs.

Isolatocereus dumortieri (synonym *Lemaireocereus dumortieri*), 20–50 ft., central Mexico, Morelos, Hidalgo, Queretaro, only 6–7 ribs, branches with constrictions.

Mitrocereus militaris (synonym *Pachycereus chrysomallus*), southwestern Mexico, reaching almost 60 ft. (11–14 ribs).

CEPHALOCEREUS COLUMNA-TRAJANI

CEPHALOCEREUS SENILIS

ISOLATOCEREUS DUMORTIERI

AGNIESZKA KWIECIEŃ

MYRTILLOCACTUS GEOMETRIZANS

Myrtillocactus geometrizans (GARAM-BULLO or PADRE NUESTRO), widespread in Mexico, to about 13 ft. tall, of interesting shape with its numerous curved branches, 5–6 rounded ribs.

Pachycereus grandis, central and south-western Mexico, barely 3o ft. tall, 9 to 11 prominent ribs, with neat, upright, "tight" branches.

Pachycereus weberi, widespread in Mexico, with numerous erect branches rising from near the base, up to 33 ft, 10 ribs, deep furrows.

Stenocereus griseus, 20–30 ft.; Mexico to Guatemala, southern Caribbean to northern Venezuela, common in Mitla; 8–10 ribs.

Stenocereus pruinosus, 13–23 ft., PITAYO, Mexico to Honduras, 5–6 prominent ribs.

AMANTE DARMANIN

PACHYCEREUS WEBERI

SCENTED CROTON

LAUREN MCLAURIN

MORNING-GLORY TREE

Morning-Glory Tree
PALO DEL MUERTO

Ipomoea arborescens
CONVOLVULACEAE Morning-Glory Family

SYNONYM *Ipomoea murucoides*
NATIVE RANGE Mexico to El Salvador and Guatemala.

Coming into Mexico from the north in wintertime, we are apt to experience the first exciting flower encounter in noticing beautiful white morning-glory trumpets in certain bare tree tops. A white-gray bark "like the hide of a hippopotamus" draws attention to the slender trunk; nary a leaf is in sight. It reminds one of the miracle of the Lady of Guadalupe, and may well have originated the story.

The tree grows up to 30 ft. in height, and is common in the Thorn Forest and adjoining zones. Depending on the species, the subsequent leaves are oblong (*Ipomoea murucoides*) or heart-shaped ovate (*Ipomoea arborescens*). The former is more common farther south.

The name **PALO BOBO** (Fool Tree) is derived from the belief in Morelos that taking one drink of the water running at its base may mean becoming deranged mentally.

Scented Croton
PICOSA

Croton ciliatoglandulifer
EUPHORBIACEAE Spurge Family

NATIVE RANGE Southern U.S.A. to Central America, Hispaniola.

The botanical name indicates the most noticeable characteristic of this medium-sized shrub: "having glandular hairs all over". The result of these tiny glands is a decided fragrance "like fresh apples or other fruit". Another, less pleasant, effect is that these hairs stick to one's hands which may get them easily into the eyes with bad results. On the other side of the ledger: PICOSA increases the flow of milk in goats browsing on it, and it is the food of a red caterpillar, which some natives eat. The leaves are fuzzy white below, which makes recognition easier. Other members of the Spurge Family include Poinsettia, Castor Bean (p. 155) and **MALA MUJER** (p. 96).

Elephant Ear Tree
GUANACASTE

Enterolobium cyclocarpum
FABACEAE Pea Family

NATIVE RANGE Mexico to southern tropical South America.

A tall, spreading tree draws attention by its enormous spreading crown and thick trunk. Even in the dry season when it is bare of leaves its numerous curiously ear-shaped black seedpods are quite evident on the picturesque smooth gray branches.

These seedpods are relished by cattle and the seeds are toasted for human food. Chiapas Indians used to survive on them in years of scarcity of beans and corn.

Small white fluffy flowers in ball-shaped heads are produced in winter, with fruit following in March and April.

The large trunks are used as boats and water troughs, being very durable in water. Its sawdust causes an allergy in some people, and it is poisonous to fish.

In Thorn Forest and Tropical Deciduous Zone, from Sinaloa to Tamaulipas, Vera Cruz and Chiapas.

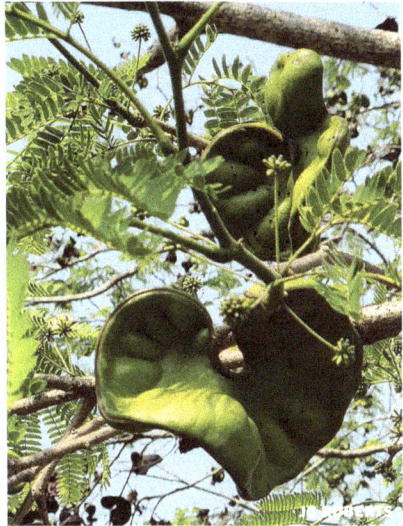

ELEPHANT EAR TREE

Borderpod "Acacias"

Lysiloma species

TEPEGUAJE   FABACEAE Pea Family

NATIVE RANGE Arizona to Central Mexico, Florida to Caribbean.

These shrubs or small trees might easily be mistaken for acacias, judging by general appearance such as the feathery effect of their compound leaves and their fluffy flower balls.

Their pods, however, are different and can be recognized by their cord-like ridge along the edges (*lysiloma* means loosening border). *Lysiloma* has no spines or prickles. Small leaf-like stipules occur at the base of each leaf on first coming out.

Several species of *Lysiloma* are restricted to Yucatán, of which **Lysiloma latisiliquum** (synonym *Lysiloma bahamensis*) is the "**Wild Tamarind**". Others occur mostly in Baja California or in southern Mexico.

Little-leaf Lysiloma

Lysiloma watsonii

QUIEBRACHA, TEPEGUAJE

FABACEAE Pea Family

SYNONYM *Lysiloma microphylla*

NATIVE RANGE Southern Arizona to northern Mexico.

This 25 ft. tree resembles an acacia but has no thorns. The heavy, cord-like margins of the broad and flat pods (4 to 9 in. long), are indicative.

Flowers are white and fluffy, ball-shaped, ⅝ in. wide, in May and June. As the leaves appear, a couple of green appendages (stipules) appear at the base of each leaf; they drop off as the leaf matures.

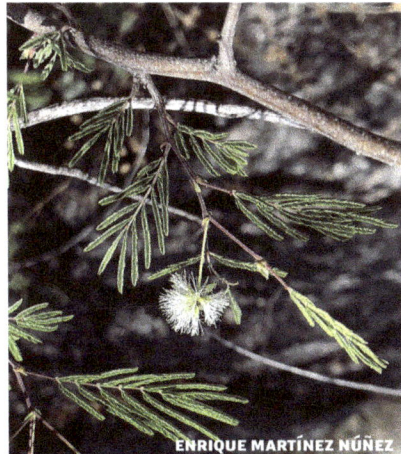

ENRIQUE MARTÍNEZ NÚÑEZ

LITTLE-LEAF LYSILOMA

KRZYSZTOF ZIARNEK

APES-EARRING

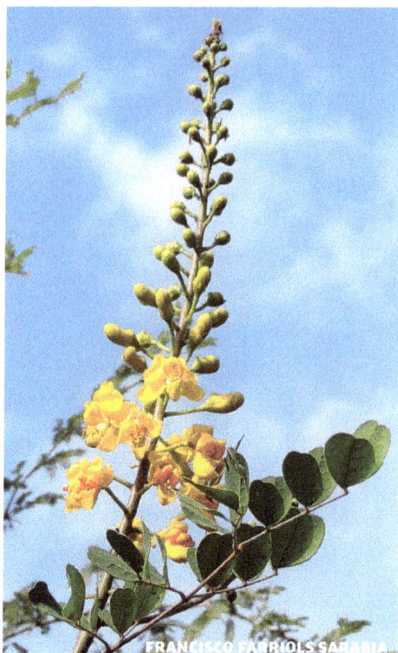

FRANCISCO FARRIOLS SARABIA

BIRD-OF-PARADISE

Bark is light brownish gray, fissured and scaly; wood hard and brittle, dark brown. The crown of the whole tree shows a dense, feathery foliage, rather attractive, due to the small and narrow leaflets crowded on four to nine pairs of featherlike divisions.

On rocky hillsides and slopes in the upper Desert and Mesquite-Grassland zones.

Apes-Earring
GUAMUCHIL

Pithecellobium dulce
FABACEAE Pea Family

NATIVE RANGE Mexico to Guyana and Peru.

It is only on close examination that the Apes-Earring shows its interesting features. From a distance the small tree impresses one by its "tight" foliage, hugging the branches. On inspection this consists of an unusual arrangement of two pairs of leaflets, with a couple of small spines at their combination stalk. Few other plants have that type of leaf.

Flowers are yellowish or greenish-white; they consist of little fluffy balls arranged along a slender stem. At the base may be seen the early twisted pods, which later turn reddish and coil like "apes earrings", whatever that may mean. The fruit is well-liked in Mexico and sold in the markets. The bark, fruit, and seeds have reputed medicinal qualities.

Four-leaf Serena
CANDELILLO, SHIHUIHUIJOYO

Senna oxyphylla
FABACEAE Pea Family

SYNONYM *Cassia oxyphylla*
NATIVE RANGE Mexico to Venezuela and Ecuador.

Sennas like a sunny exposure. Their flowers are nearly regular and generally yellow. This species (not illustrated) is found in the Thorn Forest zone; it is a tall shrub (over 6 ft. tall), has large, pale yellow flowers and fat green pods. Another name is **FRIJOL DE MONTE** (mountain bean). Other species of *Cassia* may be found in the same zone.

Bird-of-Paradise
HUISACHE
SYNONYM *Caesalpinia cacalaco*
NATIVE RANGE Mexico.

Tara cacalaco
FABACEAE Pea Family

Properly the name Bird-of-paradise should be reserved for **Caesalpinia pulcherrima** (see p. 156). Other woody native plants are similar in having large, showy, yellow-and-red flowers and double-compound leaves.

This species has fat pods, usually red on one side and somewhat constricted between the seeds. Leaflets are roundish, branches with spines. It occurs from Sinaloa to Puebla and Oaxaca, both in the Thorn Forest and the Deciduous Tropical Forest. Flowers are large, in long trusses.

ACACIAS
Vachellia species

FABACEAE Pea Family

Just what are acacias, and how can you tell them from similar plants? Originally the name was given to a thorny tree found in Egypt. Occasionally it is used for certain kinds of locusts, particularly the decorative kinds, and especially in parts of Europe.

But botanists now apply the name to over 1,000 species of a genus closely related to mimosas. Thus restricted, acacias are generally spiny shrubs with double-compound leaves, small but often showy flowers with numerous protruding stamens (up to about 400 in number), and are widely distributed in warm regions, often in more or less arid sections. Some Polynesian and Australian representatives have the leaves reduced to green, stemlike structures ('phyllodes').

Mexico has at least 60 or more acacia species, distributed over all its states. Some have immense thorns, often inhabited by vicious ants; others only small prickles. Some display beautiful ball-shaped flowerheads, often a golden yellow, but sometimes white, pink or lavender; others have the flowers arranged in cylindrical spikes (like bottle-brushes), again of various colors: white, pink, lavender or a creamy yellow (not golden). These flowers consist almost entirely of large numbers of separate stamens, with a few other inconspicuous organs added.

There are some other kinds of trees and shrubs that look somewhat like acacias. **Mesquite** (*Prosopis*) and **Mimosa** can be distinguished from Acacias by having less than ten stamens per flower, as does the **Leadtree** (*Leucaena*). **Fairy duster** (*Calliandra*, p. 30, has pink knobs on white stamens, only small feather-leaves, and no spines. *Inga* has similar flowers to acacia but once-compound leaves and no spines (p. 135). **Lysiloma**, instead of having spines at the base of its leaves, shows green leaflike ears there; it has broad pods with a distinctive cord-like ridge along their margins (p. 61). The Mexican name **GUANACASTE** is applied to the **Elephant ear tree** (*Enterolobium*, p. 60) and to **Albizia** which reminds one of **Lysiloma** but without the cord-like ridge of pods; flowers in yellowish balls. The tree is a close relative to "woman's tongue", whose persistent thin seed-pods rattle in the breeze throughout the winter (*Albizia lebbeck*).

Of the following, **Sweet Acacia** (*Vachellia farnesiana*) is all over Mexico, both cultivated and wild, and very fragrant. It has small thorns, unlike other large-thorny ones. Remember, there are many kinds in Mexico: be happy if you can recognize a few!

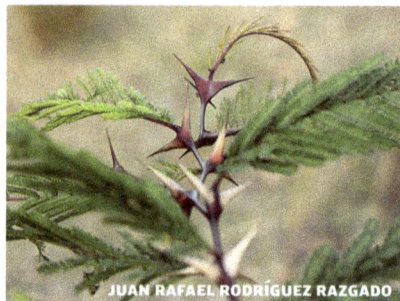

JUAN RAFAEL RODRÍGUEZ RAZGADO

BOAT-THORN ACACIA

DAVID STANG

BULLHORN ACACIA

Boat-thorn Acacia
Vachellia campeachiana

QUISACHE CORTEÑO, CUCHARITAS
FABACEAE Pea Family

SYNONYM *Acacia cymbispina*
NATIVE RANGE Mexico to Honduras, eastern Cuba.

The boat-shaped shells on the sterile branches, that might be taken for empty pods, are really a unique type of thorn, two at each node. The name **CUCHARITAS** means little spoon. There is no mistaking this particular acacia. Leaflets are very numerous, flowers are in fuzzy yellow balls, fruits over 3 in. long and blackish-brown. Found from Chihuahua and Sonora to Puebla and Chiapas.

Bullhorn Acacia
Vachellia cornigera

CUERNITOS, ISCHANAL
FABACEAE Pea Family

SYNONYMS *Acacia spadicigera, Acacia cornigera*
NATIVE RANGE Mexico to Central America.

The name indicates the type of large thorn on this shrub or small tree; they may be as long as 4 in. Not uncommonly little openings are found near the tip, punctured by ferocious ants living inside them. They feed on the nectar at the tip of the leaflets; in return they'll attack any unsuspecting person or animal molesting their host.

Flowers are yellow, in very thick, dense, cylindrical spikes, 1–1½ in. long. Fruit is a mahogany-red, thick pod at maturity. Leaflets numerous, ⅓ in. long; and nectar glands 1/16 in. long.

It prefers the warm regions of Mexico. Also called **ESPINO BLANCO** (white thorn) or **CUERNOS DEL TORO**.

Sweet Acacia
Vachellia farnesiana

HUISACHE, BINORAMA
FABACEAE Pea Family

SYNONYM *Acacia farnesiana*
NATIVE RANGE Tropical and subtropical North and South America.

For long distances ahead the fragrance of Sweet acacia draws attention to this low-topped, spreading tree with its golden yellow balls of flowers. It is widespread all over Mexico, both wild and cultivated. Small spines, pods fat, dark brown or purplish, 2 in. long.

Its names are legion, many derived from the Nahuatl **HUITZAXIN**, some referring to its aroma (**AROMA AMARILLA** in Cuba), some of unknown origin such as **Malabaila** in the southern U.S.A.

SWEET ACACIA

HAT-THORN ACACIA

So are its uses many: tannin from bark and fruit, mucilage from the exuding gum, perfume from its "cassie" flowers (a large industry in Grasse, France), and ointments and medicine from flower and fruit.

Flat-thorn Acacia (not illustrated)

Vachellia × gladiata

ISHCANAL NEGRO

FABACEAE Pea Family

SYNONYM *Acacia gladiata*
NATIVE RANGE Western Mexico.

Of hybrid origin between *V. campeachiana × V. hindsii.*

Indicative of the Flat-thorn acacia are the formidable long and flat dark thorns (1½– 2 in.), inhabited by ants. Flowers are yellow in cylindrical spikes; pods are dark brown, 4 in. long. It is a shrub or small tree, common in Sinaloa and Tepic, but found in other places as well.

Hat-thorn Acacia

Vachellia hindsii

CORNIZUELO, ISHCANAL

FABACEAE Pea Family

SYNONYM *Acacia hindsii*
NATIVE RANGE Western and southern Mexico to Central America.

A military chapeau or three-cornered hat seems to be the pattern for the inflated thorn of this acacia. The thorns are always flat, but may vary much in form and color (sometimes black); they reach 2 in. in size.

Flowers are yellow in long slender spikes, over an inch long, flowers not very densely crowded; between them are little umbrella-like structures, the purpose of which seems to be protection from moisture and fungus spores ('umbracula'). Pods are 2 in. long, beaked, more or less flat and of brown or blackish color. They open as the seeds ripen.

This is a small, glabrous tree mostly along the West coast region. It is called **CAR-RETADERA** in Sinaloa. Another ant protector and protectee.

NEPTALÍ RAMÍREZ MARCIAL
CUDJOE WOOD

FRANCISCO FARRIOLS SARABIA
RANDIA

Cudjoe Wood
SAN JUANICO, SIQUETE
SYNONYM *Jacquinia pungens*
NATIVE RANGE Western and central Mexico to Honduras.

Bonellia macrocarpa subsp. *pungens*
PRIMULACEAE Primrose Family

In valleys of the Thorn Forest or Short-tree Forest one finds a dense, symmetrical small tree, up to 20 ft. high (sometimes a shrub), with rigid, opposite, evergreen leaves, each with a small but stiff, forbidding spine.

Throughout July it carries quantities of bright orange blossoms, with five petals and five decorative stamen-like, leafy parts. They are thick and tough and can be lifted off entire and strung on a cord as necklaces or bracelets, thus keeping for years in their dry state. When submerged in water they regain some of their freshness and have a delicious fragrance. Fruit is about the size of a walnut, very hard, topped with a strong spine.

Both fruit and roots are used along the west coast for stupefying fish; its poison is called **BARBASCO**. Sometimes the fruit has a large round hole, left by an infesting beetle on coming out.

Randia
GRANJEL, CRUCECITO
NATIVE RANGE Mexico, Honduras.

Randia echinocarpa
RUBIACEAE Madder Family

A tall shrub in open sunny locations of the Thorn Forest, both in northwest and southeast Mexico, generally dropping its leaves in the dry spring season. Branches at right angles, terminating in four spines and a rosette of leaves **CRUCECITO** means little cross. Handsome, fragrant, yellow tube-flowers in clusters at the top of the stems. Fruits (on female shrubs only) are round balls, 2–3 in., with large protruding excrescences (*echinocarpa*); they are eaten by children, though bittersweet; they ripen in winter when they are filled with a black, slimy mass.

Mexico has over 20 species of *Randia*. Some are called **MALUCO DE MONTANA, PA-PACHE, TORTLLO, CRUCITO.**

MIKE MULQUEEN

FLAMEBERRY, SCRATCHBUSH

ENRIQUE MARTÍNEZ NÚÑEZ

LIGNUM VITAE

Flameberry, Scratchbush
MAL HOMBRE

Urera caracasana
URTICACEAE Nettle Family

NATIVE RANGE Mexico to tropical South America.

Both Spanish and English names sound ominous, and with reason: this small tree or shrub has stinging hairs, touching it is a most unpleasant experience. Flameberry, a member of the nettle family, comes in male and female plants; male flowers are rose-colored. Fruit is bright red at maturity. Leaves are very variable in shape.

The tree is tropical, occurring from Vera Cruz to Sinaloa, Chiapas and Tabasco, under various names. In Durango it is reported to be used to cure the effects of poison ivy!

Lignum Vitae
GUAYACAN, PALO SANTO

Guaiacum coulteri
ZYGOPHYLLACEAE Creosote-Bush Family

NATIVE RANGE Mexico to Guatemala.

At the height of the dry season, this small sturdy tree bursts into bloom with a glorious shower of fragrant, bright blue blossoms, each with 4–5 twisted petals and 8–10 stamens. In quick response to rain the first leaves are apt to appear along the trunk rather than at the tips of the branches. Later the interesting star-shaped fruit shows the family characteristics of the Zygophyllaceae, but without thorns.

Early Spaniards called it **Lignum vitae, Tree of Life,** either because of supposed medicinal properties or on account of the great strength and lasting qualities of the wood. It is used for blocks, pulleys, rulers; its tenacity, combined with the self-lubricating properties due to its resin content, makes the wood particularly adapted to underwater bearings. A most important use was for bearing or bushing blocks lining the stern tubes of propeller shafts of steamships.

Due to its slow growth the wood is very hard and heavy, and fine-grained; it is olive-brown to black in color, oily or waxy, and has a distinctive odor.

Chaparral

There is much hazy thinking about the meaning of "chaparral". It isn't the name of a plant, though derived from the word **CHAPARRO**, a dwarf evergreen oak. A thicket of these **CHAPARROS** then, is a chaparral. In more common usage it is applied to any dense, impenetrable thicket composed of stiff or thorny shrubs or dwarf trees. In southern California and Baja California, chaparral may consist of a single plant species, such as the **CHAMISAL** (*Adenostoma fasciculatum*); in Texas, many types may compose it.

Incidentally, the "chaps" of the cowboy, divided leather riding pants, are derived from the need for them in riding through the inhospitable chaparral.

The average tourist in Mexico is not apt to see much of the Chaparral: it is almost entirely confined to Baja California and the western base of the Sierra Madre Occidental. Only about 9,000 square miles of Mexico are occupied by this zone. Rainfall ranges from 14 to 30 in.

This typical chaparral contains, in addition to the abovementioned **CHAMISAL** (which is a rigid, leafy, heathlike shrub up to 10 ft. tall, with tufts of small evergreen leaves), other hardy shrubs such as sagebrush, sumac, *Ceanothus*, mountain mahogany (*Cercocarpus*), yucca, madrone, manzanita, are all dryland California shrubs that can grow in infertile soils. One yucca with large, conspicuous flowerstalk (*Hesperoyucca whipplei*) is actually called **Chaparral Yucca** for its location.

You might almost say that this Chaparral zone is an overflow into Mexico from California.

Manzanita
MANZANITA, PINGUICA

Arctostaphylos pungens
ERICACEAE Heath Family

NATIVE RANGE Southwestern and south-central U.S.A. to Mexico.

The Spanish name means "little apple"; it is used for a number of other plants as well. *Arctostaphylos* is "bearberry". It is typical of the chaparral on gravelly soils and sunny

MANZANITA

MADRONE

CHAMISE

JOJOBA

places. There are different species, varying as to leaf shape. All are evergreen shrubs (2–3 ft.) with leathery leaves, practically smooth, urn-shaped blossoms and red berries; the bark is often quite red. Leaves and fruits are noted for their diuretic qualities.

Madrone
Arbutus xalapensis
MADROÑO
ERICACEAE Heath Family
SYNONYM *Arbutus texana*
NATIVE RANGE Southern New Mexico to western Texas and Nicaragua.

A low, picturesque tree that is sure to draw attention to itself by the dark-reddish-brown, smooth bark that peels off in large thin plates. Species are variable as to the shape of leaves, but all are evergreen, thick and leathery, dark green above, pale below.

The neat, though not very large, flowers are white or pink, urn-shaped with five small lobes; they occur in regular clusters at the ends of the twigs. Fruit is dark red, granular with dry, mealy flesh; it has narcotic properties.

Found in chaparral and in somewhat humid oak forests.

Chamise
Adenostoma fasciculatum
CHAMIZAL
ROSACEAE Rose Family
NATIVE RANGE California to Mexico (Baja California).

One of the "good-for-nothing" shrubs according to stockmen who consider it a difficult pest, which crowds out palatable plants. It thrives on poor depleted soils and on dry, hot slopes. A rigid, leafy evergreen shrub, up to 10 ft. tall, with reddish-brown bark, surprisingly belonging to the Rose family (small white blossoms in June). Also fire hazard due to its resinous leaves. It reproduces quickly due to its underground, spreading root system. For that reason it does provide good protection against eroding watersheds.

This is not to be confused with the "chamisa", another name for **Rabbitbrush** (*Eriocameria nauseosa*) and with the **Fourwing saltbush** (*Atriplex canescens*), which is also called chamisa or shadscale.

Jojoba, Goatnut
JOJOBA

Simmondsia chinensis
SIMMONDSIACEAE Jojoba Family

NATIVE RANGE Southern California to central Utah and northern Mexico (including Baja California).

Jojoba is a low, attractive shrub, 3 to 5 ft. tall, at elevations from 1,500 to 5,000 ft. It is limited to northwestern Mexico on dry slopes and along washes. Also called deer-nut, wild-hazel, coffee-bush, and quinine plant.

Fruits, acorn-like, bitter but palatable, occur only on the female shrubs. Male shrubs have the same opposite, thick, bluish, evergreen leaves, and at flowering time (December to July) display round clusters of small, yellowish-green staminate blossoms (photo, right).

Jojoba is grown commercially to produce jojoba oil, extracted from its seed, and widely used in personal care products, especially shampoos and lotions.

JOJOBA, GOATNUT

Pine-Oak Forest

One of the many surprising things about Mexico's vegetation zones is the large area covered by this Pine-Oak Forest — over one-fourth of its total land surface. In early days, this area was even much more extensive. Due to its great fertility the Pine-Oak Forest has been the center of Mexico's population from time immemorial. Today, great parts of it have been altered to make way for cornfields and other crop lands.

No matter where we start, from desert regions, thorn forest, tropical deciduous forest or tropical evergreen forest, on getting into higher elevations with medium rainfall, almost invariably we find the vegetation giving way to one or more types of the Pine-Oak Forest.

Even in the northern part of Mexico, this zone does not start, in general, until an elevation of 4,000–5,000 ft. has been reached. The true pine forest is above 7,000 ft.

These elevations are raised gradually as we travel farther south. In Chiapas, for instance, oaks start at not less than 6,500 ft. and pines are unlikely below 9,000 ft. It is mainly a question of temperature and rainfall.

Where do we find this Pine-Oak Vegetation zone? It is a continuous wide strip, starting at the Arizona-New Mexico border, following the Western Sierra Madre, covering most of the Central Plateau and then following the Eastern and Southern Sierra Madre, reaching into Guatemala. Frequently the Tropical Deciduous Forest adjoins it on its lower slopes.

Recognizing the zone as you come to it is easy: conifers and oaks are unmistakable. Telling the different pines and oaks apart is another story: there are so many kinds and many of them look quite alike. Mexico boasts over 100 different species of oak (*Quercus*); no other country in the world has such a large number of oaks.

After having traveled through this zone a number of times, we begin to recognize a certain order of progression.

In general, the dryland growth is the one dominated by junipers, pinyon pine and scrubby oak brush. It joins the Mesquite-Grassland and the Desert area below it. In fact, certain desert plants like yucca, cactus, and sotol may reach up into it. The soil is often of poor quality, but warm. This portion, then, corresponds to the Upper Sonoran Zone of the arid part of the U.S.A., and adjoins it.

Then, as we climb higher, the typical Oak Forest takes over. In different regions different oaks predominate. They vary in size and shape of leaves and have different-sized and -shaped acorns.

The average tourist has little choice but to enjoy them all without all the headache of identification. Even the designation as **ROBLE** and **ENCINA** is confusing, to say the least. The Spanish adopted **ENCINO** for the live oak, reminding them of their native *Quercus ilex*, and called any deciduous oak **ROBLE**, after their *Quercus robur*. **BELLOTA** is the Spanish name for acorn. Many oaks in Mexico are evergreen, or almost evergreen.

While traveling through this oak forest, with some pines mixed in, we can often look at neighboring hills and see the almost pure pine forest higher up. There is no mistaking the character. Denser and denser they grow; in general, there is nothing but grass underneath. Only where there is an occasional sunny spot between them do we find some shrubs and flowering plants.

Again, while it is easy enough to tell a pine from other trees, it is difficult to tell them apart. (There are over 20 species of pine in Mexico). One difference is in the number of needles in a bundle, another in the size and type of cone and the way they remain on the tree. Thus, we may train ourselves to look for the widespread **Montezuma pine** with its long, drooping needles (five in a bunch), its large, attractive cones, and its interesting tall candles in the top of each tree. Then, just as we think we'll recognize it any time, here comes another pine with long slender needles, even more drooping and even longer, the **Jelecote pine** (*Pinus patula*), with needles in threes, and with smaller, very lustrous cones.

We may begin to recognize, silhouetting against the horizon, the tight cones of the three-needled **Chihuahua pine** (*Pinus leiophylla* var. *chihuahuana*), closely held on horizontal branches (three needles).

We must not forget to mention two outstanding cone-bearing evergreens that are not pines, but which have an important place in Mexico: the **Sacred ffir** or OYAMEL (*Abies religiosa*) and the famous Old-timer, **AHUEHUETE** or Montezuma Baldcypress (*Taxodium distichum* var. *mexicanum*).

OYAMEL is a high-altitude tree (7,500–9,500 ft. elevation) that really belongs to the Boreal Forest, above the Pine-Oak belt. Similarly, **Douglas fir** (*Pseudotsuga menziesii*) is a high-elevation tree). OYAMEL is as much as 150 ft. tall, 20 ft. in circumference, and has long, violet-blue cones, upright on tree. Branches are often used as church decorations — hence the name *Abies religiosa*; wood is employed for construction and for paper pulp; its resin, tapped in winter, yields balsam and a paint ingredient.

AHUEHUETE, or **SABINO** has a splendid press agent: every tourist goes to see the famous tree at Santa Maria del Tule, near Oaxaca, with a trunk circumference of 170 ft., as well as the old tree in the gardens of Chapultepec, estimated to be 500 years old. The tree under which Cortez wept, in Popotla near Mexico City, and the fine specimen near Zimapan, are also famous.

In many places **AHUEHUETE** is planted in home grounds. Perhaps the surest way to identify it is by its ball-shaped cones, up to an inch in diameter, consisting of neatly joined scales, with interesting markings. Incongruous as it may seem to us, leaves and young branches are shed in January, leaving the tree true to its name **Bald-cypress**.

This Pine-Oak Forest Zone, with rainfall ranging from 18 to 70 in. per year, corresponds to the so-called Canadian or Montane zone of more northern regions. Many of Mexico's main highways cross it in various places, often in the most scenic spots.

Curiously enough, the **Douglas Fir** (*Pseudotsuga menziesii*) is indicative of this Canadian zone, extending all the way from southern Canada to well into Mexico.

Some authorities separate the Canadian zone from the Upper Austral Zone. Our Pine-Oak Forest Vegetation Zone includes both.

Quite a number of well-known garden flowers have their origin here; such are **zinnias**, **dahlias**, **gaillardias**, **tagetes**, and **tigridias**. Others are more common in the tropical deciduous zone; some are derived from desert regions.

RAFAEL RAFAEL SALDAÑA

SACRED FIR

MEXICAN STAR

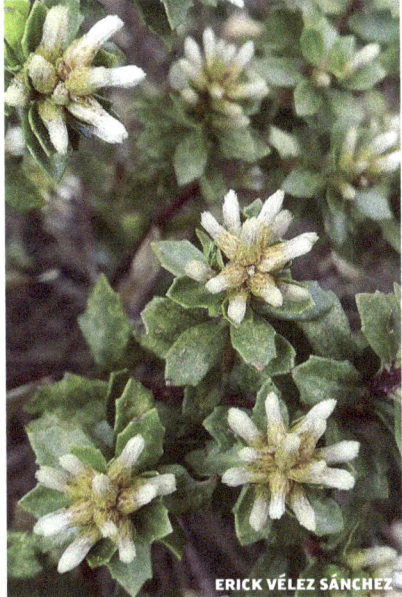

ERICK VÉLEZ SÁNCHEZ

CHARCOAL SHRUB

Mexican Star
ESTRELLITA, LILIA CIMARRON

Milla biflora
ASPARAGACEAE Asparagus Family

NATIVE RANGE Southeastern Arizona to southwestern New Mexico and Honduras.

An excellent waxy white cut-flower with green midveins, blooming in August or September in open woods and grassy slopes of this plant zone. It is a bulbous plant with grass-like leaves and fragrant flowers, 2–2½ in. across.

Charcoal Shrub
YERBA DEL CARBONERO

Baccharis conferta
ASTERACEAE Aster Family

NATIVE RANGE Mexico.

Almost invariably, as one descends from the Pine-Oak Forest, or just below it, attention is drawn to a neat shrub along the highway, with glossy, leathery leaves of a notched spatulate shape. Many of them are in small tufts at the end of the branches, each tuft surrounding an interesting bud. *Baccharis* has white or yellowish flower heads in irregular trusses.

Other species (like **Seep Willow,** *Baccharis douglasii*) are found in the Mesquite Grassland Zone (see p. 42).

Wild Dahlia
DALIA

Dahlia pinnata
ASTERACEAE Aster Family

SYNONYM *Dahlia rosea*
NATIVE RANGE Mexico.

The first dahlia introduced into European gardens was already improved, so we are not sure which was the original, but *Dahlia pinnata* is probably the parent of most of the cultivated varieties. Development of most of the spectacular modern types began in 1814.

The name comes from Andreas Dahl, pupil of Linnaeus; not be confused with Dalea, a plant of the pea family. As early as 1924 Dr. J.B.S. Norton published a list of "7000 Dahlias in Cultivation".

LEONARDO BERGAMINI
WILD DAHLIA

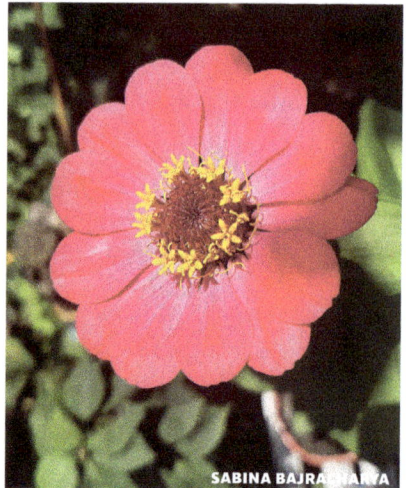

SABINA BAJRA...ARTA
ZINNIA

The **Tree dahlia** is *Dahlia excelsa*, (**GIGANTON** or **TECOTEHUE**); it is native in southern Mexico. *Dahlia coccinea*, a splendid deep red, is reported from the Lower Pine Forest in Chihuahua. See also *Hidalgoa ternata* in the Evergreen Forest Zone, p. 122, a beautiful orange vine, easily taken for a dahlia.

Zinnia
CAROLINA

Zinnia elegans
ASTERACEAE Aster Family

NATIVE RANGE Mexico to Nicaragua.

To the non-Mexican it is an unending surprise, and delight, to find well-known garden flowers growing wild. Fields of yellow and pink cosmos are not uncommon, ageratum sometimes acts as a groundcover, verbenas, marigolds and lantanas are quite at home, as is petunia. The genus *Tithonia* occurs with a number of species.

Zinnia elegans is a purple or rusty red, occurs generally in or near the Pine-Oak plant zone, and is also commonly cultivated for its showy flowers; other Zinnias are orange, yellow, white.

Wax Alder
ALISO

Alnus jorullensis
BETULACEAE Birch Family

NATIVE RANGE Mexico to Honduras.

Generally found along streams in the oak zone of Mexican mountain forests, these small trees are not too difficult to recognize by their smooth, reddish-brown branches, neatly toothed leaves, and especially by their woody little cones up to an inch long. This particular alder, named after the Volcano of Jorullo, has interesting yellow wax glands densely covering the lower surface of the leaves.

JUNIPERS AND CYPRESSES
CUPRESSACEAE Cypress Family

Few people are sufficiently interested in these two groups of coniferous evergreens to want to know individual distinctions.

Both junipers and cypresses have scale-like leaves closely held to the twig. The difference shows in the fruit: a dry, round cone in cypresses, opening up when ripe — a green

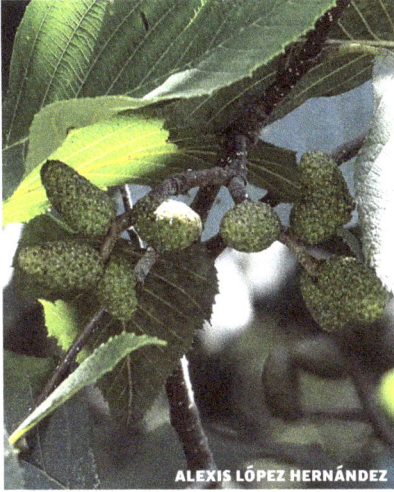

ALEXIS LÓPEZ HERNÁNDEZ

WAX ALDER

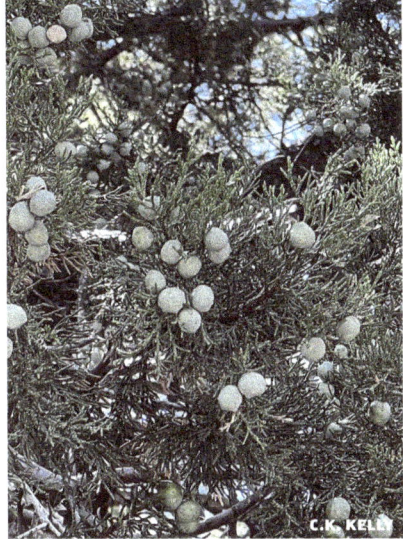

C.K. KELLY

ALLIGATOR JUNIPER

or reddish berry in junipers, that may take up to 3 years to mature and does not open up at any time.

Of the cypresses (ours formerly genus *Cupressus*), **Hesperocyparis arizonica** of the northern half extends as far south as Zacatecas; **Hesperocyparis benthamii** and **Hespero-cyparis lusitanica** are southern trees of the Pine-Oak zone. **Hesperocyparis guadalupensis** is practically confined to Baja California and the island of Guadalupe west of it. The **Italian cypress** is used as an ornamental pyramidal tree.

Juniperus californica is common in Baja California.

Mexican Juniper (*Juniperus monticola*) is scattered through almost all of Mexico in mountainous regions. It may reach 14,800 ft. in elevation, where is becomes shrub-like. Its waxy blue berries, ¼ in. wide, have sweet resinous flesh; they mature in one season and have one or two seeds each. Twigs are four-angled, as are those of **Alligator Juniper**, but the bark is ridged and stringy.

Alligator Juniper
TASCATE

Juniperus deppeana
CUPRESSACEAE Cypress Family

NATIVE RANGE Arizona to western Texas and Mexico.

Easily recognized by its rough checkered bark, red-brown, cut into nearly square plates (alligator-like), and by its dense foliage, thickly dotted with resin. Berries are dark red-brown, ½ in., often with knobby bumps; their flesh is thick, dry, mealy, sweet. Usually four seeds per berry, which is often used as food. It is a long-lived, drought-resistant tree, up to 60 ft. tall, and may live for 500 to 800 years. It grows on low dry hillsides, from Chihuahua and Sonora to Zacatecas and Puebla.

Drooping Juniper
CEDRO COLORADO

Juniperus flaccida
CUPRESSACEAE Cypress Family

NATIVE RANGE Southwestern Texas to Mexico.

The name denotes its graceful branches with slender, drooping ends. Its scale-like leaves are very sharp-pointed, light yellow-green, dying on branch with a cinnamon color.

DROOPING JUNIPER

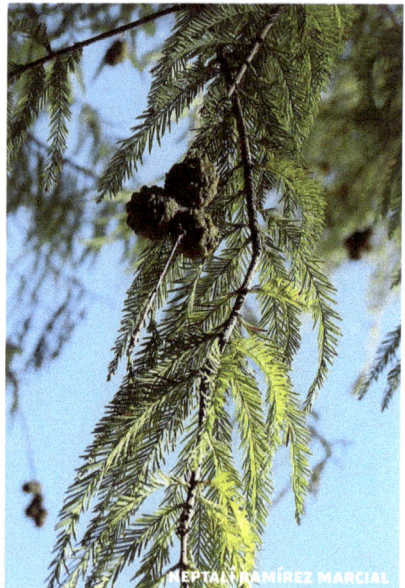

MONTEZUMA BALDCYPRESS

Berries are hard, dull red-brown, ripening in 2 years. Each contains four or more irregularly shaped, pointed seeds.

A shrub or tree up to 40 ft. tall, occurring southward from Chihuahua and Sonora at middle elevations.

Montezuma Baldcypress
SABINO, AHUEHUETE

Taxodium distichum var. *mexicanum*
CUPRESSACEAE Cypress Family

SYNONYM *Taxodium mucronatum*
NATIVE RANGE Southern Texas to Guatemala.

One of the best-known trees of Mexico (noted especially for its size and known as the National Tree), also ranks high among America's oldest living giants: some are known to be 800 years old, and others are said to reach over 1,000; height to 170 ft. They differ from their fir and spruce relatives by dropping their needles in winter, and by their roundish cones 2 in. in diameter. The male (pollen) spikes in the early part of the year are long and slender. Bark brownish-red.

These trees are most common in groves along water courses from Sinaloa to Coahuila and southward into Chiapas and Guatemala; often planted as a shade tree.

Well-known are the Chapultepec **AHUEHUETES**, the **ARBOL DE LA NOCHE TRISTE** in Popotla (under which Cortez wept), the Zimapan **SABINO**, and the giant of Santa Maria del Tule, near Oaxaca. The latter has a circumference of 160 ft., a height of 144 ft., and an age of possibly 2,000 years.

Woolly Senna, Shower Tree
RETAMA

Senna multiglandulosa
FABACEAE Pea Family

SYNONYM *Cassia tomentosa*
NATIVE RANGE Mexico, western South America.

There are nearly 300 species of *Senna*, mostly in warm regions; few can stand more than a few degrees of frost. All are sun lovers. The accepted common name is Senna, but

WOOLLY SIENNA, SHOWER TREE

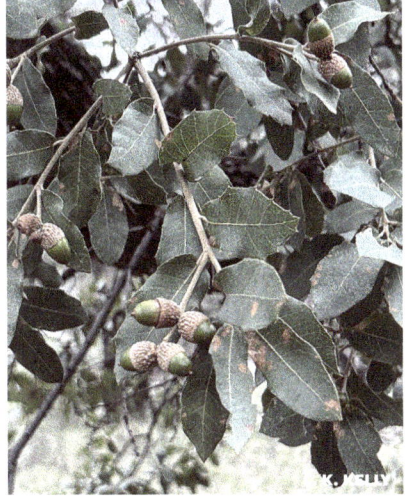

ARIZONA WHITE OAK

the spectacular flowering trees are often referred to as the Shower Trees. Brazil has pink shower and yellow shower; then there are Argentine, Burmese, Costa Rica, Honduras, Java, Kenya, Nicaragua, Siamese and Australian bush showers — and more!

All sennas have nearly regular flowers with ten stamens, many yellow; leaves are simple pinnate with a broad range of pairs of leaflets per leaf. *Senna multiglandulosa* has six to eight pairs of oblong leaflets with rounded tips, velvety-yellow underneath, green above. The entire shrub, 3–13 ft. tall, is hairy throughout. Blossoms deep golden-yellow; pods linear, hairy, 4 in. long.

It is common in thickets in the Sierra Madre. Other species are found in the same and in other plant zones.

Arizona White Oak
ENCINO BLANCO

Quercus arizonica
FAGACEAE Beech Family

NATIVE RANGE Arizona to western Texas and northern Mexico.

While this is the most common live oak of southwestern U.S.A., it also occurs in Sonora, Chihuahua, Coahuila and Durango. It is found in the same general region as the Mexican blue oak and the Emory or Black oak, on dry mountain slopes, 5,000 ft. and up, often with pinyons and junipers.

These three oaks have similar leaves, with dark upper surface (dull in *Q. arizonica*, lustrous in the other two), pale below, with stout, short stalks, and have similar acorns, about one-half enclosed in their cups.

To recognize *Q. arizonica*, remember that its toothed leaves are dull, not lustrous above, and densely hairy below; they are 1½ in. to 4 in. long, and ½ to 2 in. wide, with a conspicuous yellow midrib. Acorns ½ to ⅔ of an inch long.

The tree rarely reaches 40 to 60 ft. in height and 3 to 4 ft. in diameter. It has a large, round crown and nearly horizontal contorted branches.

Mexican Blue Oak, Chestnut Oak
ENCINO

Quercus castanea
Fagaceae Beech Family

NATIVE RANGE Mexico to Honduras.

Very widespread, small tree with medium-sized leaves (3 in. long), rather slender,

MEXICAN BLUE OAK, CHESTNUT OAK

ALEXIS LÓPEZ HERNÁNDEZ

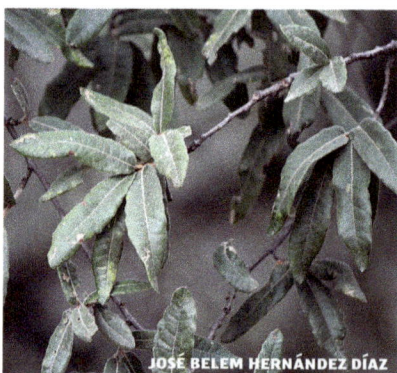

JOSÉ BELEM HERNÁNDEZ DÍAZ

MEXICAN OAK

grooved twigs, smooth brown buds, solitary or grouped annual acorns. Leaves are sharp-tipped, with veins ending in weak spines; upper surface smooth and shiny, lower white-downy.

Occurs at altitudes from 5,000 to 8,000 ft., and in states ranging from the Tropic of Cancer south. Curiously it is called white, yellow, red, and black oak depending on the location.

Mexican Oak
ENCINO

SYNONYM *Quercus mexicana*
NATIVE RANGE Mexico.

Quercus crassipes
FAGACEAE Beech Family

In general the name **ENCINO** is reserved for oaks with smaller leaves, after the Spanish holly oak, *Quercus ilex*. Large-leaf oaks are commonly called **ROBLE**, a name commonly reserved for the deciduous kind. In this case the leaves are small (1–2 in. by 4 in.) but deciduous. Identification is not easy.

It is a smallish tree, with narrow leaves, somewhat wrinkled, russet on the lower surface, having smooth or rolled edges. Acorns are small (½ in.), half-enclosed by the thick-stalked rounded cup; at the base of the cup the blunt, tight scales may show an outcurved margin. Fruit matures the second season.

Emory Oak, Black Oak
BELLOTA

NATIVE RANGE Arizona to western Texas and northern Mexico.

Quercus emoryi
FAGACEAE Beech Family

The most abundant and most typical tree of the Pine-Oak Forest in northern Mexico, e.g., Chihuahua and Sonora, from 4,000 to 7,000 ft. elevation.

It is practically evergreen, the leaves being renewed in April. The slender, rigid twigs are bright red when young; winterbuds are ¼ in. long. The leathery leaves are thick, hard, rigid, dark green above, pale below, 1 to 2½ in. long, ½–1 in. wide, with a short spiny point and a few short spiny teeth. Acorns are found on current year's wood; they are sweet and edible, ½ in. long or more, one-third enclosed by the shallow cup.

Silverleaf Oak
ENCINO BLANCO

SYNONYM *Quercus hypoleuca*
NATIVE RANGE Arizona to western Texas and northern Mexico.

Quercus hypoleucoides
FAGACEAE Beech Family

An evergreen oak that looks like an olive (due to the silvery, thick-felty underside of the leaf) occurs in the dry mountainous regions of the northern part of Mexico, extending

EMORY OAK, BLACK OAK

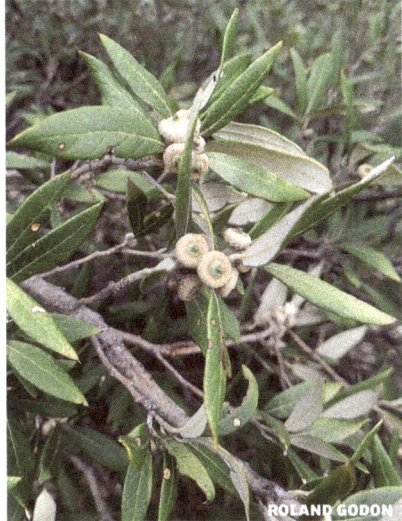

SILVERLEAF OAK

into Texas and Arizona. Less abundant than the **Emory oak**, which grows in the same general location, it is more conspicuous; its leaves are apt to be longer (up to 3–4 in.).

Thick-shelled acorns, ½ in. long, becoming light chestnut brown. Shrub or small tree on slopes and in canyons.

Mexican Blue Oak, White Live Oak
BELLOTA

Quercus oblongifolia
FAGACEAE Beech Family

NATIVE RANGE Arizona to western Texas and northern Mexico.

Has leaves seldom over 2 in. long and rarely with three teeth near the tip, none farther down as *Quercus emoryi* does. Like the latter the upper leaf surface is shining bluish-green. Leaves drop when new ones appear. Tree seldom grows over 35 ft. in height; branches are heavy and twisted, forming a round-topped crown, similar to *Q. arizonica*.

Occurs at somewhat lower elevations than *Q. arizonica* and *Q. emoryi*. White Live Oaks in general have the sweetest and most palatable acorns.

Wrinkle-leaf Oak
Quercus rugosa
ROBLE RUGOSO
FAGACEAE Beech Family
SYNONYM *Quercus reticulata*
NATIVE RANGE Arizona to Texas and Honduras.

Especially when the leaves turn a beautiful "fall" color before dropping, this oak is one of the most striking ones of the Pine-Oak Forest. An older name, *Quercus macro-*

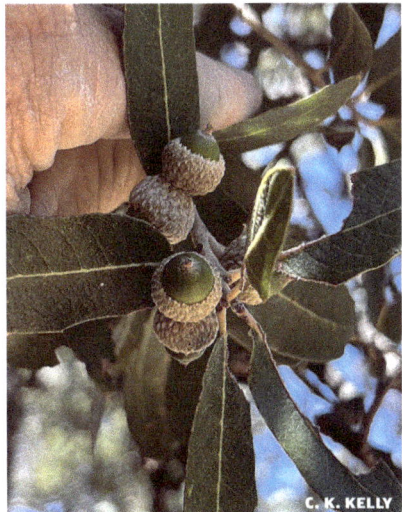

MEXICAN BLUE OAK, WHITE LIVE OAK

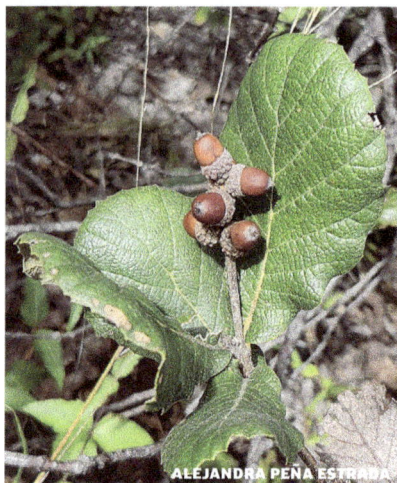
ALÉJANDRA PEÑA ESTRADA
WRINKLE-LEAF OAK

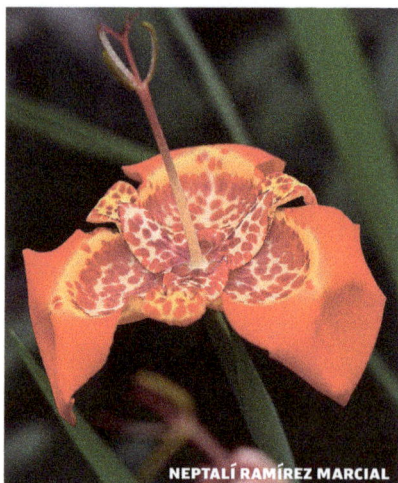
NEPTALÍ RAMÍREZ MARCIAL
SHELLFLOWER, TIGERFLOWER

phylla var. *rugosa*, indicates the large size and wrinkled appearance of the leaf. Twigs are rather stout and felty, leaves are smooth above, dingy felty and prominently veined below, with a short stubby stalk. Acorns on a long stalk, often in pairs, about ½ in. long; acorn cup shallow with sharp tight scales. Wood very heavy and close-grained, dark brown.

Shellflower, Tigerflower
FLOR DE TIGRE

Tigridia pavonia
IRIDACEAE Iris Family

NATIVE RANGE Mexico to Honduras.

If you have not actually seen this **FLOR DE TIGRE** it takes a lively imagination to visualize the brilliance of the three strikingly red, large petals and the numerous red and dark-purple "tiger" spots on the yellow background of the cup — not to mention the small "fiddle-shaped" smaller petals inside the cup. As a member of the Iris family, the whole flower is on top of the stem-like seedpod.

The entire plant comes from a single "bulb" and may grow to 2½ ft. in height. Each flower blooms from early dawn to the afternoon, but many follow each other for a period of two to three months during the rainy season in Mexico. Leaves few, pleated.

Tigridia pavonia is common around Mexico City and also in Sonora and Chihuahua. The related **Alophia drummondii** (synonym *Tigridia buccifera*), purple, white, and yellow with rounded petals, in the mountains of Jalisco. All occur in the pine forests or just below.

Cardinal Sage
SALVIA ROJA

Salvia fulgens
LAMIACEAE Mint Family

NATIVE RANGE Mexico.

A beautiful red salvia in wooded areas, quite conspicuous since it is apt to occur in colonies. Reported as characteristic of the Pine Oak Forest in the neighborhood of the **Sacred fir** (*Abies religiosa*) and *Pinus pseudostrobus*, at rather high altitudes.

It is also cultivated, as are **Salvia splendens** and **Salvia coccinea**, both red, and often cultivated as annuals. The flowers of *Salvia fulgens* are darker red than those of *S. splendens*. It is normally a perennial shrub, 2–3 ft. tall.

There are many other kinds of salvias in Mexico; some red, some blue, and scattered in various zones.

CARDINAL SAGE

LILIANA RAMÍREZ-FREIRE

ALAN ROCKEFELLER

SACRED FIR

Sacred Fir
OYAMEL, ABETO

Abies religiosa
PINACEAE Pine Family

NATIVE RANGE Mexico to western Guatemala.

Firs have flat needles and erect cones that disintegrate when the seeds are ready for distribution. This Sacred Fir's needles are slender, about 1 in. long and grooved on the upper surface. Cones are a beautiful violet-blue.

The tree is really more typical of the Boreal Forest, where it occurs at altitudes of 9,000 ft. and above, often in pure stands (as for instance on the slopes of Popocatepetl.) **OYAMEL** is particularly common on the east, west, and south rims of the Mexican plateau. (Its close relative, *Abies concolor*, **White fir**, is found in mostly northern Mexico and Baja California). The specific name, *religiosa*, refers to its use for church decoration; branches often show a natural cross. Its lumber is valuable for construction purposes and for making furniture and paper. In winter the trees are tapped for **ACEITE DE PALO** (Wood oil), for medicinal, balsam, and paint uses.

MEXICAN WHITE PINE

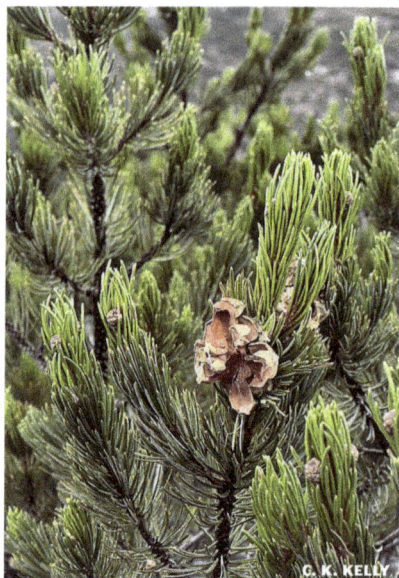

MEXICAN PINYON PINE

Mexican White Pine
PINABETE, AYACAHUITE

Pinus ayacahuite
PINACEAE Pine Family

NATIVE RANGE Mexico to Honduras.

This handsome pine, up to 100 ft. tall, with spreading, slender branches, dominates much of the lower Pine Forest, and extends all the way through the cool mountains from Chihuahua to Chiapas and Guatemala.

It resembles the limber pine and white pine of northern regions, having long needles, bluish-green in bundles of five, moderately stiff but somewhat pendulous (4–6 in.). Its cones are very large, from 8 in. up, and have thick scales and nut-like seeds, generally with a large wing; they hang down, are often slightly curved, and are pale yellowish or reddish brown.

The diameter of the trunk may well reach 3–6 ft. On exposed, dry rocky ridges it is apt to be round-topped, noticeable by its clusters of leaves at the tips of branches.

The largest of all pines, **Sugar pine**, *Pinus lambertiana*, with cones over a foot long, reaches Mexico in Baja California. It also has leaves in bundles of five.

Mexican Pinyon Pine
PINO PIÑON

Pinus cembroides
PINACEAE Pine Family

NATIVE RANGE Southeastern Arizona to southwestern Texas and Mexico.

On hot, arid mountain slopes from 5,000 to 8,000 ft. altitude, Mexican Pinyon Pine is normally associated with junipers, and sometimes with scrub oak. It occupies the zone just below the typical pine-oak woodland.

Needles are in bundles of three, different from the northern two-needled pinyon. A small squatty tree, it is most easily recognized by its irregular flattish cones, which contain the well-known edible pinyon nuts, extensively gathered and eaten.

Seldom reaching more than 20 ft. in height, the trees may take 250 to 350 years before reaching full maturity.

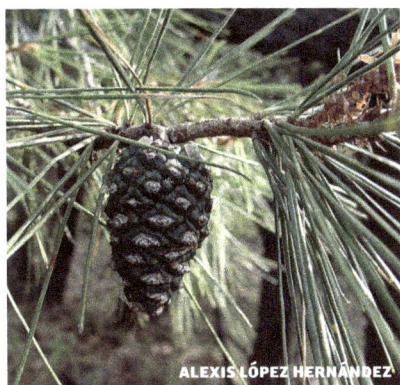
ALEXIS LÓPEZ HERNÁNDEZ
CHIHUAHUA PINE

NEPTALÍ RAMÍREZ MARCIAL
MONTEZUMA PINE

Chihuahua Pine
OCOTE BLANCO

Pinus leiophylla var. *chihuahuana*
PINACEAE Pine Family

SYNONYM *Pinus chihuahuana*
NATIVE RANGE Southeast Arizona to southwest New Mexico and north and west Mexico.

Chihuahua pines are said to reach maturity in 250 to 300 years. They can often be recognized by the number of tight cones remaining on the branches; these are about 2½ in. long, a light chestnut-brown, and lustrous, ripening the third year. The needles are in a group of three; they are about 2 to 4 in. long, slender, pale waxy-green, rough to the touch, and persist for 4 years. Chihuahua pine is restricted to a comparatively small area, on dry rocky mountain slopes of Chihuahua and Sonora. Unlike most pines it does not produce flowers until July.

Montezuma Pine
OCOTE MACHO

Pinus montezumae
PINACEAE Pine Family

NATIVE RANGE Mexico to Guatemala.

Among Mexico's five-needled pines one learns to distinguish the Montezuma Pine by its dull dark cones — 3–9 in. long — and by its interesting drooping leaves, well over 4 in. long. The top branches appear like large plumes due to this drooping habit of the leaves. It occurs from 6,500 ft. up to a little over 9,000 ft., growing from Durango and Zacatecas to Chiapas and Guatemala. The trees often have tall straight trunks extending well above the ground. At higher elevations, up to timberline, **Pinus hartwegii** is more common, with non-persistent, long, brown or black cones, and shorter leaves.

At the lower limit of the Pine-Oak Forest grows another five-needle pine, **Pinus oocarpa**, with similar drooping plumes on top of bright green leaves. Its cones are ocher-yellow, often tinged with gray or green, lustrous and persistent. It also goes by the local name of **OCOTE MACHO**, "male pitchpine".

Jelecote Pine
PINO COLORADO

Pinus patula
PINACEAE Pine Family

NATIVE RANGE Mexico.

From Querétaro to Vera Cruz and Puebla, at altitudes from 5,700 ft. up, we may find a pine with long, slender branches and with long drooping needles, so thin the hanging tassels look like green hair (the tree is sometimes called **Drooping-leaf pine**). Needles are 6 in. long or over, three in a bundle; they might be confused with those of **Montezuma**

KATE MCALPINE

ERICK VÉLEZ SÁNCHEZ

JELECOTE PINE

AZTEC PINE

pine (p. 83). The very lustrous cones are smallish, 2–3 in., dark brown and bent backward; they persist on the branches. Upper part of trunk is red. The name **JALOCOTE** or **XALECOM** is said to be applied locally to the **Aztec pine**, *Pinus teocote*.

Aztec Pine
PINO REAL

Pinus teocote
PINACEAE Pine Family

NATIVE RANGE Mexico.

Only the Aztec nobles were permitted to use the resin of this pine for incense in worship, it is said. That probably accounts for the name *Pinus teocote* (pine of the gods). It may also have something to do with the Spanish name **PINO REAL** (regal pine). Needles are in threes, 4–6 in. long, not drooping, bright green. Cones less than 2 in., spreading or reflexed, brown or somewhat lustrous. The tree produces turpentine (**TREMENTINA DE OCOTE**), used in medicine and other purposes. The tar remaining after distillation of turpentine is used for torches and for soap.

Mexican Hawthorn
TEJOCOTE

Crataegus mexicana
ROSACEAE Rose Family

NATIVE RANGE Mexico to Guatemala.

In clearings of the Pine-Oak Forest we find this well-known widespread thorny shrub, growing to about 20 ft. tall. Blossoms in July are followed in fall by large orange fruits, less than 1 in. long; these are commonly sold in public markets and are highly valued, raw or in preserves.

Leaves are thick and shiny, oblong or varying. Small leaves sometimes grow on the stout thorns. The thorns themselves are indicative of the shrub.

Named by Mociño and Sessé, the ill-fated, enthusiastic early collectors of Mexican plants.

MEXICAN HAWTHORN

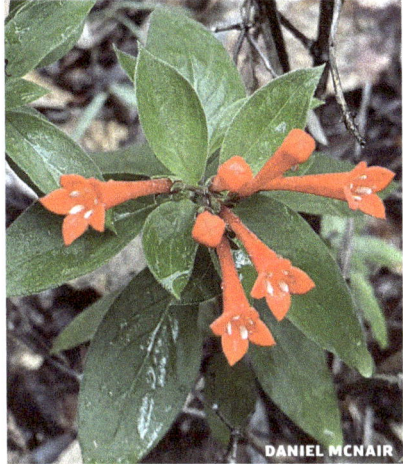

DANIEL MCNAIR

LITTLE TRUMPET

Little Trumpet
TROMPETILLA

Bouvardia ternifolia
Rubiaceae Madder Family

NATIVE RANGE Southeastern Arizona to southwestern Texas and Honduras.

This bright red, well-named flower is conspicuous in many places of the Pine-Oak Forest Zone from Saltillo to Oaxaca. The Nahuatl name is **TLACOSUCHIL**. It has three to five leaves in a whorl on the stem. Flowers are in bunches on top of the stems; they are slightly hairy. Usually herbaceous, sometimes shrubby; occasionally cultivated.

Mexican Elder
SAUCO

Sambucus mexicana
VIBURNACEAE Arrow-Wood Family

NATIVE RANGE Southwestern U.S.A. to New Mexico and Mexico (Sonora, Chihuahua).

This widespread elder is fairly common in oak forests along streams and ditches; it is sometimes cultivated. The tree reaches a height of 30 ft., and can easily be recognized by its opposite, compound leaves, its brittle branches, its peculiar odor, and, in the proper season, by its flattish, white flower clusters, followed by trusses of dark-blue berries. The edible fruit is used for pies and wine in the United States and in some parts of Mexico, according to Miranda. Found at altitudes from 6,000–10,000 ft., depending on the latitude. Mexican Hawthorn, Wax Alder, and Madrone (*Arbutus*) are apt to be found in the same neighborhood.

Blueberry Elder, *Sambucus cerulea*, a related species, extends from Canada south into Mexico between the Rockies and the Pacific coast likewise in the Pine-Oak Forest. It has normally seven leaflets instead of five, glaucous fruit, and smooth leaves.

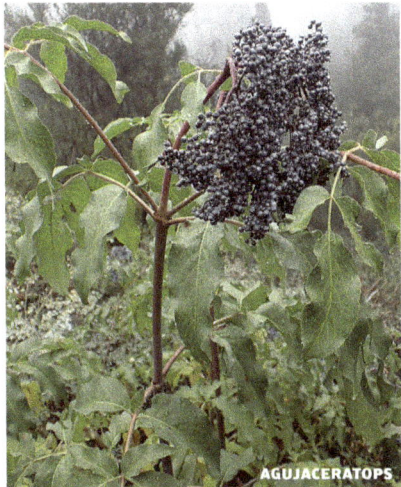

AGUJACERATOPS

MEXICAN ELDER

Boreal Forest

To find Canadian scenery — or even that of polar regions — in Mexico, all you need to do is climb up to high mountain tops, especially in its northern half. However, few people, except mountaineers, will go to the trouble; main highways seldom traverse this zone, which totals only one-half of one percent of the country.

Well-known are Mount Orizaba (Citlaltepetl), its highest peak, 18,855 ft. in elevation; Smoky Mountain (Popocatepetl), 17,888 ft.; Sleeping Lady (Ixtaccilmat1), 17,343 ft.; Cerro Malinche (Matlalcueyetl), 14,636 ft.; Volean de Toluca (Zinantecatl), 15,016; Cope de Perote (Nauhcampatepetl), 14,048 ft.; and Nevado de Colima, 14,235 ft. All of these show eternal snow. Due to the latitude, however, much of this snow melts and freezes, so that its appearance is glistening and icy, rather than soft and woolly.

Timberline varies from 13,000 to 13,500 ft. above sea level. Only two evergreens are common just below timberline: **Pinus hartwegii** and **Juniperus deppeana**. This region might be referred to as corresponding to the Hudsonian zone.

At an elevation of about 11,000 ft. on north slopes and 11,500 ft. on southern exposure, the character changes. We are now entering the so-called Canadian zone, with dense stands of **Sacred Fir** (Abies religiosa) dominating the landscape for over a thousand feet down. It is the belt of heaviest fogs. **Mexican Cypress** (Hesperocyparis lusitanica) may also be found here.

Still lower we come upon the Pine-Alder-Fir zone, mostly in lower stream valleys (7,200–8,500 tt.). The ubiquitous **Montezuma pine** (Pinus montezumae, p. 83) can be recognized with its straight trunks and plume-like tops. **Sacred fir** (Abies religiosa) is still in evidence. **Mexican white pine** (Pinus ayacahuite, p. 82), comes up from lower elevations.

Commonly associated with Sacred Fir are high-altitude species of alder, such as **Alnus jorullensis**. Together with it we may find **Senecio cinerarioides**.

All high peaks of southern Mexico display this consistent vertical order of arrangement, as indicated above. Starting at the Pine-Alder-Fir region of 7,200 to 8,500 ft., we reach the Fir Forest of **Sacred rir** between 7,500 and 9,500 ft., then come to open pine and bunchgrass between 9,500 and 11,800 ft., before arriving at timberline. Above this, trees are replaced by alpine meadows and sacatón grass. Mosses and lichens hold on to precarious life as high up as 16,500 ft.

One main highway crosses the Boreal Forest, the one from Morelia to Mexico City. Its most spectacular view is at the beautiful **"MIRADOR DE LAS MIL CUMBRES"** ('View of the Thousand Peaks') at 9,179 ft. in elevation, in the Atzimba National Park. Still higher is a point west where the road crosses the Sierra of Ozumatlan at Puerta Garnica (9,512 ft.). East of Lerma the same highway, at 10,433 ft. elevation, crosses another divide between the state of Mexico and the Federal District. Here again we find wooded mountains of the Boreal Zone.

Should you want to make a more intimate study of this Boreal Forest, you might visit the Izta-Popo Zoquiapan National Park, which covers Mexico's two famous volcanoes; it can be reached by a road branching off the main highway between Mexico City and Cuautla 1½ miles south of Amecameca.

Tropical Deciduous Forest (Short-Tree Forest)

Just below the Pine-Oak Forest Zone, which is typical of the temperate region, we find, in tropical parts, a belt of highly interesting forest land consisting mostly of trees that shed their leaves during part of the year, but include also some evergreen shrubs and trees.

Annual rainfall here varies between 24 and 60 in., most of it received in summer. We may think of this region as the more humid foothills below the pine-oak uplands. Some authorities call it the "**Short-Tree Forest**".

In general it is a strip of land following the Pacific coastline at a distance of less than 60 miles; it is often separated from the ocean by another strip of either **Thorn Forest** or of **Savanna** (which see). A smaller strip is found near the Gulf in the neighborhood of El Mante and Tampico.

In the summer, the rainy season, this Short-Tree forest presents an unbroken canopy of different tints of green. Fall shows some brilliant autumn colors; winter may surprise the unsuspecting by a sudden blossoming-out of red, pink, yellow or white flowers.

The forest canopy typically consists of three layers. A few tall trees such as *Conzattia sericea* (**PALO JOSO**), **Kapok tree** (*Ceiba aesculifolia*), and **Borderpod acacia** (*Lysiloma watsonii*) may grow up to 40–50 ft., or even higher. In southern Mexico, common high trees of this layer are species of *Bucida*, *Lonchocarpus* and *Bursera*.

The majority of trees are around 30 ft. tall, such as **Trumpet tree** (*Tabebuia*), **Pricklenut** (*Guazuma*) and **Apes-earring** (*Pithecellobium*, p. 62). **Hairbrush cactus** (pp. 57) grows up to 30 ft. or over.

The third and lowest layer seldom reaches over a height of 15 ft.; it contains trees, such as **Yellowsilk shellseed** (*Cochlospermum*), **Mouse-killer** (*Gliricidia*) and **Pinkwing** (*Alvaradoa*), and a number of shrubs. Since most of the trees of the Tropical Deciduous Forest drop their leaves during the dry season, this lower vegetation has quite a different character from the gloomy shade-lovers of the Tropical Evergreen Forest floor and that of the Rainforest.

Such beautiful flowers as **Spiderlily** (*Hymenocallis*), **Cardinal sage** (*Salvia fulgens*) and **Loose-flowered lobelia** (*Lobelia laxiflora*) are sure to draw attention in this zone. Occasionally a whole patch of ground may be covered with the Cardinal sage.

Some of the most beautiful and striking flowering trees are found in the Tropical Deciduous Forest. Such are the orchid-pink **Trumpet tree** (*Tabebuia heterophylla*), the widespread, ghostlike **Tree morning-glory** (*Ipomoea arborescens*, mentioned in the Thorn Forest on p. 60), and the amazing yellow-flowered **Yellowsilk shellseed tree** (*Cochlospermum vitifolium*), that flaunts its large poppy-like blossoms in the top of leafless trees, followed by its apple-like fruit.

Similar trumpet flowers to those of the Trumpet Tree, but in canary-yellow, are borne by **Spring bells** (*Roseodendron donnell-smithii*), again with palmate leaves.

Silk cotton tree (*Pseudobombax palmeri*) has large, beautiful, white blossoms (red in cultivated trees), followed by cotton-shedding, large, elliptical seed pods.

Large trusses of pink sweet pea blossoms, shedding easily, are borne by a tree that looks like a locust and carries the Spanish name of **Mouse-killer** (*Gliricidia sepium*). Somewhat similar, but with small, regular blossoms and shrimp-colored fruit, is the **Pinkwing** (*Alvaradoa amorphoides*), also found in the Thorn Forest.

A highly interesting, neat-looking tree might be called **Sausage tree** (*Hymenaea courbaril*) for its intriguing reddish fruit. A less attractive common name is **Stinking toe**. It can be recognized by its twin leaves.

MALA MUJER ('Bad Woman'), as the Mexicans call it, is a tall shrub with large hand-shaped leaves, often droopy, that will leave you, if you touch it, with a most unpleasant itch for a long time (*Cnidoscolus urens*). Its English name contains a warning: **Treadsoftly**.

The Bad Woman's mate, **MAL HOMBRE** (*Urera caracasana*) has similar qualities and is described in the Thorn Forest Zone (p. 67).

Equally uninviting to touch, though causing no rash, are a number of *Solanum,* near relatives of the potato. They come in whites, lavenders and yellows, and their leaves are often lobed in an odd fashion.

Yellow flowers on lower shrubs decorate a number of *Cassia*, *Senna*, and *Hoffmannseggia* species of the Pea family and of the **yellow abutilon** that reminds one of a neat hibiscus. (Cultivated **hibiscus** shrubs are found in many Mexican parks and homes).

Interesting blossoms are those of **Scarlet hamelia**, **Glorybush** (purple), **Starbell** (orange), **Rosy cups** and **Tropical blueberry** (both pink), and particularly the **Orange caterpillar** (*Combretum farinosum*), scrambling over other trees.

One of the world's most beautiful climbers is the dainty **Coralvine** (*Antigonon leptopus*). Unmistakable is a large white climbing **morning-glory** (*Ipomoea*).

This Tropical Deciduous Forest is much less awe-inspiring than the Tropical Evergreen Forest. However, in a way it is closer to those of us from temperate regions and not difficult to appreciate its beauty.

TROPICAL DECIDUOUS FOREST
Uxmal Forest, as seen from the Great Pyramid. Sitio arqueológico Uxmal, Yucatán.

COLETO

MONTANOA

Coleto

COLETO, PAPAYA CIMARRON

Oreopanax peltatus
ARALIACEAE Ginseng Family

NATIVE RANGE Mexico to Honduras.

A decorative tree, in habit and leaf somewhat resembling the papaya, hence one name given it by the natives; **CIMARRON** means wild, unruly. It grows as a small slender tree with a straight, gray trunk, mottled grayish-white, and a short, spreading crown; it is seldom over 35 ft. tall.

Its leathery, deeply lobed leaves are quite ornamental, yellowish-red below. Flowers in November dull white, in dense heads, small, numerous, long-stalked. Fruit black, round, berry-like, ripening in spring, two-celled. Wood described as "turgid and weak, with a pungent odor when broken."

Montanoa

ZOAPATLE

Montanoa tomentosa
ASTERACEAE Aster Family

NATIVE RANGE Mexico to Central America.

This much-branched shrub reaches up to 5 ft. in height. It can be recognized by its felty-white lower leaf surface and stems; leaves opposite and of an unusual shape, with three pronounced veins; they are 1 to 3 in. long.

The composite flower heads are small and white, blooming in clusters in December.

The shrub is sometimes cultivated on patios for obstetrical use.

Rosy Cups

CIHUAPATLE

Pluchea odorata
ASTERACEAE Aster Family

NATIVE RANGE Southeastern Canada to tropical and subtropical America.

Along roadsides in warm regions one may come across this lush, coarse shrub up to 6 ft. tall, with numerous pink, cup-like flowerheads in flattish trusses. Alternate, good-sized leaves, gray-hairy on the underside, on ashy-felty stems.

Its name, of Nahua origin, meaning medicine (**PATLI**) of woman (**CIHUATL**) is more commonly given to *Montanoa tomentosa* (p. 89). Other names are **CANELA**, mean-

JUDY ULRICH

ROSY CUPS

MEXICAN FLAME VINE

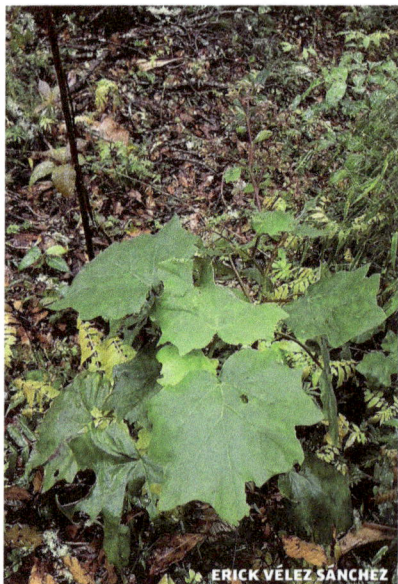

ERICK VÉLEZ SÁNCHEZ

GRAND GROUNDSEL

ing cinnamon, **CHALCHE, HIERBA DE SANTA MARIA**. In the Bahamas it is called **Sourbush** and is considered a good source of honey.

In Mexico it is fairly widespread, even into Yucatán.

Mexican Flame Vine
Pseudogynoxys chenopodioides
LLAMA TREPADORA
ASTERACEAE Aster Family
SYNONYM *Senecio confusus*
NATIVE RANGE Mexico to southern tropical South America.

Frequently we may see, from a distance, a tropical tree seemingly covered with a mass of reddish-orange daisy-like blossoms with yellow centers. On closer investigation it may well prove to be this woody vine clambering all over the branches. It is a beautiful tropical plant with thick and shiny leaves, light-green with toothed edges. Winter and spring are its blooming time.

Grand Groundsel
Roldana oaxacana
GORDOLOBO
ASTERACEAE Aster Family
SYNONYM *Senecio oaxacanus*
NATIVE RANGE Central and southern Mexico.

Over 60 woody kinds of *Roldana* have been distinguished in Mexico and Central America. Some are vines, some shrubs, some small trees. The fact that so few have local names indicates that they are not considered of great significance economically or medically. *Roldana oaxacana* is common in the neighborhood of Jalapa; typical are the large lobed leaves and many yellow flowerheads. Another species, **Roldana barba-johannis,** with a felty-white flower truss, is not uncommon.

Bloodtrumpet
Amphilophium buccinatorium
TROMPETILLA GRANDE
BIGNONIACEAE Trumpet-Creeper Family
SYNONYMS *Bignonia cherere, Phaedranthus buccinatorius*
NATIVE RANGE Mexico.

Few sights in Mexico are more spectacular than this brilliant woody vine in full bloom

JOSE ENRIQUE

BLOODTRUMPET

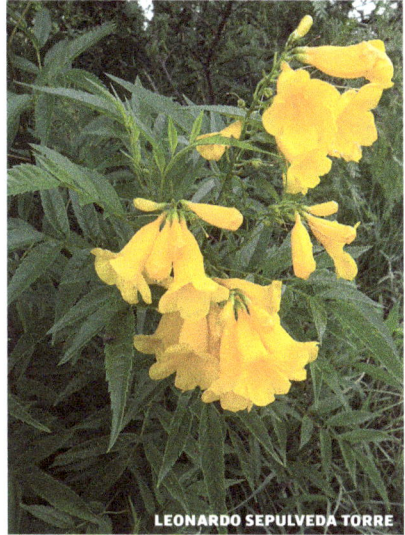

LEONARDO SEPULVEDA TORRE

YELLOW GRASS-TREE

covering high walls or scrambling up into trees to a great height. It climbs by means of branched tendrils terminating twin leaflets. Flowers are slightly curved, 4 in. long or more, with five split spreading lobes; they hang down from their stout stalks in great masses. Leaflets evergreen, variable in shape, 2 to 3 in. long, lustrous above, glandular.

Since it blooms almost during the entire year, it is a favorite cultivated vine for gardens. Other members of the Bignonia family are also found in warm regions of Mexico, some pink or purplish; none is as striking as this species.

Other common names are **CLARÍN, MEDRA BOCINA, CINATORIA**, and in English, **Mexican trumpet vine**.

Yellow Grass-tree
PALO DE AGUA

Astianthus viminalis
BIGNONIACEAE Trumpet-Creeper Family

NATIVE RANGE Central Mexico to Nicaragua.

It is seldom that similarity in leaves hints at close relationship in plants. In this case, anybody who has observed the long, slender, grass-like leaves hanging from a large **Desert Willow** (*Chilopsis linearis*) in northern Mexico (see p. 25), is very apt to guess at *Astianthus* in the south, being its relative. The funnel-like blossoms (yellow in this case) and linear seedpods verify that kinship: both belong to the Trumpet-Creeper family. *Astianthus* is at home in the Tropical Deciduous Tree zone, it parallels the Pacific coast line from Colima to Oaxaca; it is also reported from Veracruz and Puebla states; a grove of them is reported bordering Rio Amacuzac north of Taxco. It likes wet places, hence the name **PALO DE AGUA**.

The tree grows to 50 ft., with a smooth, gray or whitish bark, somewhat ridged, flowers 2 to 2½ in. long, pods 3 to 4½ in. long, leaves 8 to 12 in., often in threes. For comparison see also *Tecoma stans*, p. 93 and *Roseodendron donnell-smithii*, p. 92.

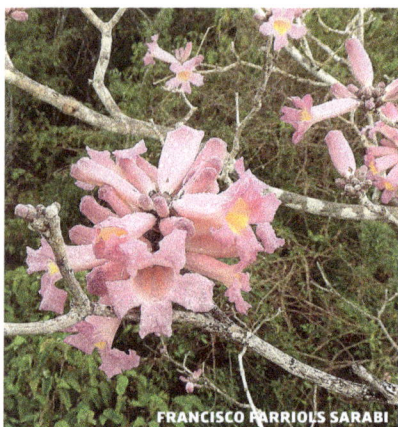

FRANCISCO FARRIOLS SARABI

TRUMPET TREE

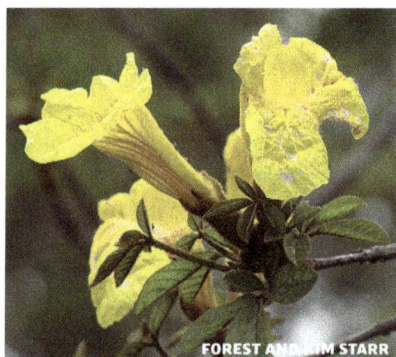

FOREST AND KIM STARR

Trumpet Tree
MACULIZ
Handroanthus impetiginosus
BIGNONIACEAE Trumpet-Creeper Family
SYNONYM *Tabebuia palmeri*
NATIVE RANGE Central Mexico to southern
tropical South America.

In March or April the Trumpet tree is one
of the most beautiful tropical trees, being
then leafless but covered with great masses

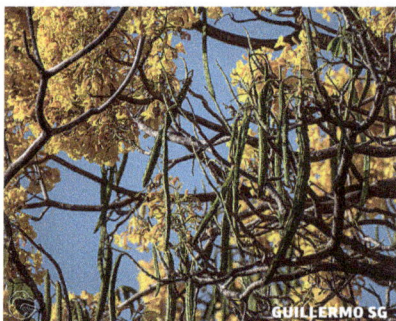

GUILLERMO SG

SPRINGBELLS

of orchid-pink or rosy, bell-shaped trumpets. It is occasionally planted as an ornamental. Its compound leaves are opposite; their five leaflets are arranged at the end of a slender stalk. They appear with the summer rains in July, lasting until late fall. Pods are long and narrow, filled with many winged, thin-papery seeds, like other members of the family.

The wood of this 18–25 ft. tree is hard and strong and used commercially for its capricious veining, especially for interior decorating.

Trumpet trees are particularly prevalent in Brazil where they go by the common name of **IPE**. Called **MATILISGUATE** in Chiapas.

Springbells
PRIMAVERA
Roseodendron donnell-smithii
BIGNONIACEAE Trumpet-Creeper Family
SYNONYMS *Cybistax donnell-smithii, Tabebuia donnell-smithii*
NATIVE RANGE Southern Mexico to southern Venezuela.

One of the most beautiful trees in Mexico is this one, called "Spring" in Spanish (**PRIMAVERA**). Even from a distance the tall tree with a smooth and almost white bark draws attention with its large clusters of canary-yellow, trumpet-shaped blossoms. In winter they are bare and ungainly. It may reach 100 ft. in height and over 3 ft. in diameter.

Its opposite leaves, which come after the flowers, are palmately compound, with seven oblong leaflets. On older trees the leaflets are arranged along a central stalk (pinnate). The long narrow pods, five- or six-ribbed, are typical of the family.

The exceptionally fine timber, lightweight and used for interior decorating, is in such great demand that the tree is becoming rare in Central America. Its older name is *Tabebuia*. Other English names are **Gold and Sunshine Tree**.

YELLOW TRUMPET, YELLOW ELDER

SERENELLA LINARES

MARILYNE BUSQUE-DUBOIS
LIPSTICKTREE

Yellow Trumpet, Yellow Elder
Tecoma stans
TRONADORA BIGNONIACEAE Trumpet-Creeper Family
NATIVE RANGE Tropical and subtropical North and South America.

A most attractive tall shrub with golden yellow tube flowers, and yellow-green, opposite, compound leaves. Its long slender pods (6 to 8 in.) with flat, winged seeds indicate its family relationship with **Desert willow** (p. 25) and the **Trumpet Tree**, (p. 92).

Found in many places in Mexico (in well-drained areas), both in the Deciduous Tropical Forest and the Mesquite-Grassland Zone. Sometimes cultivated for its beautiful blossoms; blooming profusely from August to November, but often twice a year. Its reputation for controlling diabetes has been disproved.

The name **CANDOX**, used for it in Chiapas, may mean tongue (**TOTZ**) of tiger (**KAN**) , according to Miranda.

Lipsticktree
Bixa orellana
ACHIOTE BIXACEAE Lipsticktree Family
NATIVE RANGE Mexico to southern Tropical South America.

Sometimes an unassuming tree or shrub, as this is, has a hidden surprise True enough, a certain curiosity may be aroused by the brownish-green, soft chestnut burs that surmount the large, long-petioled, heart-shaped leaves, but it is only on opening them up that we find the striking red-orange pulp around the small angular seeds. It contains the annato dye, with which ancient warriors used to paint their bodies, and that is now a common coloring matter for butter and cheese. It is also used for dyeing silk, not to mention "lipstick" use.

In November there are large pink flowers, 2½ in. in diameter, quite ornamental, par-

ANDRÉS RAMÍREZ-BARRERA

ROSA SCHULZ

STARBELL

DOMINIK MAXIMILIÁN RAMÍK

YELLOWSILK SHELLSEED

ticularly since the leaves are evergreen. It is considered a desirable garden shrub of the tropics.

Yellowsilk Shellseed
Cochlospermum vitifolium
TECOMASUCHIL, POMPOSHUTI
BIXACEAE Lipsticktree Family

NATIVE RANGE Mexico to southern tropical South America, Cuba.

This is one of the least-publicized flowering trees of Mexico, while among its most beautiful ones. Large golden cups adorn the tops of small trees during the leafless season; inside are numerous curly, orange-yellow stamens, hiding the pistil. The outside of the calyx is dark brown, which adds interest to the opening bud. Following the flowers is a crop of apple-shaped green fruit, changing to brown.

The English name refers to the silky down of the spoon-shaped seeds; the Latin name (*Cochlospermum*) means spoon- or shell-seed. Leaves do not appear until the flowers are gone.

Mexican names are **CHUUM, COCRRO, ROSA AMARILLA** (yellow rose), **APOMO, PAN-GOLOTE, POCHOTE, MADERA DE PASTA** (paste wood), **HUARUMBO, QUIERIGA, FLOR IZQUIERDA** (crooked flower), **POMPOSHUTI, TECOMASUCHIL**, and others.

Starbell
Cordia dodecandra
CUPAPE, ZIRICOTE
BORAGINACEAE Borage Family

NATIVE RANGE Central Mexico to Guatemala, Cuba.

This pretty orange-colored, tube-like flower, consisting of a 12–16-pointed star flaring out toward its mouth, decorates a tree which may at times grow as tall as 90 ft. or more. It is frequently cultivated in the Mexican Isthmus for its edible fruit, which is yellowish and fleshy, 2 in. long and rather acid; it is generally used in sweets. The leaves, 3 to 5 in. long, are harsh, and used as a substitute for sandpaper or for cleaning dishes. The wood

ALAN ROCKEFELLER

LOOSE-FLOWERED LOBELIA

ALEXIS LÓPEZ HERNÁNDEZ

FRANCISCO EMILIO ROLDÁN VELASCO

ORANGE CATERPILLAR

is hard and heavy and takes a fine polish which makes it desirable for the making of furniture and saddletrees. A syrup of its bark, flowers, and fruit is considered a good cough medicine.

Loose-flowered Lobelia
CHILPANXOCHITL

Lobelia laxiflora
CAMPANULACEAE Bellflower Family

NATIVE RANGE Southern Arizona to Colombia.

Issuing from the crevices of a rock (as it often does) this graceful plant has beautiful red-and-yellow two-lipped blossoms, which hang down in unpredictable angles as from a thin thread. Each flower comes from the axil of a narrow, sharp-pointed leaf. Its dark-red calyx is equally striking, as is the long pistil which extends beyond the slit in the flower. Color blends from the yellow top part to a blood-red lower portion. The plant is what is sometimes called a "sub-shrub", not quite woody, and grows to 3 ft. tall.

Other lobelias occur in the Pine-Oak Forest, some blue-, some red-flowered.

Orange Caterpillar
PEINETA

Combretum farinosum
COMBRETACEAE West Indies-Almond Family

NATIVE RANGE Mexico to Central America.

PEINETA is an ornamental comb dressing up a lady's hair; it is quite appropriate for this long, orange-red flower-brush, which shows numerous stamens hanging down from each floret. The inelegant English name is suggested by its similarity to a large hairy caterpillar crawling over the plant. Once noticed, it is easily recognized: to make sure, look for the opposite leaves, scaly underneath, and for the scaly calyx (*farinosum* means "mealy").

What apparently looks like a tree is found to be a woody scrambler upon close investigation; it decorates its host tree. The showy flowers are full of sweet nectar. Thirsty travelers avail themselves of the large amount of water oozing out from cut limbs.

Extending from Sinaloa to Chiapas and Veracruz, it goes by various names, such as **CARAPE, COMPIO, ANGARILLA, QUIETZINE**; in Central America many names refer to the honey (**MIEL**) as **PAPA-MIEL, CHUPA-MIEL, ABACÁ-MIEL**. The name **CEPILLO** simply means brush.

Giant White Morning-Glory
CAMPANILLA, OLOLIUQHQUI

Ipomoea species
CONVOLVULACEAE Morning-Glory Family

There are dozens of morning-glories (*Ipomoea*) in Mexico, ranging from the ethereal **Morning-glory tree** (p. 60) and the cultivated **Sweet potato vine** (*Ipomoea batatas*), to various white, pink or purple flowering vines.

Treadsoftly
MALA MUJER

Cnidoscolus urens
EUPHORBIACEAE Spurge Family

NATIVE RANGE Mexico to Tropical America.

Sometimes **Poison Ivy** has been given the name **MALA MUJER** ('Bad Woman'). More often it is reserved for this rank-growing nettle spurge with large hand-shaped leaves. In any case it has reference to the unpleasant quality of giving a stinging nettle rash to the person touching the 'bad woman'.

It is fairly common in the tropical deciduous zone, where it reaches 6 to 8 ft. in height with an equal spread and large, drooping leaves.

Like other members of the spurge family it has milky sap and the typical pendant pistillate flowers in not-too-conspicuous flower clusters. Stinging hairs are present on the leaf surface and on the long leaf stalk.

Hungry Spurge
COJAMBOMÓ

Euphorbia schlechtendalii
EUPHORBIACEAE Spurge Family

NATIVE RANGE Mexico to Central America.

All euphorbias have a peculiar flower arrangement: a stalked pistillate flower surrounded by single-stamen florets among sticky glands, and the whole surrounded by (often colorful) bracts that look like petals. The poinsettia is a good example. Most have milky sap.

For the rest there is an enormous difference in habit, shape and size. This spurge has apparently four or five-parted yellowish-white "florets" in close clusters, the showy parts again being bracts. Leaves are small and in whorls. It is a small tree or shrub, never over 20 ft. tall, with reddish bark and abundant milky sap, which might be made into rubber except for the difficulty of separating the rosin.

Found in dryish spots of the Tropical Deciduous Zone.

MOUSE-KILLER

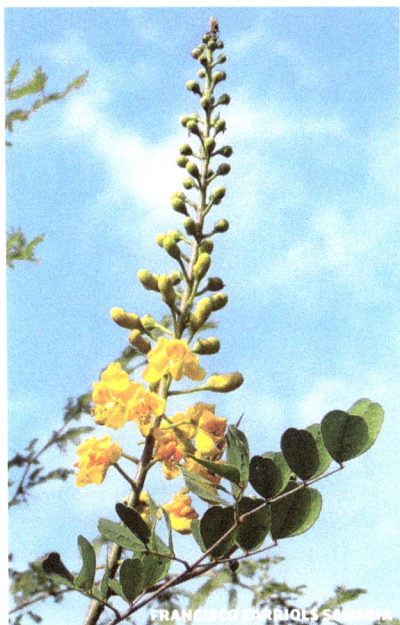

MEXICAN CAESALPINIA

Mexican Caesalpinia
RETAMILLA

Caesalpinia mexicana
FABACEAE Pea Family

NATIVE RANGE Texas, Mexico.

Showy yellow blossoms with attractive protruding stamens are apt to indicate Caesalpinia. One of the most decorative ones is the **Dwarf poinciana** (*Caesalpinia pulcherrima*, see p. 156). It has 5–11 pairs of leaflets.

Mexican Caesalpinia has less than five pairs of leaflets, which are almost circular in shape. The shrub is 6 ft. tall or over, and has flat pods. It occurs from Sinaloa to Tamaulipas and Guerrero; varies in different regions. **TABACHIN DEL MONTE** is another common name.

Mouse-killer
MATA RATÓN

Gliricidia sepium
FABACEAE Pea Family

NATIVE RANGE Mexico to Colombia.

Looking like a pink locust this small tree is bound to draw attention along the roadside. On being picked the pea-shaped flowers drop in large quantities. They are pink and white, fragrant, in long clusters. Seedpods are 4 to 6 in. long.

The tree is used for fencing (and sometimes called **Fence-post Tree**), having exceedingly durable wood (**MADERA NEGRA**), and as a shade tree for cacao plantations.

Bark and leaves, ground with cooked corn, are used for rat or mouse poison. Also poisonous to dogs, but cattle eat the leaves with immunity.

Widespread from Sinaloa to Veracruz, Yucatán and Chiapas, and into northern South America.

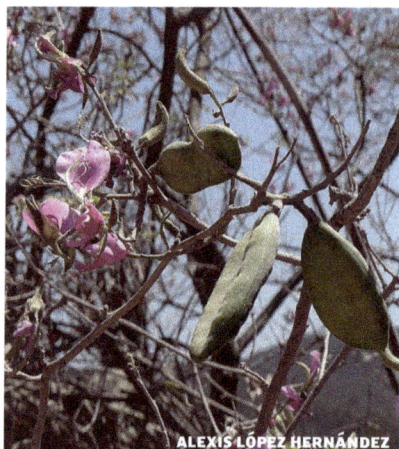

ALEXIS LÓPEZ HERNÁNDEZ

HAIL TREE

ANNIKA LINDQVIST

SAUSAGE TREE, STINKING TOE

Hail Tree
PALO GRANIZO

Harpalyce arborescens
FABACEAE Pea Family

NATIVE RANGE Mexico to Nicaragua.

This close relative of the Ironwood, Pink locust, and Mouse-killer can be distinguished, even without its hanging trusses of large pea-flowers, by its very odorous, leathery, definitely wrinkled leaves. The odor is due to numerous reddish or yellowish glands on the lower surface of the 7 to 11 leaflets. Pods are short and broad, of a reddish-black color, and rather conspicuous.

We failed to find out the reason for the name **PALO GRANIZO** (**GRANIZO** means hail).

Sausage tree, Stinking Toe
CUAFINOLE

Hymenaea courbaril
FABACEAE Pea Family

NATIVE RANGE Mexico to tropical South America.

When you are intrigued by seeing some reddish-brown "sausages" hanging from the ends of the twigs of a tall, large tree (up to 80 ft. with a trunk of 6 ft. with buttresses), the chances are you have come across this tree. Look for the glossy, evergreen, leathery leaves and see if they aren't arranged in twins. That will indicate the botanical name *Hymenaea* in allusion to the paired leaflets, 2 to 4 in. long. The name **COURBARIL** refers to its fragrant amber-like resin, also called American copal. This gum exudes from the trunk, and is found more abundantly in the roots.

Flowers are large, yellow, striped purplish, at end of twigs.

White Popinac Lead-tree
GUACIS

Leucaena leucocephala
FABACEAE Pea Family

NATIVE RANGE Mexico to Central America.

Many similar-looking trees and shrubs belong to the Acacia sub-family of the Pea family. Some have flowers in balls, others in elongated fluffy catkins; fruits generally resemble bean pods. The Thorn forest has many of them; others are at home in the Desert and Mesquite-Grassland zones. *Acaciella*, spread over many of the drier parts of Mexico, is always spineless, and has white, densely ball-shaped heads, and double-compound leaves;

EGOR DYUKAREV

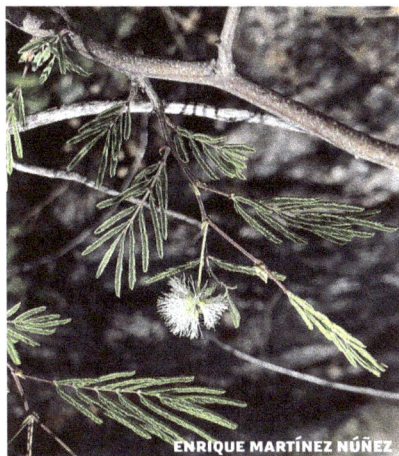
ENRIQUE MARTÍNEZ NÚÑEZ

WATSON BORDERPOD

Y. LIU

WHITE POPINAC LEAD-TREE

the pods are flat, bean-like, from 4 to 10 in. long, with transverse seeds.

Leucaena leucocephala, growing to 30 ft., has pods in green or brownish clumps hanging on at all seasons. Seeds are used for necklaces and sometimes eaten.

Watson Borderpod
Lysiloma watsonii
TEPEGUAJE
FABACEAE Pea Family

NATIVE RANGE Southern Arizona to northern Mexico.

Along canyons of Sonora and Chihuahua we are apt to become pleasantly aware of this picturesque shrub or low tree (over 25 ft.), projecting from the hillside, extending its horizontal, feathery branches far out from the trunk. Both leaves and twigs are densely hairy, the latter covered with small, wart-like bumps. Flowers are in dense, greenish-white balls; pods are 4 to 8 in. long, with heavy cordlike margins. The tree is in the same region as Trumpet tree.

Related, not quite so tall, and with non-hairy leaflets, is **Lysiloma divaricatum**, one of the most abundant trees in the Short-Tree Forest, less extensive in the Thorn Forest. Pods are ½ in. by 4½ in. White flowers in August.

Twin-flowered Senna
Senna pallida
RONRON
FABACEAE Pea Family

SYNONYM *Cassia biflora*
NATIVE RANGE Mexico to tropical South America.

Most species of Senna have showy yellow blossoms, almost regular, and no spines. The leaves are simple–compound. Even botanists find it difficult to tell the different species apart. *Senna pallida* is a slender shrub, 3–7 ft. tall, often found in the undergrowth

NEPTALÍ RAMÍREZ MARCIAL

TWIN-FLOWERED SENNA

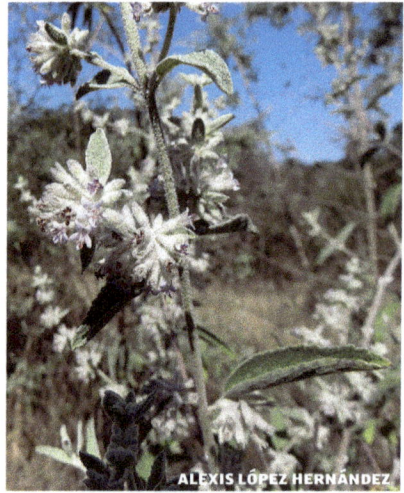

ALEXIS LÓPEZ HERNÁNDEZ

BUSHMINT

of deciduous tropical forests, especially where the ground has been disturbed. The showy yellow flowers bloom in pairs; notice the curved pistil. Pods are linear, 3–4 in. long. Leaflets are usually in four to eight pairs.

Since it is a persistent bloomer, from October to April, the traveler is almost sure to find it. It is widely distributed in tropical America, and also occurs in the Thorn Forest.

A number of other caesalpinias are found (several dozen); all are showy and all have double-compound leaves; the latter characteristic distinguishes them from the otherwise similar cassias.

Bushmint
Condea albida

SALVIA REAL
LAMIACEAE Mint Family

SYNONYM *Hyptis albida*
NATIVE RANGE Mexico.

Again and again, especially along the highways in Central Mexico, we are sure to notice a tall, white-hairy shrub, up to 6 ft. or more, that has all the earmarks of the Mint family (it is, indeed, used locally for flavoring food). Small, blue, two-lipped flowers are almost hidden in tight, hairy clusters along the square branches; they can be found from late fall to spring. It is one of the shrubby *Condea*; there are also a number of herbaceous ones. The popular name **SALVIA REAL** is rather misleading: it is neither a true salvia, nor royal-looking. **OREGANO** is another name. It is said to be good for earache and for rheumatic pains. A good bee plant.

Red Parrot Flower
Psittacanthus calyculatus

CHUJQUEN
LORANTHACEAE Showy Mistletoe Family

NATIVE RANGE Mexico to Venezuela.

A beautiful woody parasite on certain tropical trees, such as **Spanish plum** (*Spondias purpurea*) and *Vachellia pennatula*. It has handsome, large blossoms, red or orange, square stems, and opposite fleshy leaves. The places where the parasite enters the host plant swell and form star-shaped scars, looking like a decorative wooden flower afterwards.

The sticky fruits and stems are used for catching live birds, as its European relative mistletoe used to be (therefore called "bird-lime"). Nayarít to Chiapas and Yucatán. A common name for it is **MUERDAGO**, the Spanish name for mistletoe.

RED PARROT FLOWER

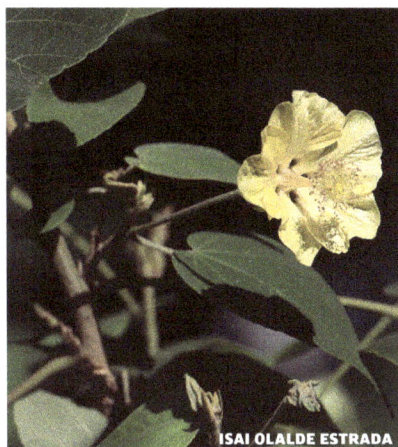

ISAI OLALDE ESTRADA

ABUTILON

Abutilon
CANASTILLA

Bakeridesia notolophium
MALVACEAE Mallow Family

SYNONYM *Abutilon notolophium*
NATIVE RANGE Mexico to Guatemala.

Imagine a golden-yellow cup-shaped flower with petals 1 in. long and, in the center, a yellow brush on a slender stalk. Place a number of them on a medium-sized shrub with decorative, heart-shaped leaves. Add a few broadly winged, basketlike fruit (like a "little canasta" according to its name), and you get an idea of this Mexican Abutilon, fully as lovely as the cultivated "Flowering Maple". You'll find it together with **Scarlet Hamelia** (p. 106), **Hail Tree** (p. 97), and **Tropical Blueberry** (p. 102).

Pricklenut
GUACIMO, CUAULOTE

Guazuma ulmifolia
MALVACEAE Mallow Family

NATIVE RANGE Mexico to tropical South America.

Except for the black, hard, prickly nut this medium-sized tree along arroyos would be hard to recognize, though fairly abundant in the secondary growth of the tropical forest. Its leaves are like those of an elm, in flat planes of rather heavy foliage, deciduous in spring. Flowers are small, fragrant, yellowish-green.

Reported from many parts of Mexico, often in company with the Morning-glory tree. It is said that this tree yields medicinal preparations, good for "endless types of sicknesses."

GIOVANA A. VALENCIA

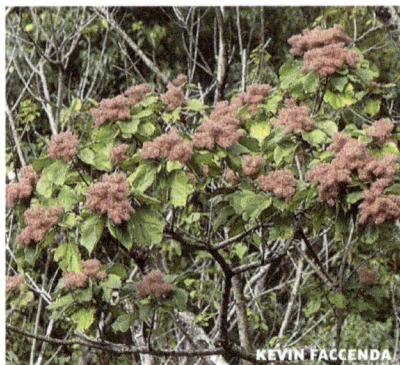

KEVIN FACCENDA

SUNFRUIT, WHITE MOJO

FRANCISCO FARRIOLS SARABIA

SILK COTTON TREE

Sunfruit, White Mojo
FRUITASOL, AGUAJPO, JONOTE
Heliocarpus americanus
MALVACEAE Mallow Family

SYNONYM *Heliocarpus tomentosus*
NATIVE RANGE Mexico to southern tropical South America.

Both the Spanish and the former Latin name indicate the outstanding characteristic of the fruit by which this medium-sized tree of the tropics can be recognized. The numerous bristles of the quantities of small fruits with red glands radiate from the center like the rays of the sun. When in bloom the flower trusses have a brownish appearance; individual florets are quite small.

Leaves are fairly large, alternate, with russet lower veins; they resemble those of the linden tree in whose family they belong.

This particular species is found most commonly in Puebla, Oaxaca and Veracruz. The other dozen or so species are spread over other tropical areas of Mexico. **JOLOCIN** (*Heliocarpus donnellsmithii*) of Tabasco, is known for its bark from whose fibers are produced paper and twine, so far on a small scale.

Silk Cotton Tree
CUAJILOTE, CLAVELLINA
Pseudobombax palmeri
MALVACEAE Mallow Family

SYNONYM *Bombax palmeri*
NATIVE RANGE Mexico.

Such broad-crowned, thick-trunked giants as the silk cotton trees just don't grow in the temperate zone! Often they have large buttresses at their base, anchoring the huge load. Many of these trees have a smooth, light-colored bark.

Flowers of *Pseudobombax*, coming out while the tree is leafless, are most spectacular, with petals well over 4 in. long, white in native trees, red in cultivated varieties, with numerous pink stamens, and later, pods bursting with brownish cotton.

Leaves are palmately compound, the leaflets broad in this species, narrower and stalked in **Pseudobombax ellipticum**, which grows farther south in more humid regions, where it is called **SOSPO**.

While it produces kapok, the true kapok of commerce comes from **Ceiba pentandra**, described in the Tropical Evergreen Forest on pp. 125.

Tropical Blueberry
LOLITO, CANALLITO, PUPU
Miconia xalapensis
MELASTOMATACEAE Melastome Family

SYNONYM *Conostegia xalapensis*
NATIVE RANGE Mexico to Colombia, Cuba.

EDUARDO A. BOLAÑOS VARGAS

TROPICAL BLUEBERRY

JUAN CARLOS FONSECA MATA

STRANGLER FIG

By far the most common representative of the Melastomataceae family (Greek for black-mouth, alluding to the color left in the mouth on eating the berries) is this Tropical Blueberry. It is a shrub or "awkward" small tree, with good-sized opposite leaves, easily recognized by their five curved veins running from top to bottom. Many leaves are brownish-hairy below, others vary in their hairiness. Small pink blossoms in plume-like clusters, each with 5 petals and 10 stamens. Buds open by a kind of cover-lid. Fruits are small but of good flavor, resembling blueberries, blue or purple. Common in tropical thickets.

Strangler Fig
MATAPALO, NACAPUL

Ficus cotinifolia
MORACEAE Mulberry Family

NATIVE RANGE Mexico to Central America.

Mexican figs, unlike the European edible fig, *Ficus carica*, have simple, unlobed leaves. All have milky sap which yields a kind of rubber. All have edible fruit, some too small and dry to be palatable for human taste.

Many are known by the common name **AMATE** in Mexico, from the Nahuatl **AMATL**, meaning paper. The ancient use of paper in pre-colonial days was connected with **BRUJERIA**, withcraft, and with native ceremonies. For its production the bark is stripped from the tree, treated in lye water, then washed, beaten, and dried in the sun. From early records we find that many thousands of rolls of paper were exacted as tribute to the government.

Many species of figs are "strangler figs"; the seed, sprouted in a crotch of its host, sends roots down and finally this epiphyte may strangle the host. It is not unusual to see a palm tree dying in this fatal embrace by a strangler fig. Examples of such figs are *Ficus obtusifolia*, *Ficus pertusa* (see p. 127) and *Ficus cotonifolia*.

Ficus cotonifolia is a gray-barked tree, which may reach a height of 45 ft. (generally less), with a thick trunk (3 ft.) and few branches. Often it sends out secondary roots from the trunk, enveloping whatever is in their way. It occurs in all but a few parts of Mexico.

NEPTALÍ RAMÍREZ MARCIAL

PINKWING

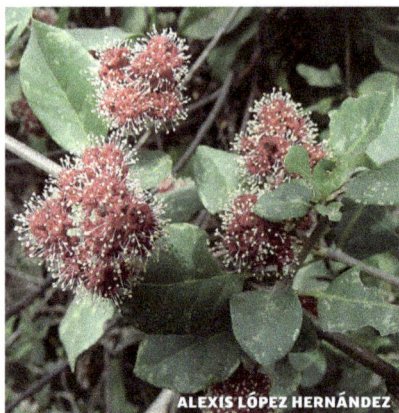

ALEXIS LÓPEZ HERNÁNDEZ

GARABATO

Garabato
BAINORO

Pisonia capitata
NYCTAGINACEAE Four-O'clock Family

NATIVE RANGE Southern Arizona to Mexico.

This relative of bougainvillea and four o'clock (*Mirabilis*) is a compact, spreading, spiny shrub forming dense thickets. It may climb around in other trees like a liana, up to 30 ft. above the ground. Small dark red flowers (February and March) on the male plants and brownish, sticky fruit on the female ones may help to identify it, together with the vicious curved spines and the opposite roundish leaves.

It is sometimes planted for the sake of creating a barrier on unwanted paths. Reported in sandy soil from Sonora to Tepic in canyon bottoms and arroyo margins, reaching into the Thorn Forest to a certain extent. Other names are **KALOKA, GARAMBULLO, GARABATO PRIETO**.

Pinkwing
CAMARÓN

Alvaradoa amorphoides
PICRAMNIACEAE Bitterbush Family

NATIVE RANGE Mexico to Central America, Florida to Cayman Islands.

It looks somewhat superficially, by its compound leaf and its hanging flower-truss, like a locust tree. But the small greenish or yellowish-white florets are regular, and the shrimp color which has suggested the Spanish name **CAMARÓN** for shrimp, comes later from the color of the numerous, winged fruit. That color makes one think of the seed clusters of Tree-of-heaven (*Ailanthus*).

Staminate and pistillate flowers occur on separate trees.

Common on rocky banks both in the Thorn Forest and the Short-Tree Forest.

Other names are **BEEZINIC-CHE** and **PALO DE HORMICA** (ant tree).

Pepper
CORDONCILLO, HOJA SANTA

Piper species
PIPERACEAE Pepper Family

NATIVE RANGE Tropical and subtropical areas worldwide.

There are over 2,400 species of *Piper* in the world. **Black pepper** (*Piper nigrum*) comes from the Old World tropics, **Cubeb** (*Piper cubeba*) from the East Indies, the **Betel nut** (*Piper betle*) from the Eastern tropics. The latter is chewed with lime, coloring teeth black.

The numerous species found in Mexican grow in moist tropical regions, especially in the southern part. Some are in very restricted areas, and it takes an expert botanist to

BLACK PEPPER

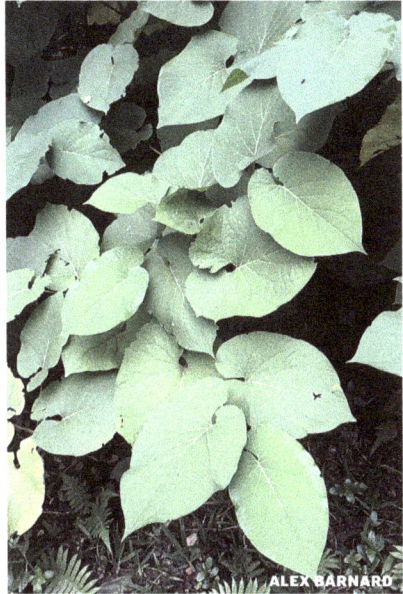

EARED PEPPER

tell them apart; classification is by the location of flower clusters and the number of stamens in each floret.

Eared Pepper
HIERBA SANTA

Piper auritum
PIPERACEAE Pepper Family

NATIVE RANGE Mexico to Guianas and Ecuador.

Easily distinguished by its leaves that are very unequal at the heart-shaped base (3½ in. wide), and by the swollen nodes of its stem. It is a shrub or small tree up to 25 ft. in height, sometimes planted at homes as a headache remedy and, in Veracruz, for seasoning tamales.

Coralvine
BELLISIMA

Antigonon leptopus
POLYGONACEAE Buckwheat Family

NATIVE RANGE Mexico to Central America.

One of the most highly ornamental tendril vines in the world is found in most parts of Mexico, both wild and cultivated. It may climb into the highest trees or clamber over shrubs. While losing its leaves in dry periods, its flowers draw attention: borne in festoons of delicate sprays which spring from the leaf axils; they are a bright rosy-red (and not coral-red as the name might indicate).

It forms edible tubers which may reach 15 lbs. in weight, nut-like in flavor. Also propagated from seed. The many names indicate is popularity: **ROSA DE MONTANA** (love chain), **CORONA DE LA REINA, ROSA DE MAYO, FLOR DE SAN DIEGO, SAN MIGUELITO.**

SCARLET HAMELIA

SWEETWOOD

Scarlet Hamelia
Hamelia patens
CORALILLO, SANGRE DE TORO
RUBIACEAE Madder Family
NATIVE RANGE Tropical and subtropical North and South America.

Comparatively few trees or shrubs have leaves occurring in threes from a node, as Hamelia does usually. Its flower clusters of narrow, tube-shaped, orange-red flowers, that stay on for lengthy periods, have suggested the name "firebush" and **CORALILLO**. Even the calyx and part of the flower stalk are reddish. Handsome black berries follow the blossoms; they are acidic but edible; the entire tree, at times, takes on a purplish hue. Fairly common tree or shrub up to 12 ft. tall. Another common name is **PIE DE PÁJARO**, meaning birds-foot.

Sweetwood
Xylosma flexuosa
BRUJO
SALICACEAE Willow Family
NATIVE RANGE Texas to northern Venezuela.

Xylos means wood, *osme* is odor, referring to the aromatic wood of some species. Long spines and red berries in April are the only outstanding characteristics of this small bushy tree of the Willow family. Leaves are somewhat holly-like. Flowers are small, yellowish and occur in close bunches; there are male and female trees. Other names are **HUICHICHILTEMEL, MANZANILLO**, 'little apple', (referring to the ¼ in. fleshy fruit), and **CORONILLA**.

Mullein Nightshade
Solanum erianthum
BERENJENA, SACA MANTECA
SOLANACEAE Potato Family
SYNONYM *Solanum verbascifolium*
NATIVE RANGE Tropical and subtropical North and South America.

This shrub or small tree, from 6 ft. up, is found in almost all regions of Mexico and extends farther south. Its large leaves (up to 10 in. long) are white woolly below, light yellowish above, alternate; branches are also felty-white. The many white blossoms are

KENGHUNG

MULLEIN NIGHTSHADE

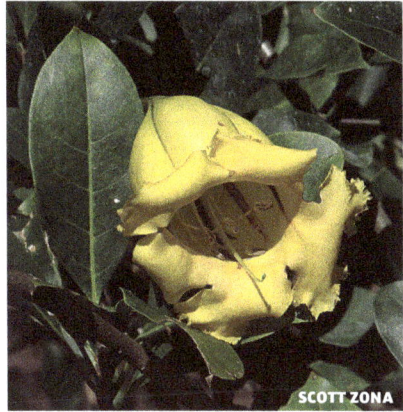

SCOTT ZONA

MILKCUP CHALICE VINE

produced in early winter; they are attractive—though small—and have red stamens. Their total flower cluster is whitish felty. Fruits are small and globe-shaped.

It is reported that the large leaves are used for washing dishes and as a hot compress to relieve headaches. Names are many, ranging from wild eggplant and wild tobacco (**BERENJENA CIMARRONA** and **TABACO CIMARRÓN**) to **GUARDOLOBO, XTUHUY, SOSA**, and **GALANTEA**.

Milkcup Chalice Vine
COPA DE ORO

Solandra grandiflora
SOLANACEAE Potato Family

SYNONYM *Solandra nitida*
NATIVE RANGE Central Mexico to Venezuela, Caribbean, Brazil.

This showy shrub or woody vine, native of tropical Mexico and south, is often culti-vated. In the jungle it may climb up to 60 ft. Its fragrant blossoms change from huge waxy buds to light cream to golden-yellow and finally to apricot orange, all in four days' time. Notice the dark brown lines inside the cup and the interesting way in which the corolla lobes fold back. Flowers are almost 9 in. in diameter and correspondingly deep. Leaves are from 3 to over 6 in. long, lustrous, and with long stalks.

Cup of gold (**COPA DE ORO**) is a natural designation for a number of yellow, cup-shaped flowers. **Golden Trumpet** (*Allamanda cathartica*) is likewise a woody vine (see p. 147), **Shellseed** (*Cochlospermum*) on p. 94 a small tree, **Luckynut** (*Cascabela*, p.120) of the Evergreen Forest, a shrub or small tree. In each case the leaves and the stamens are distinguishing marks.

Additional related species are described below.

NIGHTSHADES (*Solanum*)
SOLANACEAE Potato Family

It is not difficult to tell a solanum from other plants; the flowers are more or less wheel-shaped, with five well-defined lobes, often white, sometimes purple or yellow. The fruit is a roundish berry with two distinct cells. Many species have a distinctive "solanum" odor. The common "Irish" potato is a typical species.

Worldwide, there are over 1,200 species of *Solanum*, varying from herbs and shrubs to vines and trees. In addition to the potato, **Solanum tuberosum**, which originated in the Andes, well-known examples are the **eggplant**, from Asia and Africa, **Solanum melongena** (called **BERENJENA** in Mexico), and the **Jerusalem cherry**, *Solanum pseudocapsicum*, from the Old World, with its showy scarlet fruit. Mexico alone has well over 100 species, with both prickly and non-prickly types. Among the non-prickly kinds we should mention the vine from Brazil, **Solanum laxum** (see p. 169), the **black nightshade**, *Solanum nigrum*, and the **mullein nightshade**, *Solanum erianthum*, p. 106.

Among the prickly solanums we find the original host of the Colorado potato beetle, a yellow sprawling weed, usually called **Buffalo-bur**, *Solanum rostratum*. The solanums described below, often with showy flowers, are difficult to identify positively:

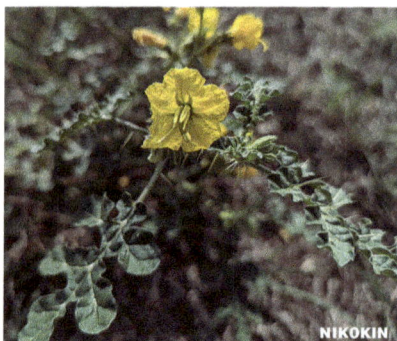

NIKOKIN

BUFFALO-BUR

A yellowish-white flower, between Salina Cruz and Oaxaca, thornless, with simple leaves, apparently **Solanum pubigerum**, called **HIERBA DEL PERRO**.

A white thorny plant east of Veracruz, common, called **SOSA** in Mexico, apparently **Solanum torvum**.

Small, orange-colored fruit on very prickly stems, also with many prickles on the underside of the leaves: **Solanum asperolanatum**. It is likewise called **SOSA** in Michoacan and Guerrero. It was collected in dry areas in Nayarít, near trees of Sabal palm.

Purple-colored solanums are found in both the northwestern and southern dry regions of Mexico: **Solanum hindsianum** from the neighborhood of Guaymas; it has simple leaves and prickles, and large blossoms. A very prickly lobed-leaf kind is also found. A strikingly large-and-yellow-fruited solanum with prickles on both stems and leaves was found north of Ciudad Victoria. Its leaf is much lobed and stalkless; probably **Solanum refractum**.

Solanum diversifolium, as its name indicates, has variable leaves. Blossoms are white or bluish, fruit up to ½ in. in diameter; throughout Mexico.

Solanum candidum, is a coarse giant, with leaves well over a foot long, and branches

CSTOBIE

SOLANUM MAMMOSUM

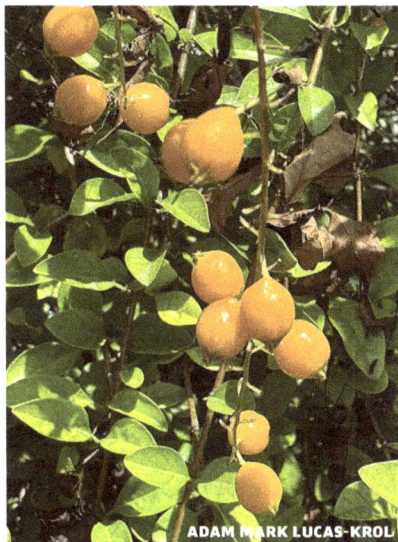

SKYFLOWER, PIGEONBERRY

with dense, long, stout prickles; fruit covered with fine, golden hair.

Solanum mammosum, (**CHICHIGUITA**), has leaves nearly as broad as long, 4–6 in., long stout prickles, large purple flowers, large orange fruit, pear-shaped with five smaller nipples at the base.

Solanum macranthum (or *Solanum crinitum*), sometimes called **Potato-tree**, has beautiful large pale lavender blossoms with darker stripes, up to 1½ in. broad; it is a climbing shrub with yellowish-brown prickles.

Skyflower, Pigeonberry

Duranta erecta

VELO DE VIUNDA

VERBENACEAE Verbena Family

NATIVE RANGE Mexico to northern South America, Caribbean.

Few ornamentals produce handsome flowers and fruit at the same time, almost continuously, as does this widespread tropical evergreen shrub (up to 15 ft. tall) with lavender flowers and persistent golden berries. For that reason it is frequently cultivated and is considered one of the most beautiful shrubs in Mexico (with or without spines).

Its branches are four-angled and are inclined to droop gracefully, especially when weighted down by its waxy berries. Its five-parted flowers are apt to be somewhat irregular, ½ in. in diameter, with two darker lines on two of its lobes; throat yellow.

A white variety is called **VELO DE NOVIA** (Sweetheart's veil), as distinguished from the Widow's veil (**VELO DE VIUDA**) when blue. Other names are **LLUVIA** (rain), **ADONIS MORADO, CELOSA** (jealous lady), **ESPINA BLANCA** (white-spine), **CÓLERA** (rage) **DE NOVIO** (bridegroom), **ZARZA, XCAMBOCOCHE**, Golden dewdrop.

Reported from Baja California and Sinaloa to Chiapas, Puebla, Veracruz and Yucatán.

Savanna and Flat Coastal Region

Due to their relatively small area, we are lumping together some plant zones that strictly speaking, could be further separated. In addition to the Savanna proper we are adding the **MANGLARES** and **PALMARES**, the Mangrove Woodland and the Sabal Palm groves.

The name Savanna is of Caribbean origin, referring to the flat coastal plains along both Mexican coasts in tropical and subtropical regions. A few interior marshy basins have a similar character. Extreme changes in groundwater levels—from marshy to dry—make plant growth unique; drainage is generally poor. The result is a cover of coarse tropical grasses with some scattered trees. Many of the latter have twisted trunks, roots that penetrate to great depths, and leaves that are leathery to withstand periods of drought.

During the dry season the grass gets so inflammable that the slightest spark will start a savanna fire; smoke clouds will appear like huge layers of fog, darkening the sky. It is likely that more trees would gradually invade the savanna if fire were kept in control. Uncontrolled, the barren area is enlarged year by year, leaving isolated islands of trees.

Dominant trees of the Savanna, which has a rainfall ranging from 34 to 100 inches, are **Gourd tree** (or **Calabash**, *Crescentia alata*), **Pickle tree** (*Byrsonima crassifolia*), *Curatella americana*, and *Vachellia pennatula*. In the isolated "islands" mentioned before, we find *Microdesmia arborea*, *Hymenaea courbaril*, (p. 97), *Bursera simaruba*, and *Andira inermis*. **Figs** follow watercourses.

The **Gourd tree** is easily recognized by its large round fruit, as large as a small grapefruit, growing tight on the larger limbs (see p. 113). **Pickle trees** might be recognized by their beautiful clusters of yellow flowers, turning reddish, followed by bunches of fleshy yellow fruit (see p. 115). *Curatella* is a small, crooked tree, somewhat resembling an oak in its general aspect; large, rough, hard leaves, inverted egg-shaped, are used as a substitute for sandpaper; numerous ill-scented white flowers, small fruits.

In spots the only tree is the **Oaxaca palmetto** (*Sabal mexicana*, see p. 113) with fan-shaped leaves; it can stand periods of prolonged drought.

All along the coast we find **coconut trees**, in many places wild, in others cultivated. On sandy seashores the interesting **Seagrape** (*Coccoloba uvifera*) should be looked for. Its round, large and thick leaves, often with a red midvein, are unique (see p. 116), as are its long trusses of edible grape-like fruit.

For representatives of the Mangrove Woodland see **Mangroves, Red** (p. 116) and **Black**, (p. 111), and **Stinkwood** on p. 114, (not to be confused with another tree of that unsavory name, *Gustavia*, an evergreen from Brazil). *Annona glabra*, **Pond apple** or **Alligator apple**, a poor relative of Custard apple, p. 146, is also found here.

Farther from the coast we may find magnificent palm groups; the tallest and most showy being the **Cohune palm** (*Attalea cohune*, p. 111). The spiny *Cryosophila nana*, and **Pishan** (*Brahea calcarea*), **broompalm**, are in the mountains.

Depending on the adjoining vegetation zones we may find other representatives in the savanna region. Some of the savannas have developed gradually at the expense of the Pine-Oak Forest, the Tropical Evergreen Forest, or the Thorn Forest. Thus we find the **Bullhorn acacia** (*Vachellia cornigera*, p. 64) in the savanna, *Hymenaea courbaril* (p. 97), and the beautiful **Guiana chestnuttree** (*Pachira aquatica*, p. 115, 167). Even the striking **Yellowsilk shellseed** (*Cochlospermum vitifolium*, p. 94), may occasionally be found; it is not typical of the savanna proper.

COHUNE PALM

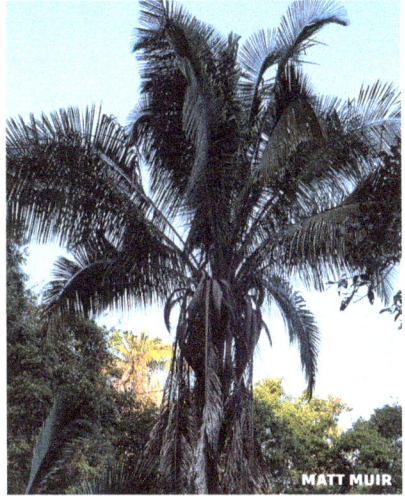

BLACK MANGROVE

Black Mangrove
MANGLE PRIETO

Avicennia germinans
ACANTHACEAE Acanthus Family

SYNONYM *Avicennia nitida*
NATIVE RANGE Southeastern U.S.A. to South America.

In addition to *Rhizophora*, Mangrove swamps (along both coasts) are apt to have *Avicennia*, *Conocarpus* and *Laguncularia*. Leaves are similar (leathery) in all, though the latter two belong to the Combretum family (Combretaceae) and *Avicennia* to the now placed in the Acanthus family (formerly in Verbenaceae). Strangely enough, it is called both white and black mangrove (**MANGLE BLANCO** and **MANGLE PRIETO OR NEGRO**). It does not have "stilt-roots" but sends out vertical rootlets above the water to breathe. Seeds, as in *Rhizophora*, may sprout while on the tree. On falling they are kept afloat until finding a likely place to grow, along the shoreline. Flowers are small, white, and contain much nectar. The tree (up to 75 ft. tall) is often lopped for firewood, reducing it to low shrubs.

Conocarpus has alternate leaves and clusters of persistent, round fruit, *Laguncularia* has oblong, leathery, 10-ribbed fruits.

Cohune Palm
COQUITO DE COLIMA

Attalea cohune
ARECACEAE Palm Family

SYNONYM *Orbignya cohune*
NATIVE RANGE Southern Mexico to Honduras, Colombia.

This is the tallest and most showy of all Mexican palms (*attalus* means magnificent). Its leaves are over 20 ft. in length. Fruit resembles a small coconut 2½ in. long, much eaten by cattle; its seeds are used for human food, especially for sweets. They contain 50% oil, which is used for soap, candles and machine oil. Flowers have a heavy, unpleasant odor. Trunk and leaves are spineless, unlike some related genera such as *Acrocomia* and *Astrocaryum*, both armed with vicious, needle-like spines. In Chiapas *Attalea* is locally known as **COROZO**.

COHUNE PALM

COCONUT PALM

Cohune palms grow generally at low levels where the ground water is near the surface, in tropical regions from San Blas to Guatemala and Yucatán. A very useful palm whose leaves are used for thatch, trunks for building purposes, buds and seeds for food, young leaves for making hats. Also known as **GUACOYUL, MANZANILLO, COYOL, PALMA REAL, MONACO,** and other names.

Bactris is lower, generally spiny. **Date palms** (*Phoenix dactylifera,* introduced) are common in the states of Sonora and Sinaloa. See below for **Coconut palm**, for **Mexican sabal** see pp. 113.

Chamaedorea is a large genus, imperfectly known, of slender, shade-loving palms, most of them in the mountainous tropical region. Stems are mostly ringed or jointed like reeds. Leaves may be slender, with few divisions, or even like a fish-tail (*Chamaedorea ernesti-augusti*).

Coconut Palm
COCOTERO

Cocos nucifera
ARECACEAE Palm Family

NATIVE RANGE Central Malaysia to southwestern Pacific.; introduced in southern Mexico and northern South America.

In Mexico, the coconut palm is the best known and most important of all palms, widely distributed along both coasts, as far north as climate permits: it prefers an average temperature of 78º F. and an elevation less than 650 ft., according to Martinez.

Once we become familiar with the typical slant of the trunk, enlarged at the base, the feathery leaves and the clumps of fibrous large fruits just below the crown of its leaves, there is no mistaking it. The trunks are used for building dwellings and rafts, the leaves for roofs, the shells of the nuts for cups, the meat for food and for **DULCES** (candies), the milk for a drink and for medicine, and even the sap from trunk and inflorescence is made into **TUBA,** an intoxicating drink.

GOURD TREE

OAXACA PALM, MEXICAN FAN PALM

Oaxaca Palm, Mexican Fan Palm
PALMA REAL

Sabal mexicana
ARECACEAE Palm Family

NATIVE RANGE Southern Texas to Central America.

Often found in extensive, though not dense, groves (**PALMARES**) , this fan palm makes us realize that palms are not necessarily confined to tropical places of high rainfall. Its trunk may grow to a height of 30 to 50 ft., at first covered with the persistent leaf stalks, later becoming naked.

The greenish blossoms are found in thin, much-branched clusters arising from the top of the tree. Black fruit about ⅓ in. in diameter, flattened, ball-shaped.

A close relative is *Sabal palmetto*, commonly planted in southern portions of the United States as a shade and avenue tree.

Gourd Tree
CUAUTECOMATE, MORRO

Crescentia alata
BIGNONIACEAE Trumpet-Creeper Family

NATIVE RANGE Mexico to Central America.

The large fruit of this tree resemble a green grapefruit on heavy limbs of what at first glance looks like a "mulberry tree". Leaves have a most interesting winged-cross pattern: a sure way of identifying it.

The peculiar fruit is first olive green, then turns brownish as it gets hard and light. It is reported that the rind, from early times, was used for making **JICARAS** (chocolate cups), decorated artistically and provided with gold handles, so beautiful that "the king himself could drink out of them without repugnance".

Sandboxtree
HABILLA DE SAN IGNACIO

Hura polyandra
EUPHORBIACEAE Spurge Family

NATIVE RANGE Mexico to Central America, Ecuador.

Rather widespread large tree (45 ft. tall), often planted, with a broad crown and sharp, cone-shaped spines on young trunk and branches. It belongs to the Spurge family, having copious milky sap, irritating to the skin. For that reason special precaution has to be taken when a tree is cut for its attractive wood.

Leaves deciduous, smooth, with long stalks. Flowers are of two types, on the same tree: the staminate on a long stalk, the pistillate like a showy octopus. The latter changes into a 3 in. pumpkin-like fruit, which explodes with much force when ripe, scattering its

SANDBOXTREE

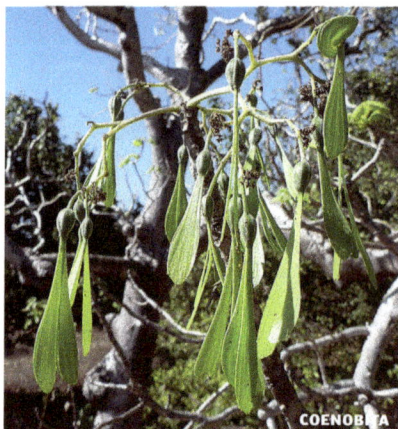

STINKWOOD, PROPELLER TREE

seeds widely (its Aztec name **QUAUHTLATLATZII** means explosive tree). The seeds are poisonous. On the west coast the poisonous milk is used for stupefying fish.

The name **Sandboxtree** dates from the time when fine sand was used for blotting ink: the empty pumpkin was its container.

Other native names are **CHICOMUSELO, JABILLA, HABA**.

Stinkwood, Propeller Tree
SAN FELIPE

Gyrocarpus americanus
HERNANDIACEAE Mago Family

NATIVE RANGE Central Mexico to Venezuela.

In the marshy region not far from the savanna country proper I came across a twig with a number of two-winged fruits. It was enough to be recognized as "stink-wood", even without its smelly leaves. The wings are almost a foot long, evidently ideal for seed dispersal and self-planting.

The tree is up to 60 ft. tall, with smooth, whitish bark. Leaves are quite large, 12 in. wide or more, with three to five lobes and heart-shaped base, alternate with long leaf-stalks. Flowers small, greenish, unisexual. Wood soft, white and very light, used locally for making drums, toys and light boxes; takes paint and varnish well.

Found commonly in swampy deciduous forests. Also called **QUITLACOCTLI, BABÁ, XKIS**, or **CUS**.

The tree belongs to the Hernandia family, named after the first important, very capable plant collector in Mexico, Francisco Hernandez (died January 28, 1578).

Beetlesage Cuphea
CLAMERIA

Cuphea jorullensis
LYTHRACEAE Loosestrife Family

NATIVE RANGE Mexico.

An older name, *Parsonsia tricolor*, had reference to the orange-red "flower", 1½ in. long, (really a calyx), which becomes first pale-yellow and then white toward its mouth. About 10 stamens show from this opening, together with the small white petals. The plant is a shrubby perennial, rough-hairy, much-branched, about 2½ ft. high. Leaves are opposite, flowers borne in a one-sided spike. The cultivated **Cigar-flower** is *Cuphea ignea,* also from Mexico. The name *jorullensis* is derived from the fact that it was described from the now extinct volcano Jorullo in Michoacan. In general it is found together with **NANCHE** and some acacias, in the arid lower tropical regions.

BEETLESAGE CUPHEA

JULIEN RENOULT

PICKLE TREE

GUILLERMO HUERTA RAMOS

Pickle Tree
NANCE

Byrsonima crassifolia
MALPIGHIACEAE Barbados-Cherry Family

NATIVE RANGE Mexico to tropical South America.

Medium-sized or small tree with opposite, broadly elliptic evergreen leaves, yellowish underneath. Yellow, rather pretty flowers in long clusters, turning red in age. Fleshy, yellow fruit with a sour fermented taste, used raw with salt, in soups, sweets and pickles or for stuffing meat; it is offered for sale in the marketplace. The name **NANTIZINZOCOTL** means 'sour fruit for mothers and aged'.

Guiana Chestnut, Shaving-brush Tree
ZAPOTE DE AGUA

Pachira aquatica
MALVACEAE Mallow Family

NATIVE RANGE Mexico to southern tropical South America.

Imagine an ethereal white blossom topping a small tree with its feet in the water. The flower is almost 1 ft. long, with numerous delicate stamens in the center, and the five petals gracefully curved back. The flower may have a pinkish tint and the stamens are reddish brown: a truly beautiful sight. Leaves are also decorative: usually of seven leaflets attached to a slender stalk; they measure about 10 in. across.

Since it reminds one of a huge shaving brush with the buds appearing like a shaving stick, the flower was humorously remembered as belonging to the "Shaving-brush Tree".

ALEXIS LÓPEZ HERNÁNDEZ

MADELEINE CLAIRE

EGOR DYUKAREV

SEA GRAPE

The flowers show up best in the morning and in the early part of spring, when the leaves have not yet appeared. The fruit is large, 7–15 in. long, light brown or grayish. When it opens up, at maturity, the seeds float in the water until germination.

Sea Grape
UVA DE MAR

Coccoloba uvifera
POLYGONACEAE Buckwheat Family

NATIVE RANGE Florida to Peru, Caribbean to northern South America.

A small seashore tree, up to 45 ft., of crooked but ornamental habit, easily identified by its large, thick, circular leaves with red veins; they may be 5 to 7 in. wide. Slender spikes of small, fragrant, white flowers are borne above the leaves; they are followed by strands of edible, reddish-purple, pear-shaped berries, ½ in. and over in diameter; they are somewhat sour and astringent.

The wood is hard, dark brown and takes a good polish. In Central America it is valued highly for cabinet work. It resembles in color that of **MADROÑO**, but is stronger.

During the early colonial wars, when paper and ink were scarce, the Spaniards used the leaves of sea grape like paper. Messages were scratched into the leaf surface, the letters resembling white scratches. They could then be dispatched by the Indians.

Other names are Platter-leaf, **UVA DE LA PLAYA** (beach), **NIICHE, PAPATURRO, CARNERO**. There are a number of other *Coccoloba* species, and a related herbaceous groundcover may be found in similar places, with stalked leaves and single berries.

Red Mangrove
MANGLE

Rhizophora mangle
RHIZOPHORACEAE Red Mangrove Family

NATIVE RANGE Southern Florida to tropical South America.

This is one of those fairytale trees, that "walk on stilts through the marshes". Its name, *Rhizophora*, means root-bearing, refers to the seed germinating while still attached to the tree, and before it drops to start its new plant.

Leaves are evergreen, opposite, tough, dark-green, of an elliptic shape like so many tropical trees. Flowers are also leathery, fair-sized, yellow, of four parts with 8 to 12 stamens, blooming in late summer. Wood is reddish-brown, heavy. New roots form on the lower end of trunks, growing down into the marsh and acting as stilts, which again help to catch debris. In this way the shoreline is extended.

RED MANGROVE

Jamaica Feverplant
ABROJO

Tribulus cistoides
ZYGOPHYLLACEAE Creosote-Bush Family

NATIVE RANGE Introduced in southern Mexico and Central America.

A pretty yellow blossom on a delicate vine or groundcover on sandy beaches in the tropics is apt to draw our attention. It may lose its appeal when our bare feet come in contact with its sharp-pointed seedpods. It is a close relative of the **Puncture weed** (*Tribulus terrestris*) dreaded by children on some playgrounds.

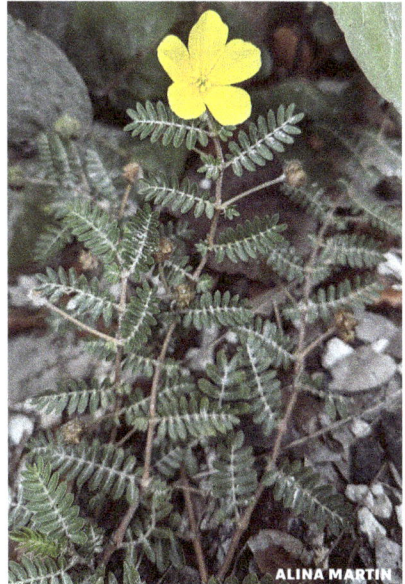

JAMAICA FEVERPLANT

Tropical Evergreen Forest

Now we are really in the tropics! Here you will find yourself surrounded by tall broadleaved evergreen trees, palms, ferns, huge leaf shapes, lianas (vines), and more. This happens, for instance, when you arrive in Tamazunchale, having come in from the north on the Pan-American Highway. Again you experience the same exhilaration of being overwhelmed by lush plants on going to Veracruz from Mexico City or Pachuca, upon crossing the Isthmus of Tehuantepec on the highway, and in a few places on the Pacific Coast.

No distinction here between winter cold and summer heat, only a change from the rainy to the dry season, with perhaps some change in plant growth, but never a total dormancy.

The humid tropical region of lower altitude in Mexico logically divides itself into three different vegetation zones, based mostly on rainfall:

• The **RAINFOREST** with the highest rainfall and the most luxuriant growth of broadleaved evergreen trees (see pp. 132).

• The **TROPICAL EVERGREEN FOREST**, a little less humid, with dense but lower stands of evergreen trees, with a few losing their foliage during a brief period of drought.

• The **SAVANNA** and neighboring coast area with the least rainfall (34 to 100 inches annually), and limited to flat coastal plains, as described on pp. 110.

There is no hard and fast line between Rainforest and Tropical Evergreen Forest: one intergrades with the other, and species typical of rainforest occur in the Tropical Evergreen Forest, though in fewer numbers and only in certain areas.

There is a little more area in the Mexican rainforest (7.3% of the total land surface) than in the Tropical Evergreen Forest (5.5%), but the former is much more inaccessible by automobile, and you have to make special exploration trips to see it. A good chance to study plants from both zones is in the Botanic Garden at Tuxtla Gutierrez, with well-kept and well-labeled specimens.

SELVA is the Mexican word for this evergreen forest, as distinguished from the **BOSQUES** of temperate zones. The latter have comparatively few dominant trees, all deciduous, with few exceptions.

In the **SELVA** we find many tropical trees that do not have well-known common names, except locally. Here are colorful epiphytes like **orchids** and **bromeliads**, that live on trees but not off them—they are not parasites. And here, from tree to tree, is a veritable maze of climbing plants — **lianas** — some of them almost like trees themselves. Often, on examining a beautiful flower, it becomes difficult to tell which belongs to the tree itself, and which to an epiphyte or a climbing vine. (Yes, and there are also a few real parasites among them, with gorgeous flowers).

The Tropical Evergreen Forest can be considered as a transition between the dripping rainforest and relatively drier zones like savanna and tropical deciduous forest regions. Some of it, in fact, may be a transitional formation, caused by human intervention during centuries of cutting.

In other words, it is now mostly a secondary scrub forest in which some of the following trees predominate: *Ficus, Cedrela, Cecropia, Apeiba, Ceiba, Lonchocarpus*.

Tree heights range from 25 feet to 70 ft. Below the more or less dense canopy grow number of shrubs, palms, and perennial herbs.

To a person from a temperate zone, where plant leaves remain of "temperate" sizes and shapes, it is quite an experience to be suddenly confronted with a "Poor Man's Raincoat" (**CAPA DE POBRE**), *Gunnera insignis*, having up to 5- or 6-foot leaves with beautifully modeled lobes. (They are being introduced into ornamental gardens all over the world).

Then there is another giant-leaf, hanging down, smooth and shiny. It is an **Anthurium** species, called **CONTE CINCO DEDOS**, "Five-finger-eating-plant," which is big enough and neat enough to serve as a dining cloth.

Monstera deliciosa, with the common name of Ceriman, but often referred to as a philodendron, is almost as gigantic. It is well-known as a tropical houseplant.

The "leaf that weeps blood" (**LLORA SANGRE**), *Bocconia arborea* and *Bocconia frutescens*, with large triangular lobes (p. 128) and orange sap, a large-leaf plant, shows up again and again along the highway, once you come to recognize it. Soon you begin to look for it by the large trusses of flowers topping the plant. Its juice has a toxic quality which makes its use possible as a quick local anaesthetic.

Another enormous leaf should be mentioned, though it seems to prefer somewhat drier locations: it surprises one by peeking out of dry rock walls along the road, even out of masonry structures. It is not as beneficial a plant as the previous ones mentioned: one of its local names is **QUEMADORA**, the burning plant, another **ORTIGA** or nettle. Both names refer to the unpleasant stinging hairs covering the plant. If you decide to pick one of its leaves, you'll be sorry for some time after, depending on how susceptible you are to this nettle rash. Anyway, the leaves are so large there is hardly room enough in the car for it and passengers as well; the dusky violet flowers are not much to boast about. Its scientific name is *Wigandia urens* (see p. 122).

LEAF GIANTS
Anthurium and Gunnera

Tropical plants thrive on moisture and an even, warm temperatures; where the two are combined we can expect prodigious growth. We may find these leaf-giants in clearings of the evergreen tropical forests, the rainforest and higher into the cloud forest.

Anthurium (*not illustrated*)   *Anthurium titanium*
CONTE CINCO DEDOS   ARACEAE Arum Family
NATIVE RANGE Mexico (Southeastern Chiapas), western Guatemala.

Anthurium have found their way into house plant favorites, some for their showy red flower spathes that look as if they had been varnished (called Flaming flowers), some for their equally striking leaves. Worldwide there are over 1,300 species.

Anthurium titanium has enormous, glossy, "upside-down", vertical leaves. The name **CONTE** comes from the Tzeltal language, meaning **COME-BOCA** ('eat-mouth'); it is used for other plants as well, like *Philodendron* and *Monstera*. The **CINCO DEDOS** have to do with five fingers.

Gunnera   *Gunnera insignis*
CAPA DE POBRE   GUNNERACEAE Giant-Rhubarb Family
NATIVE RANGE Nicaragua to Panama.

The Spanish name, 'Poor Man's Coat', refers to the use that is made of the leaf in a sudden tropical shower. This highly decorative perennial grows up to 6 ft. tall and has roundish, much-lobed leaves 3 to 6 ft. wide. Reddish flower clusters are hidden below these leaves. Fruits are small fleshy stone fruits. In disturbed soil of tropical evergreen forest, extending to the cloud forest. The cultivated *Gunnera manicata* is still more spectacular, the crown of leaves measuring 25 to 35 ft. across.

GUNNERA

Bomarea
YATZÍ

Bomarea acutifolia
ALSTROEMERIACEAE Parrot-Lily Family

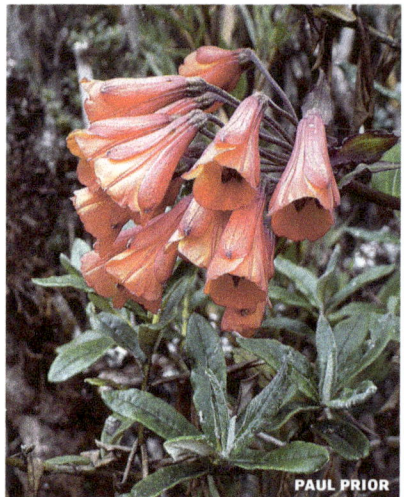

NATIVE RANGE North-central Mexico to Central America.

A conspicuous twining plant with pink and green flowers in large terminal, pendant clusters, somewhat like an amaryllis. It is found in shady woodlands, not only in this zone but also in oak-woods and in the tropical deciduous zone. Its tuberous roots are edible, and in Chile, starch is made from them. Many Bomareas have short twisted flower stalks. Some are cultivated as pot-plants.

The name YATZÍ is derived from YA (excrement) and TZÍ (dog), not a compliment to its smell. Widespread, but not abundant in most places; fairly plentiful in the Valley of Mexico.

Luckynut
CODO DE FRAILE, CHILCA

Cascabela thevetia
APOCYNACEAE Dogbane Family

SYNONYM *Thevetia peruviana*
NATIVE RANGE Mexico to southern tropical South America.

This tropical yellow trumpet flower is of lighter color and more informal character than the cultivated **Golden Trumpet**, *Allamanda* (p. 147). Like it, it is often grown in gar-

LUCKYNUT

CERIMAN

dens; but it is found native in San Luis Potosi, Tamaulipas, and from Veracruz south, either as a shrub or as a small tree to 25 ft. tall. Leaves narrow with interesting markings; sap milky, poisonous, as are the seeds.

Tradition says that carrying the seeds in your pocket brings good luck and good health, and a cure for whatever ails you. **CODO DE FRAILE** means friar's elbow, referring to the fruit. **Yellow oleander** is another name for it.

Ceriman
PIÑANONA
Monstera deliciosa
ARACEAE Arum Family

NATIVE RANGE Mexico (Veracruz, Oaxaca, Chiapas) to Guatemala.

It's an amazing experience to meet our well-known houseplant with large, shiny, perforated leaves, rambling wild in the tropical jungle, pushing out aerial roots, blooming like a yellow calla lily, and producing edible fruit. Its roots are tough enough to be used as rope and for the making of hats, chair seats, baskets.

Ceriman grows to 18 ft. long, the leaf blades to 20 in. broad, the flowering "spadix" is 7 to 8 in. long. It is believed that the holes in the leaf help protect it from being torn in the wind.

Philodendron
MUTUSAY
Philodendron radiatum
ARACEAE Arum Family

NATIVE RANGE Mexico to Colombia.

Philodendrons are so well-known as house plants that all plant lovers are apt to recognize them. The name means tree-lover, a most appropriate name, since most of them are climbing epiphytes growing on and around the tropical evergreen trees.

Philodendron are relatives of Jack-in-the-pulpit, as their flower arrangement shows. This philodendron has very large, leathery-fleshy leaves, much-lobed. Its abundant aerial roots are very flexible and tough, and therefore often used as a tying material.

RICARD BUSQUETS REVERTE

PHILODENDRON

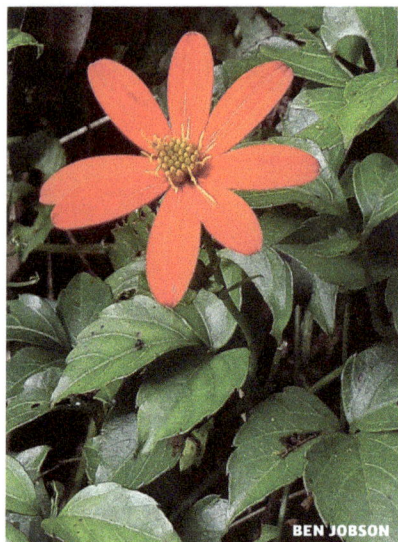

BEN JOBSON

CLIMBING DAHLIA

Since they naturally grow in the dark lower story of the tropical evergreen forest, they survive in deep shade and high humidity.

Climbing Dahlia
DALIA

Hidalgoa ternata
ASTERACEAE Aster Family

NATIVE RANGE Mexico to Central America, Ecuador.

In the evergreen forest we may be suddenly attracted by a vibrant, orange-scarlet blossom up in a tree, resembling a single type of dahlia. On investigation it proves to be a climbing vine, with opposite, compound leaves, again similar to a dahlia. It climbs by means of the leaf stalk, often coiled at the base. Leaflets have reddish brown-tipped teeth. *Hidalgoa* is closely related to *Dahlia* and *Coreopsis*, but it has fertile ray flowers.

Wigandia
ORTIGA GRANDE, QUEMADORA

Wigandia urens
BORAGINACEAE Borage Family

SYNONYM *Wigandia caracasana*
NATIVE RANGE Mexico to Trinidad and Peru.

Once you have begun to recognize this coarse, large-leaved, violet-flowered shrub or small tree, it peers at you from the most unlikely overhanging rocks, or old walls, usually where dryish and warm. Leaves are as large as 3 ft., and covered with stinging hairs like nettles, most unpleasant for a long time after touching it.

ORTIGA GRANDE means 'large nettle', **QUEMADORA** is 'stinger'. Flowers are violet with a white tube.

Prodigious Bromeliad
TECOLUMATE

Tillandsia prodigiosa
BROMELIACEAE Airplant Family

NATIVE RANGE Mexico.

Most bromeliads, like most orchids, are air-plants or "epiphytes", living on trees but not off them; a few live on the ground. This species has leaf stalks with a red base, dark red flower spikes and blue tips (see also *Tillandsia imperialis* on p. 134). Seeds are carried in the air by means of soft hairs, and start new plants, often in crotches or on branches

WIGANDIA

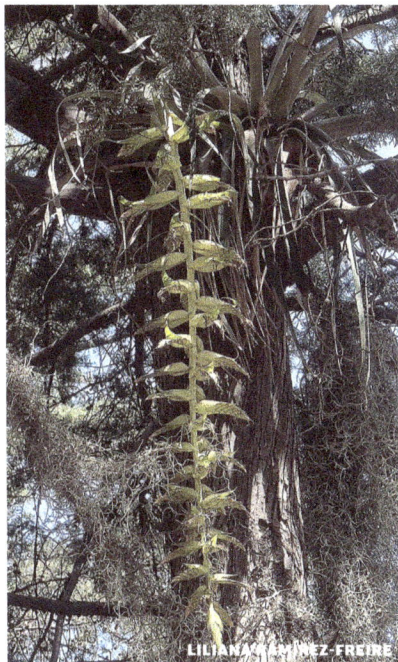

PRODIGIOUS BROMELIAD

of trees—especially in the tropics—but sometimes in oak forests. Since the leaves are in a tight cluster, water collects after a rain, available for thirsty travelers. Spanish moss, is *Tillandsia usneoides*; Pineapple, *Ananas comosus*, also belongs to the Bromeliad family.

Coralbean
COLORÍN
Erythrina americana
FABACEAE Pea Family
SYNONYM *Erythrina coralloides*
NATIVE RANGE Mexico.

The name draws attention to its bright red flowers and seeds. Even the name *Erythrina* comes from the Greek for "red". *Erythrina* are small tropical trees or shrubs, much used for ornamental planting on account of their blooms, although most of them blossom while the leaves are off.

The coral beans are often gathered and used for beads. A paralyzing extract is used for "lazy fishing". On account of the spiny branches, coralbeans are often planted as hedges. Leaves look like a large cloverleaf with blunted points. A common name **PITO** (whistle) refers to the use children make of the flowers.

FRANCELI MACEDO

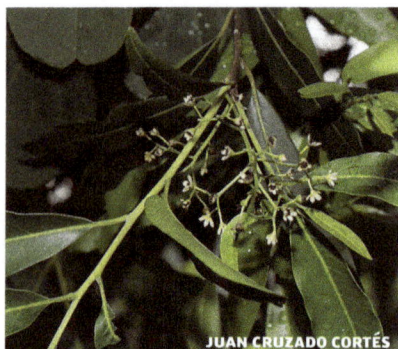

JUAN CRUZADO CORTÉS

MEXICAN LAUREL

SEBASTIÁN DE JESÚS HERRERA BUENFIL

LANCE POD

Lance Pod
GUAMA DE MEXICO, BALCHE

Lonchocarpus longistylus
FABACEAE Pea Family

NATIVE RANGE Central Mexico to Honduras.

Typical of the Tropical Evergreen Forest are a number of lance pods, so called after the shape of the fruit. They are graceful trees or tall shrubs, occurring primarily in Chiapas, Yucatán, Veracruz, Guerrero, Oaxaca, and Jalisco.

This tree resembles a thornless locust tree, with numerous violet, purple, white or pinkish, pea-like blossoms. It blooms for 3 weeks in fall, with 6 to 10 in. flower-trusses, lavender with a greenish-white spot at the base of the "standard" petal; the calyx is inflated and reddish-purple. Seed pods are flat, one- or two-seeded, 3 in. long, with thin margins. Compound leaves, from 8 to 12 in. long, with some 15 leaflets, paler on the underside. Long, slender branches, leaves borne horizontally.

The Mayans used to make a fermented drink from the bark, used in religious ceremonies (**BALCHE**). **Rotenone** (a natural insecticide) is produced from some South American species.

Mexican Laurel
LAUREL

Ocotea tampicensis
LAURACEAE Laurel Family

SYNONYM *Phoebe tampicensis*
NATIVE RANGE Eastern Mexico.

To the Laurel family belong the **European Laurel** or **Sweet Bay** (*Laurus nobilis*), cultivated in Mexico as well, the **Camphor tree** (*Camphora officinarum*), **Cinnamon-tree** (*Cinnamomum verum*), known as **CANELA** in Mexico, and the **Avocado** (p. 157).

Mexican Laurel has evergreen, glossy leaves like the European laurel, but the leaves are narrower. Flowers are white, densely hairy. Fruit glossy black on long stalks. The tree, also called **PALO DE HUMO**, reaches 45 ft. in height, and can be seen in the neighborhood of El Mante and Tampico on the east highway.

KAPOK TREE

Kapok Tree
POCHOTE

Ceiba pentandra
MALVACEAE Mallow Family

NATIVE RANGE Mexico to tropical South America.

An enormous tree with spreading crown and over 120 ft. tall, 6 to 8 ft. in diameter above the large buttresses. Young specimens have large conical spines on the trunk, bark of mature trees is smooth and light gray.

The palmately compound leaves drop during the dry winter season. New leaves often have a rich reddish-brown color. Fleshy, greenish-brown, fragrant flowers in February, followed in late March by the woody pod, 3–4 in. long, containing the fluffy kapok.

For commercial use, kapok is gathered from pods dried in the sun to open; seed has to be removed. Most kapok now comes from Java. In Mayan times the tree had a religious significance and was seldom cut. Like *Pseudobombax* it is often cultivated in plazas and around homes.

Glorybush
MISTELAJOYO, ENTRODELIA

Chaetogastra longisepala
MELASTOMATACEAE Melastome Family

SYNONYM *Tibouchina spathulata*
NATIVE RANGE Mexico to Guatemala.

Triplets of most handsome royal purple flowers with hooked stamens and a peculiar sickle-shaped pistil — no wonder they draw attention to themselves in the humid tropics! This shrub is apt to occur in clearings of either evergreen or deciduous tropical forests. Leaves are opposite, long and leathery, and have usually five nerves running parallel from top to bottom. Even the

CIGARBOX TREE

GUMTREE

urn-shaped fruit is striking for its long brown spurs. Flowers of most species are pink or white.

The Mexican name combines the well-known drink **MISTELA** (made with wine, sugar and cinnamon) and the Indian Zoque name **JOYO** meaning flower.

Cigarbox Tree
CEDRO

Cedrela odorata
MELIACEAE Mahogany Family

SYNONYM *Cedrela mexicana*
NATIVE RANGE Mexico to tropical South America.

Next to the mahogany this is the most important tree of the American tropics. Even though it grows very fast when young (except in dense shade), it may reach 24 ft. in height in the second year from seed. However, it has been much over-harvested and is quickly disappearing in its native Yucatán, Veracruz, and Nayarít.

It is a tall tree, up to 135 ft. when fully grown, and to 3 ft. in diameter. Its bark is smooth and gray. The alternate compound leaves have 5 to 10 pairs of leaflets; leaves drop at the end of the dry season. The fragrant, greenish-white small florets bloom in trusses in July. The brown woody fruits, over 1 in. long, mature the following April and May, opening up to let the winged seed escape.

Wood is fragrant, durable, easily worked, pinkish or reddish brown, and remarkable for its great strength in proportion to its weight.

Gumtree
HULE

Castilla elastica
MORACEAE Mulberry Family

NATIVE RANGE Mexico to Central America.

In some regions the tropical evergreen forest has been cut so heavily that a secondary growth springs up. The Gumtree is particularly common in such clearings. It is a rather tall, but not spreading, tree, 60 ft. or more, with a straight, grayish, smooth trunk. Leaves are leathery but hairy, up to a foot or more long. An interesting phenomenon of this tree is that the early horizontal side branches drop off and are replaced by others at an acute angle. The fruit is a tight group of of 15 to 20 individuals, orange-red in color.

Gumtree's copious milky sap is the source of Panama rubber, made into rubber coats and capes. The Mayans and Aztecs used it for making the rubber ball (**PELOTA**) for their game called **TLACHTLI** in Nahuatl. For its coagulation the juice of *Ipomoea* (synonym *Calonyction*) is often added. It is inferior to Para rubber, derived from *Hevea brasiliensis*.

ALEXIS LÓPEZ HERNÁNDEZ

PLUMLEAF FIG

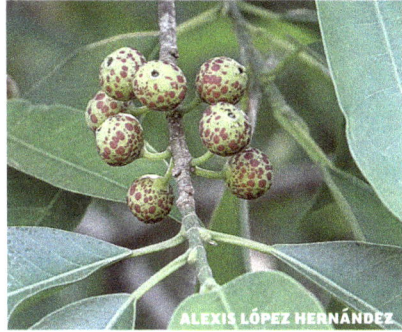

ALEXIS LÓPEZ HERNÁNDEZ

WILD FIG

Wild Fig
AMATE

Ficus insipida
MORACEAE Mulberry Family

SYNONYM *Ficus glabrata*
NATIVE RANGE Mexico to southern tropical South America.

Unlike the common edible fig brought in by the Spaniards at an early date, which has lobed leaves (see p. 161) all Mexican native figs have simple leaves with smooth edges. Many are **MATAPALOS** (tree-killers), beginning their life from seed lodged on another tree, then enveloping and often crushing it. Their aerial roots often assume fantastic forms, hugging rocks or other trees.

Since pre-conquest days, bark paper (**AMATE**) was made from fig trees. It was used by the Aztecs for records and correspondence, as well as for witchcraft. For the latter purpose it was cut into forms of humans and animals (**MUNECOS**); to work injury they were buried in front of a house or in a corral. A few other trees were used in a similar way.

Over 20 species of figs are recorded for Mexico, some with edible fruit, some with rubber-like milky sap. Belonging in the same Mulberry family is the gum-plant, *Castilla elastica*, p. 126.

Plumleaf Fig
CAMICHIN

Ficus pertusa
MORACEAE Mulberry Family

SYNONYM *Ficus padifolia*
NATIVE RANGE Mexico to tropical South America.

"One of the handsomest of Mexican trees, often with an immense crown of dark green leaves" (Standley). Its bark is yellowish but brownish on the slender young branches. One of the most abundant of strangler figs, it has generally numerous trunks and aerial roots, one way of recognizing it.

Fruit is usually tinged or spotted with red or purple; it is eaten by children and birds, and sometimes found for sale in public markets. Being widely dispersed in Mexico, it is much varied in leaf form, lance-leaved to egg-shaped, and in leaf size, 1½ to 4 in. in length.

Local names, for the same reason, vary from **CAMICHÍN** to **COZAHUIQUE**, **JALAMATA**, **CABRA-HIGO**, **SAMATITO**, or even **PALO DE COCO**. For another strangler fig, more common in the tropical deciduous zone, see *Ficus cotinifolia*, p. 103.

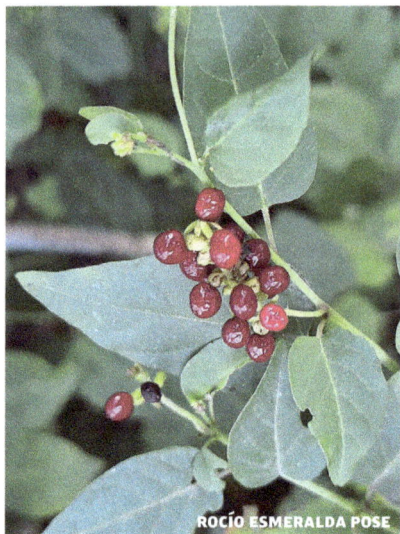

ROCÍO ESMERALDA POSE

ROUGE PLANT

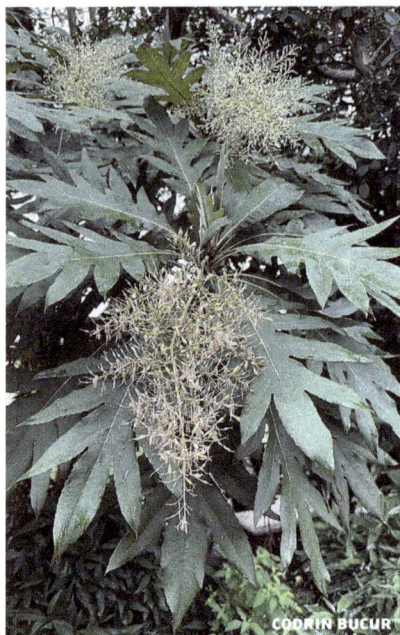

COORIN BUCUR

TEARS OF BLOOD

Tears of Blood
Bocconia frutescens

LLORASANGRE, CHAPULHUACAN
PAPAVERACEAE Poppy Family

NATIVE RANGE Mexico to northwestern Argentina, Caribbean.

Even without its red sap this *Bocconia* would be remembered for its large, deeply divided leaf: it may be as much as 1½ ft. in length. Its lower surface is generally reddish-hairy; the midrib is quite prominent. Plants may reach 25 ft. in height as a tree, though more commonly it is found as a large shrub. The purplish flowers are small but in large filmy clusters; seeds often over ¼ in. long.

Medical studies have been made about the toxic and anesthetic properties of both *Bocconia arborea* and *B. frutescens*, similar in many respects. *B. arborea*'s leaf has long slender lobes.

Rouge Plant
Rivina humilis

UCUQUIRO
PETIVERIACEAE Guinea-Hen-Weed Family

NATIVE RANGE Tropical and subtropical North and South America.

The name "rouge plant" is probably due to the small pink or red berries (occasionally orange), which follow the small white or pinkish flowers. This is a partially woody plant up to 2 ft. or more, sometimes vine-like. Leaves are 1 to 3 in. long; flower racemes not infrequently pendulous. This plant is often seen in the Tropical Deciduous zone as well.

Sweet-and-Vile Vine
Agdestis clematidea

TRIPAS DE JUDAS
PHYTOLACCACEAE Pokeweed Family

NATIVE RANGE Central Texas to Nicaragua.

This plant is told by its very sweet-scented, filmy-whitish blossoms, vile-smelling though attractive leaves, an enormous tuber (growing half out of the earth), of gray-granite color that looks like a rock and may weigh over 100 lbs., and a quick-growing red-

SWEET-AND-VILE VINE

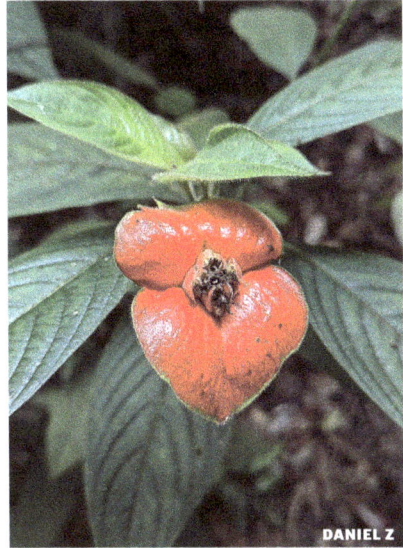

RED TWINCUP

dish stem. No wonder this climbing shrub was given the name *Agdestis* who was a mythical hermaphroditic monster.

Even the genus is said to be an anomalous one of its family. The Spanish name is equally uncomplimentary as the Latin one: **TRIPAS DE JUDAS**, which can only be vulgarly translated as Judas-guts.

In addition, here is a well-meant bit of advice, quoted: "on account of its ill-smelling foliage it cannot be recommended for veranda decoration; but it is a fine plant for covering unsightly objects and outhouses". Regardless, it grows as much as 50 ft. in one season, and makes a lovely and long-lasting effect in flower arrangements when stripped of foliage.

Red Twincup
HIERBA GALLINA

Palicourea tomentosa
RUBIACEAE Madder Family

SYNONYM *Cephaelis tomentosa*
NATIVE RANGE Southern Mexico to tropical South America.

The dark red "flowers" of this interesting tall shrub are merely modified colorful leaves (as they are in the Poinsettia, for instance); the small white star-faced tubes in the center are the real flowers. The entire plant is hairy, not entirely woody, but typical of the lush growth that we associate with colorful tropical or semi-tropical regions.

This plant is a close relative of **Ipecac** (*Carapichea ipecacuanha*) exported in large quantities from Brazil, as an emetic in medicine.

GRETE PASCH
JUNGLE QUEEN

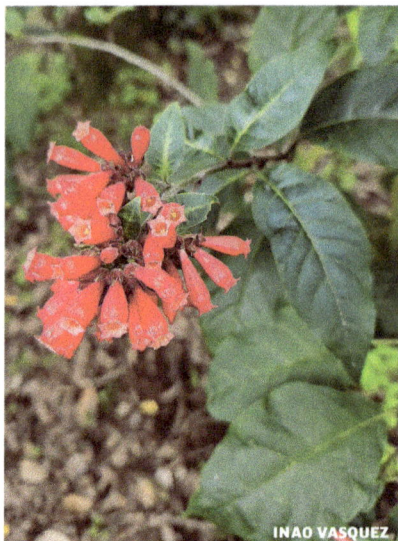
INAO VASQUEZ
EARLY CESTRUM

Jungle Queen
CANGREJO

Rogiera cordata
RUBIACEAE Madder Family

SYNONYM *Rondeletia cordata*
NATIVE RANGE Southern Mexico to Central America.

Most attractive dense shrub (3 to 6 ft.) of Guatemala and Mexico, blooming with clusters of showy, fragrant, waxy, pink or red flowers with a yellow throat; the flowers at the end of the branches. Leaves opposite, thick, leathery, shiny green, occasionally in whorls of three.

Early Cestrum
HIERBA DEL PERRO

Cestrum fasciculatum
SOLANACEAE Potato Family

SYNONYM *Habrothamnus fasciculatus*
NATIVE RANGE Mexico.

The old name, *Habrothamnus*, meaning "graceful shrub", is indicative. It grows to 4 or 5 ft. in height, with leaves 4 to 5 in., and with attractive, dense clusters of purplish-red tube flowers, about ¾ in. long. These flowers have a distinctive inverted urn-shape, with a swelling and constriction close to the five-parted opening, hairy. Good-sized roundish berries, almost ½ in.

Other cestrums are white or greenish, one of them **Cestrum nocturnum** with a heavy night fragrance. **Cestrum elegans** is an old-fashioned shrub or vine of greenhouses, with red-purple flowers blooming almost continuously. Mexico's species are all from tropical regions.

MADELEINE CLAIRE
CESTRUM NOCTURNUM

PUMPWOOD, TRUMPET TREE

Pumpwood, Trumpet Tree
GUARUMBO, CHANCARRO

Cecropia peltata
URTICACEAE Nettle Family

NATIVE RANGE Mexico to northern Brazil, Jamaica to Barbados.

Silhoueted against the sky with a few awkward horizontal branches, carrying long-stalked, hand-shaped leaves at their tips, and with a green or white, prominently ringed trunk — we may easily recognize Pumpwood. It is probably called that name because the cut trunks, being hollow, are often used for conducting water. Many native inhabitants of tropical America used them also for making a kind of trumpet. (Be careful: the hollow branches are often the home of furiously biting ants).

The large leaves are easily recognized: deeply lobed and white on their lower surface. Flowers are very small, in cylindrical heads, many arranged in a star shape.

PUMPWOOD, TRUMPET TREE

Rainforest

Here is the "forest primeval", with all that the concept brings to mind: huge trees, 160 ft. tall or more, the mystic half-shade underneath, luxuriant growth of lianas, some 500 ft. long, large leathery, dark evergreen leaves with fascinating "cut-outs", orchids and bromeliads nestling on tree trunks and branches.

It really is primeval, resembling the original vegetation of the earth, when 200 in. of annual rainfall was nothing unusual and when eternal summer created the luxuriant plant paradise that existed millions of years ago.

The ice ages pushed back what we might call "vegetation at its best" — back to the equatorial belt from 3–10 degrees north and south of the equator. There it continues to thrive.

In reality there are three layers of plants in this rainforest, each layer a world in itself, yet each dependent, in a way, upon the others. From a plane flying over it, the rainforest appears like a huge carpet of dark green trees, with a regular canopy from 60 to 120 ft. above the ground. Only from a distance, at an oblique angle, can the topmost layer be differentiated, made up of the huge emergent trees referred to above.

Best known among these tall trees is the **Mahogany** (*Swietenia macrophylla*), which reaches 230 ft. in height and over 10 ft. in diameter. **Canshan** (*Terminalia amazonia*) is equally tall. A little-known giant, **Ulmus mexicana,** (p. 142) is said to grow up to 295 ft., with a diameter of almost 20 ft. (it is really more typical in cloud forests and tropical deciduous forests). Another tall tree, called **MILADY BLANCO** in Guatemala, is a close relative of the oleander; it is *Aspidosperma megalocarpon*, known for its large, winged seed, measuring 3 in. in diameter.

A dozen dominant trees form most of the main canopy, with a height of from 75 to 120 ft. Among them is the **Chicle** or **Chewing-gum tree** (*Manilkara zapota*, see pp. 139, 167), **Cacao tree** (*Theobroma cacao*) and **Ramon bread-nut tree** (*Brosimum alicastrum*, p 138). Many of these rainforest trees are still imperfectly known. And yet, the multiplicity is astounding: it is said that a square mile of rainforest may well support over 200 species.

In the half-shade of the "ground-floor" is a mixture of highly luxuriant growth: palms, bamboo, shade-enduring leafy plants, lianas scrambling upward, epiphytes like orchids, and bromeliads, aroids and even cacti. A number of them have spines or fish-hook structures by which to climb to the light.

The popular idea that these rainforests are a labyrinth of impenetrable jungle, through which humans can only hack their way laboriously, is not accurate. Such spots are only the areas of secondary growth, resulting from despoliation of the original forest. In such cases the prolific tropical vegetation crowds in quickly. A similar chance is afforded by the tumbling down of one of the forest's giant trees, whereby a light opening results.

What is true, are the fabulous and varied root supports of some of these immense trees. Their roots are fairly small and close to the surface, providing insufficient leverage. Buttresses of an Andira tree may spread over a diameter or 80 ft., and may well reach 12 ft. in height on the trunk.

Smaller trees may have a number of "stilt roots" emerging from the trunk at intervals up to 10 ft. above the ground. These kinds of supports are flattened or triangular in such a way as to provide the best props.

Air roots are not uncommon in lianas and in certain epiphytes. Some strangler figs, and their relative, *Coussapoa*, send air roots down to the ground and subsequently may easily kill their hosts in time by surrounding them. They are appropriately called tree-killers (**MATAPALOS**)

"Climbing" trees, shrubs and palms, on the other hand, seldom do damage to their supports; they merely try to reach more light.

How to identify this maze of plants becomes a problem. Even the best botanists have difficulty with trees that may not flower annually, since floral analysis is required. On the other hand, an observant nature lover may begin to recognize them by their trunks and other characteristics. With the help of a local practical naturalist, they may begin to name them first by their Aztec or Nahuatl designation and thus arrive at the botanical name.

Trunks, for instance, while straight and tall, in general, differ from light to dark, smooth and rough, and may be gray, black, yellowish or even bright red, as in case of the tree that is called **MULATO** or "Naked Indian" (**INDIO DESNUDO**) locally, *Bursera simaruba*.

Equally effective for recognition might be the color of their sap, which, again, is blood-red in some trees, milky in others, black, yellow, or gummy.

While a great many trees have the stereotypical oval shape, green-glossy and thick-ened, there are others with more distinguishing characters. Hand-shaped leaves are apt to have a variety of lobes, more or less deeply cut. Compound leaves may have leaflets arranged like a feather (*pinnate*) or a fan (*palmate*); others, especially of the Pea family, are doubly compound. When the leaf-stalk is attached to the leaf center we call the leaf *peltate* (shield-form).

Occasionally a compound leaf has wings along the main stalk, as in *Inga* species (see p. 135).

"Drip tips" (pointed and elongated for shedding water) are not at all uncommon in evergreen leaves of wet climates.

Another fascinating feature of certain rainforest plants is of interest to the thirsty traveler. Lianas particularly are apt to contain large reservoirs of water for easy supply to the leaves at their extreme ends. Workers in the forest know they can tap them by making two cuts some distance apart in a thick stem of 3 to 5 in. diameter: there will be enough good drinking water forthcoming to quench their thirst. A particular grape, **Vitis bourgaeana**, is known for this.

The average tourist sees little of the rainforest in Mexico: most of it is quite inaccessible, although a paradise for the study of tropical fauna. It is said that no habitat on earth harbors so many tree-living animals as the rainforest. In Spanish it is called **SELVA ALTA SIEMPRE VERDE**, the evergreen tall jungle. The South American type is named *hylaea*, from the Greek word for wood.

A classic novel of the rainforest is W. H. Hudson's *Green Mansions*.

MULATO, NAKED INDIAN

GUILLAUME DELAITRE

SCARLET-STAR

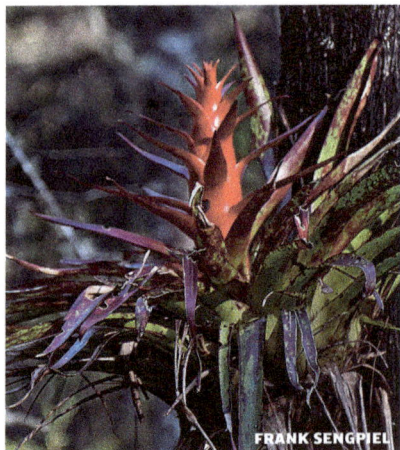

FRANK SENGPIEL

AIR PINE

Scarlet-Star
PIÑUELA

Guzmania lingulata
BROMELIACEAE Airplant Family

NATIVE RANGE Southeastern Mexico to tropical South America.

Many tourists visiting tropical humid regions for the first time call any colorful epiphyte (a plant growing on another plant for support but not food), an "orchid". The fact is that a large number of these airplants belong to the Bromeliad family, which have no resemblance to orchid flowers but which are related to the pineapple, one of its representatives. Much of the brilliant color is apt to be in the channeled leaves and bracts.

Worldwide, there are about 200 species of *Guzmania*, many of them difficult to identify. Other important members of the family are *Vriesea, Billbergia, Aechmea*. See also p. 122 and 134 for *Tillandisa*.

Air Pine
GUACAMAYA

Tillandsia imperialis
BROMELIACEAE Airplant Family

NATIVE RANGE Mexico.

This bromeliad is commonly found for sale in flower markets in winter. The whole plant can be used as a lasting cutflower, with its roots in water. It is properly called *imperialis*, topping most other bromeliads: the entire stalk—leaves, flowers and all—is a brilliant red clear down to the bottom. The flowers proper peep out of the red bracts; they are small, purplish and yellow. The lower leaves remind one of its relative, the **pineapple**, *Ananas comosus*.

When seen native in the rainforest, it is sure to attract attention. See also p. 122 for the **Prodigious bromeliad** (*Tillandsia prodigiosa*), its close relative.

Many bromeliads are able to store a great deal of water in the "cups" formed by the rosette of leaves, helpful in nourishing the plants, many of which have no proper roots.

Nargusta Terminalia
CANSHÁN

Terminalia amazonia
COMBRETACEAE West Indies-Almond Family

NATIVE RANGE Southern Mexico to southern tropical South America and Trinidad.

Abundant in the rainforest, this enormous tree reaches occasionally 230 ft. in height and almost 5 ft. in diameter, sometimes with large buttresses. Its bark is somewhat wrinkled and of a yellow-gray color. (**CANSHÁN** means **SHÁN** for palm and **K'AN** for yellow.

NARGUSTA TERMINALIA

OXHORN BUCIDA

The wood, as well, is yellowish; it is fairly hard and takes an attractive polish. The fruits are a golden color, not large, but abundant; they have three or four wings of unequal size. Flowers are very small, fragrant, and of a greenish-tan color, appearing in February at the end of the then leafless branches. Leaves almost evergreen, 1½ to 3 in. long, bunched at the end of the slender branches.

Paul Allen says that you can generally recognize the tree by its slender whip suckers with their characteristic leaves at the lower portions of the trunk. Other names are **VOLADOR, AMARILLO, MEMBRILLO, GUAYABO** (different from **GUAYABA** p. 163).

Oxhorn Bucida
Terminalia buceras
PUK-TÉ
COMBRETACEAE West Indies-Almond Family
SYNONYM *Bucida buceras*
NATIVE RANGE Central Mexico to Colombia (San Andrés Island), Caribbean.

This tall, broad-spreading tree that may attain 3 ft. in diameter, is found in the rainforest in Campeche and Tabasco (and also probably in Yucatán). It has a scaly gray bark, and is armed with spines, as long as ¾ to 1 in. Leaves are alternate, crowded at the end of branches, evergreen and leathery. Flowers an inconspicuous green, followed by ovoid and small fruit.

Not too easily identified except on close inspection of the leaves and branches, and especially by the oxhorn spines.

Star Tree, River Koko
Inga vera
CUAJINICUIL
FABACEAE Pea Family
SYNONYM *Inga spuria*
NATIVE RANGE Mexico to Venezuela and Bolivia, Caribbean.

A highly interesting tropical tree with numerous white star-shaped blossoms, easily identified by the winged leaf-stalk of the compound leaf. It grows especially along water courses, and is reported from Tepic to Tamaulipas, Veracruz and Chiapas, as a small tree up to 45 ft. tall, with a wide-spreading crown. The long narrow pod, 1 ft. long, is somewhat squarish and covered with a dense, yellowish velvet. Pulp around the seeds is edible.

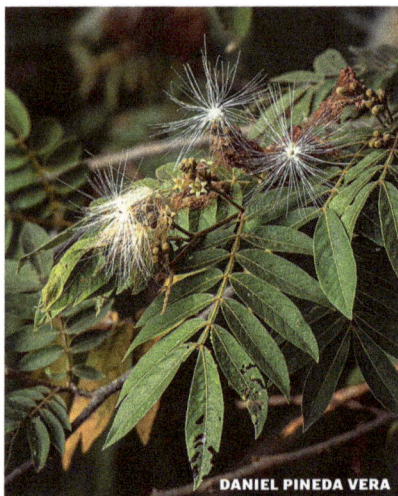

DANIEL PINEDA VERA

STAR TREE, RIVER KOKO

NYANATUSITA BHIKKHU

BALM TREE

Balm Tree

Myroxylon balsamum

BALSAMO

FABACEAE Pea Family

NATIVE RANGE Mexico to southern tropical South America.

A tall tropical forest tree, 90 ft. and more, common in Central America and found in Mexico mostly from Veracruz and Oaxaca to Yucatán and Chiapas. It is the source of the famous fragrant, dark reddish-brown, viscid liquid, misnamed **Balsam of Peru**, now shipped mainly from El Salvador, used as a drug and for perfumery.

Alternate compound leaves, with 5 to 11 lustrous, leathery leaflets (1 to 3 in. long) that show translucent dots and lines. Flowers white in trusses, fruit winged, with a thick, one-seeded tip, totaling 2½ in. in length.

Balsam is collected from the crushed, live bark in spring before the rainy season. Wood is a beautiful reddish-brown with a pleasant aroma.

Pre-colonial Aztecs cultivated the tree in the royal gardens and the Court exacted jars of the balsam as one of the regular items of tribute. Spanish explorers shipped the balsam to Europe via Peru: it sold at prices ranging from $20 to $200 an ounce. As early as 1562 Pope Pius IV authorized the clergy to use **BALSAMO NEGRO** in the preparation of the chrism. It was declared a sacrilege to injure or destroy the trees.

Lobster Claw Heliconia

Heliconia bihai

TANAY

HELICONIACEAE False-Bird-of-Paradise Family

NATIVE RANGE Southern Mexico, Caribbean, Colombia to northern South America.

This looks like a "small" banana plant (it may at times reach 18 ft. in height); it is, in fact, a close relative, but has dry fruit. Leaves are long-stalked, the blades 3 to 5 ft. long. Its red and orange flowers are in a very large, scarlet and black blossom sheath, with boat-shaped parts. The total effect is both bizarre and beautiful. "Lobster-claw" is an appropriate name; also called **BALISIER**. It is plentiful in wet, shady spots of the forest.

Apparently a number of varieties have been derived from this species, with ribs and veins yellow-striped or pink or red. *Heliconia latispatha* is more slender, resembling **Bird-**

WILLIAM STEPHENS

LOBSTER CLAW HELICONIA

SCAUP

CACAO TREE

of-Paradise (*Strelitzia*, p. 173). It is generally called **PLATANILLO**, and is quite abundant in clearings of the rainforest.

Cacao Tree
CACAO

Theobroma cacao
MALVACEAE Mallow Family

NATIVE RANGE Costa Rica to southern tropical South America.

Theobroma means "food of the drink of kings and nobles; its seed gods". Long before the advent of the Spanish, **CACAO** furnished the drink of kings and nobles; its seed was widely used as money: in Nicaragua a slave was worth 100 seeds, a rabbit, 6. In English the name "cacao" refers to the plant and the raw product, "cocoa" is the manufactured product, "chocolate" the chief commodity.

CACAO is a small tree, grown in fertile foothills of tropical regions with more than 70 in. annual rainfall. Production is particularly high in Chiapas, and from there along both coasts, reaching as far north along the Gulf as Tampico. Shade is usually provided by legu-minous trees, then called **MADRE DE CACAO**; they are needed until the cacao tree is well-established. It blooms after 3 or 4 years, and then fruits can be harvested both in midsummer and midwinter.

The fruit grows out of the trunk, is reddish or yellowish, 10 in. long, 10-ribbed, and has a thick, hard, leathery rind; each of its cells contains 5 to 12 "beans" in a row, em-bedded in a white or pinkish pulp. Leaves are large, 8 in. long or more, with thick leaf veins. In addition to *T. cacao*, there are two other species from which cocoa is derived: ***Theobroma angustifolium*** and ***Theobroma bicolor***. The latter produces an inferior quality of cocoa.

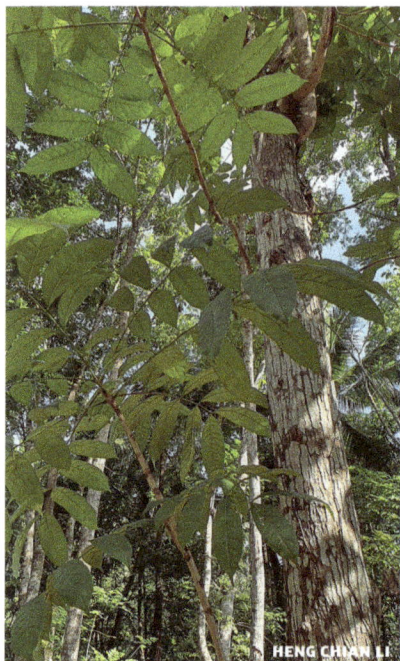
MAHOGANY TREE *fruit*

RENJUS BOX

HENG CHIAN LI

MAHOGANY TREE *leaves*

Mahogany Tree
CAOBA

Swietenia macrophylla
MELIACEAE Mahogany Family

NATIVE RANGE Mexico to Bolivia and Brazil.

Even in Mexico the true **CAOBA** is pointed out with pride to the visitor; it is the tall tree from which the handsome hardwood mahogany comes, so much valued for furniture and interior finishing. At one time mahogany was cut to such an extent in the tropics that, for instance, the city of Belize in British Honduras (now Belize) is reported to have been built on a stagnant pool, filled up with mahogany chips and gin bottles!

Swietenia are typical of the rainforest zone in tropical Mexico; the original mahogany, *Swietenia mahogani*, does not occur in Mexico. *S. macrophylla* has particularly large leaves, up to 7 in. long; they are opposite, compound, glossy-evergreen, high up in the tree. Trunks are immense, with thick, dark gray, splotchy bark.

The peculiar woody, ovoid fruits, over 4 in. long, with curved stalks, resemble buzzard heads, hence the name "buzzard-head-tree" in Nahuatl, **ZOPILO-ZONTECOMA-CUAHUITL**. The winged fruit is said to be poisonous.

Ramon Bread-Nut Tree
MOJU, CAPOMO

Brosimum alicastrum
MORACEAE Mulberry Family

NATIVE RANGE Mexico to Central America, Caribbean.

"The fruits of moju have a nutritious value halfway between maize and beans" according to a well-known Mexican botanist (Miranda). In addition, the milky sap, which resembles cream, makes a good substitute for cow's milk after being diluted with water; it does, however, contain considerable rubber. Leaves and young branches are cut for fodder. All-in-all, the tree is among the most important trees of Yucatán.

RAMON BREAD-NUT TREE

SIDDARTH MACHADO

CHICLE, SAPODILLA, NASEBERRY

GERRY VAN TONDER

It grows to a height of 75 ft. or over, in dense stands, called **MUJUALES**, in limestone soils, often with large buttresses; the bark is gray or reddish, not smooth. Evergreen leaves are leathery and shiny on top, 3½ to 6 in. long. Inconspicuous small white flowers in September or October are followed by yellow, plum-like fruit, 1 in. long, in early spring. Its pulp is edible; the seeds can be boiled (the taste being like potatoes or chestnuts, according to different authors), or ground into meal for the making of bread or tortillas. Wood valuable for timber. Another name is **OJOCHE**, ox.

A close relative is *Brosimum utile*, **PALO DE VACA** (**Cow-tree**), first described by Alexander von Humboldt.

Chicle, Sapodilla, Naseberry
CHICOZAPOTE

Manilkara zapota
SAPOTACEAE Sapodilla Family

SYNONYM *Achras zapota*
NATIVE RANGE Mexico to Colombia.

A very useful tree: it furnishes hard and very durable wood, (found in excellent preservation in Mayan ruins); latex for the making of chewing gum; and a fruit that has been called variously "the best of all fruit"; "a more luscious, cool and agreeable fruit is not to met with in this or any country in the world"; "melting, and with a perfume of honey, jasmin and lily-of-the-valley". Chicle is now cultivated all around the globe.

Its fruit is roundish, with the color of an Irish potato, the flesh yellow-brown and translucent with small seeds. Leaves are stiff and glossy-green, clustered at the end of the branches. Flowers are pinkish-white, small.

This is a typical tree of the rainforest, up to 120 ft. in height, of a beautiful shape and good wind-resistance. For other Sapotas see p. 166.

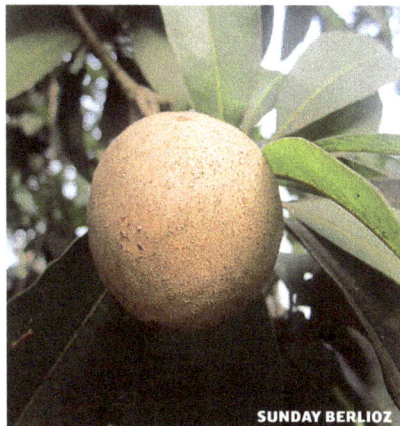

CHICLE, SAPODILLA, NASEBERRY

SUNDAY BERLIOZ

Cloud Forest (Temperate Rainforest)

What do you notice about the character of the tropical plant growth when you climb up into the mountainous country? In general, the effect is similar to that of going north: latitude and altitude have corresponding changes in temperature. In the tropics, however, summer and winter hardly exist, even on the higher mountains. Again, the length of day varies little here, even though you climb above 5,000 ft., the altitude of the Cloud Forest. Its upper limit is around 7,500 ft. above sea-level.

While the temperature is low, it does not go down to freezing. Fogs are the inevitable result of heavy rainfall and cold air. In many cases precipitation reaches 100 in. per year (occasionally twice that amount). In this respect it matches the rainforest.

Some interesting characteristics in which the Cloud Forest differs from the Rainforest are:

• Lower height of the trees: from 50 to 65 ft.
• The almost complete absence of **Strangler figs** here; in their stead we find *Oreopanax* and *Blakea*.
• **Tree ferns** are sure indicators of this zone; they are scarce in other tropical forests.

In a way we might say that two zones are wrapped up in this region: an extension southward of northern trees, and a tropical undergrowth of low trees, shrubs, and vines.

The northern "relic" consists of pines and oaks, accompanied by a number of trees more commonly associated with the southeastern United States. Such include the *Liquidamber* or **Sweet gum**, with its gorgeous fall color (see p. 141), the **Sour** or **Water gum** (*Nyssa*), **Hornbeam** (*Carpinus*) and **Hop hornbeam** (*Ostrya*). Even **Beech**, **Linden** and **Flowering dogwood**, that naturally belong in the temperate rain belt of the middle-eastern U.S.A., show up here in this "Temperate Rainforest" of Mexico. It looks as if they had simply jumped across the Gulf of Mexico to find a new congenial home. They occur as far as Chiapas and Guerrero.

We might think of the second part of this zone as a relic of a prehistoric geological age (as it well may be). **Tree ferns** here may grow up to 30 ft. in height. The low trees of other types have shiny dark green leaves. There are even giant **horsetails** (*Equisetum*) among them, that strengthen the prehistoric illusion.

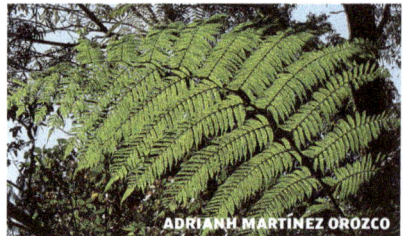
ADRIANH MARTÍNEZ OROZCO

TREE FERN

Begonias, bromeliads and lovely orchids thrive in the semi-shady mysterious atmosphere of this lower story; so do mosses and lichens. Locally, in Guerrero, are such unusual trees as *Ternstroemia* and *Verbesina*.

Curiously enough, Mexico's tallest tree, *Ulmus mexicana*, **BAQUETA** or **Ramrod Tree**, on p. 142, thrives in the cool parts of the Cloud Forest. In the valleys we may even encounter some Arizona cottonwoods. Truly, here is a vegetation zone of surprises!

All-in-all, the area of the Cloud Forest occupies only one-half of one percent of Mexico's area. No main highway crosses it. San Cristobal and the town of Orizaba are fairly close to it.

The usual Spanish name for it is **SELVA BAJA SIEMPRE VERDE**, or sometimes **SELVA DE MONTANA**.

SWEET GUM

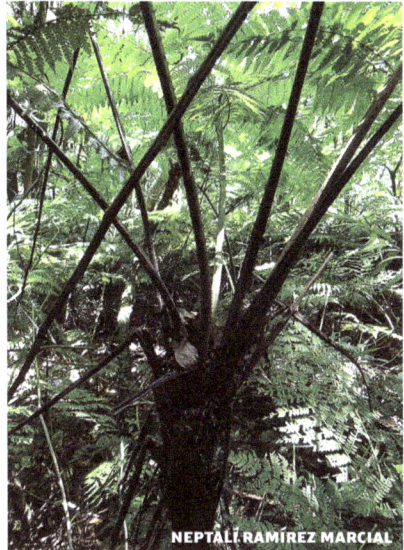

NEPTALÍ RAMÍREZ MARCIAL

TREE FERN

Sweet Gum
Liquidambar styraciflua

LIQUIDAMBAR, OCOZOTE
ALTINGIACEAE Sweet-Gum Family

NATIVE RANGE Central and eastern U.S.A. to Central America.

This handsome deciduous tree of the rich bottomlands of the southeastern part of U.S.A. appears again in eastern Mexico, together with **Tupelo** (*Nyssa*), **Hop hornbeam** (*Ostrya*), and **Hornbeam** (*Carpinus*). It may grow up to 140 ft. tall and 4 to 5 ft. in diameter. Its highly distinctive leaf turns into a riot of color in fall.

Balsam liquid amber, forming in cavities of the bark when injured, is used in soaps and for incense, although the more common incense comes from Oriental trees.

Pollen-bearing flowers are in catkins, seed-bearing ones in heads on the ends of slender twigs. Most trees show wing-like projections on the bark of their smaller branches.

Its wood is a pleasant reddish color with a satin luster and is used for furniture and interior decoration. The tongue-twister Nahuatl name, **XOCHIOCOTZOCUAHUITL**, means "tree of aromatic rosin".

Tree Fern
Alsophila firma

RABO DE MICO
CYATHEACEAE Fork-Sori Tree Fern Family

SYNONYM *Cyathea mexicana*

NATIVE RANGE MExico to Ecuador.

Locally abundant but confined to those mountainous regions near the Gulf of Mexico with an equable moist climate, the stately tree ferns are a remnant of the carboniferous age. They are the most typical plant of the Cloud Forest and easily recognized by their 6 to 9 ft. long fern fronds arising from the top of a tall tree trunk (up to 30 ft.), with scars of the old leaf stalks showing. The leaf blades are armed with a few sharp, conical, shiny-black spines.

The spiral unfolding of the leaves has given rise to the name **RABO DE MICO** ('monkey tail'). Another name is **OCOPETATE**, and **TZIMUY**. Tree trunks can be used for temporary construction. Pieces of them make a good growth medium for ornamental orchids.

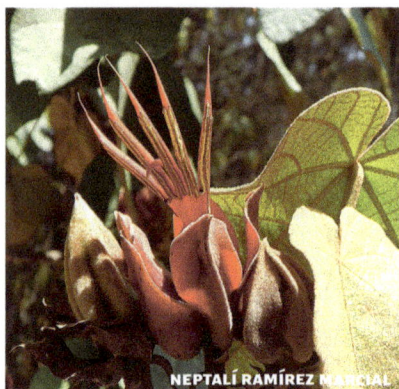

NEPTALÍ RAMÍREZ MARCIAL
HANDFLOWER TREE

SCOTT HARRIS

Handflower Tree
MANO DE DRAGON

Chiranthodendron pentadactylon
MALVACEAE Mallow Family

NATIVE RANGE Mexico to Honduras.

The Aztec kings used to plant this tree in their gardens; they venerated it for its curious blossoms which show a set of red stamens resembling a human claw; at its base the style extends like a thumb. At one time an ancient tree near Toluca was erroneously believed to be the only one of its kind in the world.

Flowers are leathery, reddish brown on the outside, intensely red inside. Fruit large, elliptical, woody, five-angled. Its alternate velvety leaves are 6 in. long; they resemble those of the Sycamore (*Platanus*).

Ramrod Tree
BAQUETA, OLMO

Ulmus mexicana
ULMACEAE Elm Family

SYNONYM *Chaetoptelea mexicana*
NATIVE RANGE Mexico to Central America.

Probably the tallest tree of Mexico, reaching a height of 285 ft. and a diameter of 20 ft. (The tallest measured redwood tree in California is 380 ft. high).

It is common in the cool parts of the Cloud Forest and Tropical Evergreen Forests, often replacing **Sour gum** (*Nyssa*) which grows farther south.

In many ways it has the appearance of the familiar elm of North America, in the shape of its leaves and its flat, small fruit. The latter has no wings but a hairy fringe around the edges; it has two teeth at the top. Leaves are somewhat leathery but deciduous.

The tree has an open crown, ascending branches, and a scaly, cracked bark, which is astringent and used against cough. The wood is used for wheels, doorsills, and lintels, being hard, heavy, and strong.

NEPTALÍ RAMÍREZ MARCIAL

Introduced and Cultivated Plants

How can you tell whether a plant, now commonly found in Mexico, has been introduced through the ages or is native from the "beginning"? The answer in general is: "You can't!". Mexico's climate is so varied and the country has been so hospitable to so many plants from all parts of the world.

Even the ever-present **Bougainvillea** came from Brazil originally. Cultivated **figs** and **dates** were brought in by the Spanish; they had been grown in Europe for thousands of years. **Coffee** comes from Arabia, **bananas** from India and the Pacific, via Spain; all members of the orange-lemon family (**citrus fruit**) came from China and India to begin with, and then to Mexico via Spain. The **coconut**? Authorities are not all agreed, but the majority feel that the nuts floated in from the ocean.

To help the bewildered visitor in this dilemma we are attempting to divide these "newcomers" and some native cultivated plants into four groups, depending on location and use:

• **ALONG MEXICAN HIGHWAYS** we find — quite commonly — ornamental trees planted by public agencies. Such are **Peppertree, Blue-gum, Beefwood** (*Casuarina*), **Flamboyant tree**, and even **Oleander**. Some native trees, such as **Tree Tobacco**, are also used for highway planting.

• In **PARKS** and **PRIVATE HOME GROUNDS** we find a large number of beautiful ornamentals, for instance: **Orchid tree, African tuliptree, Chinaberry, Tropical almond tree, Glossy privet, Crape myrtle, Frangipani, Fern tree, Cannonball tree, Heartflower tree, Traveler's tree, Golden trumpet, Dwarf poinciana, Castor bean**, and a variety of vines and "house plants".

• **USEFUL PLANTS**, for fruit or other purposes, including medicinal, are grown on both home grounds and commercially. Thus we find, in the proper climate and environment, all kinds of citrus fruits, bananas, papayas, coffee, sugar cane, some date palms and European figs, avocados, mangos, breadfruit, and quite a number of **SAPOTES** (see pp. 166). Bamboo is important; so is cotton. Agaves, often referred to as century plants, occupy a most important place in Mexican life. There are **MAGUEYS** for liquor such as **PULQUE** and **TEQUILA**, for fiber as **HENEQUEN** (sisal) and **ZAPUPE**, and for fencing purposes (see p. 151).

In addition to cotton, coffee, cacao (p. 137) and others before-mentioned, we should draw attention to the large crops of maize (corn), rice, wheat, FRIJOL (Mexican bean), GARBANZO (chick-pea) and **CACAHUATE** (peanut). No tourist should fail to look over the local markets: they will be rewarded by seeing what the Mexican PAISANOS grow and buy.

• **LONG-TIME INTRODUCTIONS** are most confusing: many of those plants that were "exotics" to begin with have found conditions in their new home so much to their liking, that they have now gone apparently "wild".

Here is a surprising illustration. In tropical forests you may suddenly come across a colony of so-called "air-plants", fleshy leaves that sprout new plants along their edges, with fleshy stalks of pinkish-red bells hanging down in quantities. It is *Kalanchoe pinnata*. There is nothing to intimate that they really came from Africa originally: they seem so thoroughly naturalized in Mexico.

The common **bamboo** is now such a typical plant of Mexico tropics that it looks perfectly wild. In reality it is introduced.

In Mexican markets the **Calla lily** (*Zantedeschia aethiopica*), originally from South Africa, has become perfectly naturalized.

It is known that the Spaniards took to the new world oranges, lemons, limes, olives, figs, sugarcane, ginger, mulberries, as well as grapes, apricots, peaches, pears, wheat, barley, lettuce, cabbage, onions, parsnips, and turnips. Captain Bligh's mission was to bring breadfruit from Tahiti to the West Indies on H.M.S. *Bounty*. After the mutiny he completed the job with another ship.

Even before the Spaniards came, Montezuma had introduced into the tropical garden at Huaxtepec many balled plants from the tropical coast region. Planted after 8 days of fasting, being anointed with blood from human ears and dead quail, with sacrifices to the god of flowers, they blossomed luxuriantly after 3 years. This was soon after Montezuma's ascension to power in the year 1450.

Dr. Hernandez, the Spanish physician and botanist, visited these royal gardens of Huaxtepec between 1570 and 1577, and described some of the remarkable trees and flowers in them. Even Cortez said: "Spain has never seen a finer kind of pleasure garden". Sad to say, at present nothing remains to testify to this beauty in the first tropical botanical garden on the American continent.

A number of beautiful flowering trees and vines now found in Mexico came from Central American and farther south. **Fern tree** (*Jacaranda*), with showy violet blossoms, now more and more planted in parks and gardens, came from Brazil; so did **Bougainvillea**, called **BUGAMBILIA** in Mexico, and a number of the "**Shower trees**" (*Cassia, Senna*).

Brazil was also the original home of the pineapple; Columbus found it on the island of Guadeloupe; most people now associate it with Hawaii.

CALLA LILY

MAYA LODHIYAL

MANGO

TIM HARRIS

PEPPER TREE, PERUVIAN MASTIC TREE

Mango
MANGO

Mangifera indica
ANACARDIACEAE Sumac Family

It does not take long, after having reached tropical Mexico, before we encounter this stately, decorative, evergreen tree with its ample, rounded top. We may recognize it by the coppery-red color of newly leafed portions and by the attractive, large, yellowish-filmy flower clusters, sometimes almost covering the tree.

Later in spring or summer, clusters of red and yellow luscious fruits (they may grow to 4 or 5 lbs.) dangle down from the twigs. They taste "like a deliciously resinous peach". Others say the taste is like apricot and pineapple. The *World in Your Garden* recognizes "mangophiles" and "mangophobes" depending on the variety and ripeness of the mango they have tasted. What makes the tasting all the more difficult is the slippery character of the flesh, and some serve mangoes with a corkscrew to be inserted into the large flattened stone.

Leaves are leathery, dark green when mature; they emit the odor of turpentine when crushed. Mangoes are related to cashew nut and sumac, also belonging to the Sumac family. They are as important a fruit in the tropics as apples are in the temperate zones.

As the scientific name indicates, the mango came from the East Indies. The Portuguese probably carried it to East Africa, where it is now common, and introduced it into America. They planted it at Bahia (Salvador), Brazil, about 1700. It reached the West Indies some 50 years later, and Mexico early in the 19th century. Not until 1889 was a choice variety introduced in the U.S.A. to bear fruit 9 years later.

Pepper Tree, Peruvian Mastic Tree
PIRÚ

Schinus molle
ANACARDIACEAE Sumac Family

Few ornamental shade trees are as much used along Mexican highways as this introduction from Peru. It is now thoroughly at home in all warm countries. Beautiful at any

CUSTARD APPLE

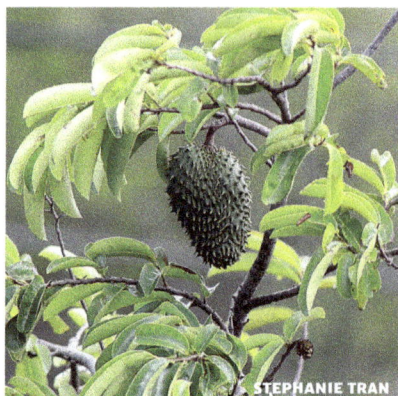

SOURSOP

time for its graceful hanging branches and filmy leaves, the female trees are particularly attractive when they are bearing their large trusses of pink berries in mid-winter. It is, however, subject to black scale which makes it a real menace to orchards of citrus fruits, the reason why it is banned in some regions. The **Brazilian pepper tree** (*Schinus terebinthifolia*) seems to be free of pests and has red berries, very dark aromatic foliage, and is stiffer in habit.

Custard Apple
CHIRIMOYA, POOX

Annona cherimola
ANNONACEAE Custard-Apple Family

One of the most delicious fruits in Mexico; it originated in Peru but was naturalized at a very early date. It is a low tree, 13 to 20 ft. in height, with yellowish soft-hairy young growth and leaves velvety below.

Flowers are fragrant; greenish-yellow with purple spot at base of the inch-long petals. Apple-sized fruit are roundish with warty U-shaped lumps; pulp soft, white, pleasantly acid, with a number of black seeds embedded—which seeds are poisonous.

This **CHIRIMOYA** is the best of the many species of *Annona*; it does best in the cooler tropics with a long dry season, and in sandy, well-drained soils. There are several different types, depending on the character of the rind.

Among other notable species:

Annona purpurea, **SONCOYA**, abundant on the Isthmus of Tehuantepec, very fragrant and edible, orange-colored with mango flavor;

Annona muricata, **Soursop**, eaten fresh, or in beverages, jelly, tarts, or preserves; both fruit skin and leaves are ill-smelling;

Annona squamosa (includes **Annona glabra**), **Sugar apple, Sweet apple, Sweetsop**, of excellent flavor, eaten alone or made into sherbets, attractive greenish-yellow fruit, the size of an orange; also called cork-wood, since the light, spongy roots are used to make bottle corks and floats for fishing nets.

Annona macroprophyllata (synonym *Annona diversifolia*), **ILANIA**, with delicious pink-tinted pulp (Acapulco and Colima).

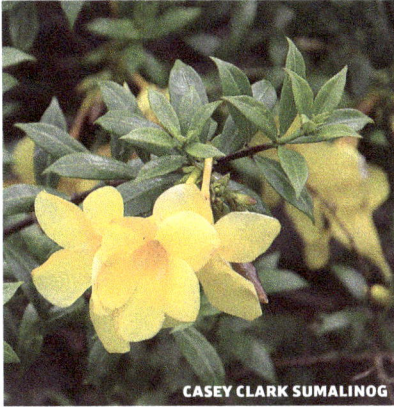

CASEY CLARK SUMALINOG

GOLDEN TRUMPET

PEAK99

HERALD TRUMPET

Golden Trumpet
TROMPETA DE ORO

Allamanda cathartica
APOCYNACEAE Dogbane Family

Some woody vines, like this Golden Trumpet, disguise themselves almost like shrubs. It can be told by its handsome, large golden flowers; and its good-looking glossy, evergreen leaves that come in fours, and are somewhat wrinkled. Flowers are followed by spiny pods that open in two parts.

On casual observation this flower might be confused with that of **Yellowsilk shellseed** in the Tropical Deciduous Forest (see p. 94), which opens up much wider, and with **Lucky nut**, *Thevetia*, p. 120, which is of a lighter color, but also belongs to the Dogbane family. Like it, it has milky sap.

This striking, vigorous vine is of very easy culture and can be propagated by cuttings. It is widely grown as an ornamental, both in the open in the tropics and in greenhouses and conservatories all over the world.

Herald Trumpet
BEAUMONTIA

Beaumontia grandiflora
APOCYNACEAE Dogbane Family

In the tropics we accept such an anomalous sight as Easter lilies on woody vines, and formed in the first months of the year. They come in heavy clusters and are fragrant, 5 in. long, milky-white, sometimes tipped with pink and veined with green.

The plant is native of India-China, cultivated in Mexican gardens, and belongs to the Dogbane family, together with *Thevetia*, *Plumeria*, *Nerium*, and *Tabernaemontana*, all strikingly beautiful. Flowers have five lobes each, with ruffled edges. Leaves hang down (6 to 9 in. long), are dark glossy green, leathery but supple, with wavy margins; they die-off and drop during the blooming season.

Oleander
LAUREL-ROSA, TRINITARIA

Nerium oleander
APOCYNACEAE Dogbane Family

Although introduced from the Mediterranean area, Oleander is now a very popular ornamental in Mexico, planted in patios and along highways. It is easily recognized by its pink or white funnel-shaped blossoms, by the leathery leaves that come in threes along the stem (**TRINITARIA**), and by its pleasant fragrance.

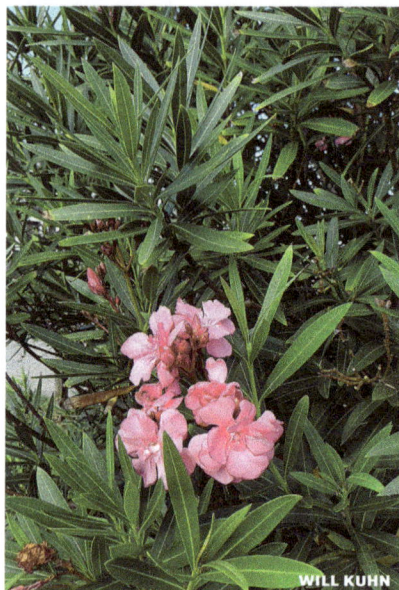

FRANGIPANI, MEXICAN PLUMERIA

NICK H.

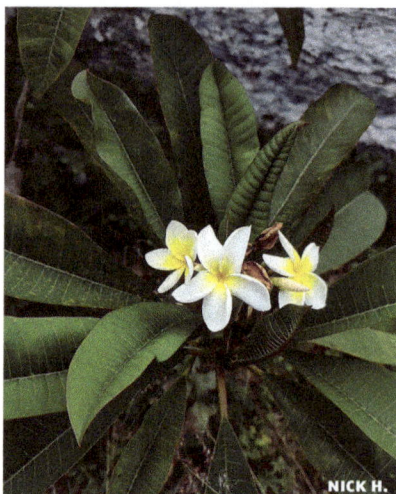

OLEANDER

WILL KUHN

The entire plant, however, is quite poisonous, the leaves, particularly, containing a strong cardiac poison, occasionally used as a stimulant. Like all members of the Dogbane family it contains milky juice.

Frangipani
FLOR DE MAYO

Plumeria rubra
APOCYNACEAE Dogbane Family

In April and May in tropical regions, every **FIESTA** uses the strikingly beautiful and fragrant flowers of Frangipani. While native in Mexico in the tropical deciduous forest, it is also widely cultivated, in white, yellow, red, and variegated colors.

Trees are small to medium-sized, with abundant milky sap; leaves are thick, large, and clustered, with an interesting vein pattern. When flowers are at their best, leaves are mostly absent.

"Century Plants"
MAGUEYS

Agave species
ASPARAGACEAE Asparagus Family

NATIVE RANGE Central and eastern U.S.A. to Venezuela, Caribbean.

To many, the mental image of Mexico almost immediately is associated with the highly decorative **MAGUEY** which we find predominating many picturesque landscapes. The name *Agave* is derived from the Greek *agauos* meaning admirable. One author says: "No genus of plants in America furnishes so many suitable decorative plants".

More than 280 species of *Agave* have been described, largely from the Mexican tableland, but some from the West Indies islands.

The name "Century Plant" was given in the belief that it took 100 years for a plant to mature, after which it would bloom and then die. It is an intriguing idea but it is not true. Some agaves do follow the general pattern; their life, however, is more typically 18 to 20 years, at the end of which they send up a huge flower stalk, which may reach 25 ft. in height, then mature their seed, followed by the death of the whole plant. It is doubtful whether any agave would ever reach as many as 50 years. Other agaves flower from each year, still others only occasionally.

Generally the leaves are in a close rosette, stiff and fleshy, persisting from year-to-year; their margins are mostly armed with teeth; and a sharp spine, sometimes as long as 2 in., tips the end. Spines and teeth may be reddish (as in *Agave tequilana*), black, green or gray.

Depending on the arrangement of the flowers, *Agaves* may be divided into two groups; in each flowers are all tube-shaped, with six stamens.

Two subgenera are of note, designated as the Candelabra type (subgenus *Agave*) and the spike-bloomers (subgenus *Littaea*).

The candelabra type or true agave develops a number of flower clusters extending from the main stalk at regular intervals; it is by far the more ornamental kind. To this group belongs the typical **MAGUEY**, *Agave atrovirens*.

The spike-bloomer type (*Littaea*) has the flowers arranged, often in pairs, like an enormous bottlebrush. Here belong the **LECHUGUILLAS**, rather common in northern Mexico.

The normal color of agave flowers is yellow or white; occasionally — as in **Agave kerchovei** (synonym *Agave inopinabilis*) — a claret color lends charm.

Leaves are sometimes tinged with purple, as in **Agave angustifolia var. rubescens** and **Agave dissimulans**, or may have a yellow margin, as some forms of **Agave americana**. They may be narrow or very broad and thick. **Agave atrovirens** has leaves from 12 to 16 in. wide and 8 ft. or more long, sometimes reaching 12 ft. On the other hand, the whole plant of **Agave x pumila**, the smallest of all, is only 2 in. in diameter.

A number of species may be restricted to certain parts of Mexico: Baja California alone has about 25 species. Others, on the other hand, are cultivated all over Mexico, and in other parts of the world, like the Philippines, India, the Azores, and the Mediterranean countries.

The following list of names connected with *Agaves* may be useful in the maze of Mexican terminology. We might call it an "Agave dictionary".

AGUA MIEL — the unfermented sap of maguey, collected in the cavity hollowed out of the center when it starts blooming.

AMOLE — plant used as a soap substitute, often **Agave schottii** and **Agave filifera**.

CANDELILLO, meaning little candle, is applied to **Agave karwinskii**, which has a trunk becoming 13 ft. tall.

HENEQUEN— particularly applied to **Agave fourcroydes**, with a trunk 6 ft. tall, the source of the larger part of Sisal hemp, used for hammocks, etc.

IXTLE — the fiber from **Agave angustifolia** (synonym *Agave endlichiana*) and **Agave americana** (synonym *Agave gracilispina*), as well as from some bromeliads, commonly used for cordage, basketry, etc. (see also **LECHUGUILLA**).

SULA VANDERPLANK

CANDELILLO

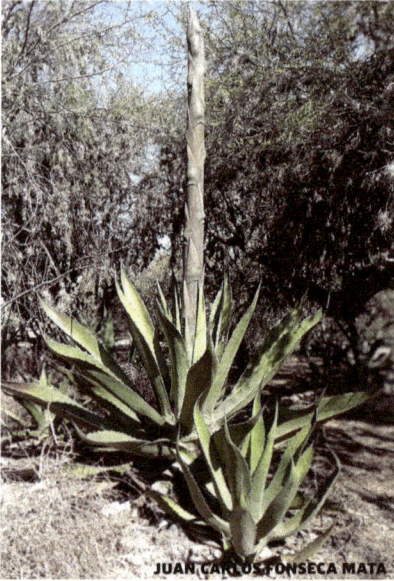

JUAN CARLOS FONSECA MATA

QUIOTE

JAY8085

STAN SHEBS

RIGHT **AGAVE TEQUILA**
UPPER Cultivated plants,
LOWER Plant base used in making tequila.

LECHUGUILLA — diminutive of **LECHUGA** (lettuce), particularly used for *Agave lechuguilla* of northern Mexico; its fiber is used for cordage, brushes, bagging, etc. exported as **IXTLE**.

MAGUEY — applied specifically to *Agave atrovirens*, the principal source of the pulque industry, but also to some similar species, such as *Agave americana*; sometimes extended to all members of the *Agave* subgenus.

MEZCAL — colorless intoxicating drink, distilled of mash from the stalk of *Agave longisepala, Agave tequilana, Agave angustifolia*, and others. **MEZCAL** also designates the food, obtained by roasting their stem end in pits. Mescalero and other Apaches used **MEZCAL** for food.

PITA — *Agave* fiber. In the Azores, *Agave americana* is cultivated from which the **PITA** used in the drawn work of those islands is procured.

PULQUE — national drink of Mexico: fermented **AGUAMIEL**, principally from **MAGUEY VERDE GRANDE** (*Agave atrovirens*). **MEZCAL DE PULQUE** is distilled from **PULQUE**. It is also derived from *Agave americana* and others.

QUIOTE — flower stalk of *Agave salmiana* (synonym *Agave quiotifera*), for sale on the streets, cut to be chewed like sugar cane. It grows to a height of 18–19 ft.

SISAL HEMP (from Sisal, a port of Yucatán) — comes particularly from the fiber of *Agave sisalana*. See also **HENEQUEN** and **IXTLE**.

TEQUILA, properly **MEZCAL DE TEQUILA** — distilled liquor from the stems of *Agave tequilana*.

ZAPUPE — any of the various Mexican agaves yielding fiber somewhat similar to **HENEQUEN**, primarily from varieties of *Agave angustifolia*.

Yucca, Sotol and Beargrass (*Nolina*) also belong to the Asparagus family.

Pulque Agave
MAGUEY

Agave atrovirens
ASPARAGACEAE Asparagus Family

NATIVE RANGE Mexico (Oaxaca to Veracruz).

Agave atrovirens has dark green, very thick and large leaves 12–16 in. wide (and occasionally 13 ft. long), growing in a rosette. The top-spine is gray and long-conical, teeth are triangular, 4 in. long. Cultivated magueys bloom and die after 8 to 10 years, the flower stalk growing very quickly if allowed to develop, and reaching 10 ft.

For the production of **PULQUE** the stalk is cut and the collecting sap is gathered daily for fermentation. The process, simple and effective with the aid of a bulky pipette, is well worth watching.

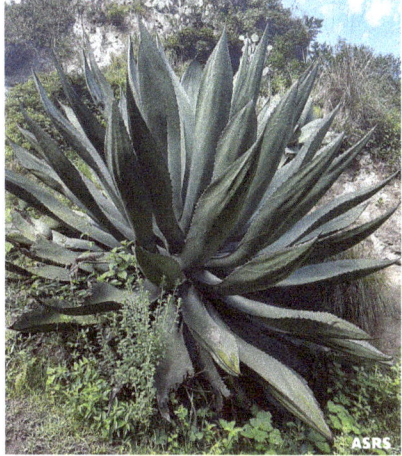

MAGUEY

True Aloe, Bitter Aloe
ZABILA, AZIBAR

Aloe vera
ASPHODELACEAE Onionweed Family

NATIVE RANGE Oman (Hajar Mountains).

If you thought you saw a maguey growing wild along the Mediterranean, it would be more apt to be an Aloe—they are similar as far as the leaves are concerned. Aloe flowers, however, are quite different: yellow or red tubes hanging down from a central stalk, with stamens barely showing outside this tube.

This aloe is naturalized from southern Europe and Africa; it now grows commonly in large clumps on dry parts of the Mesa Central. It is the source of "Barbados aloes" of commerce, a bitter resinous juice, used as a laxative and for treating sunburn. *Aloe vera* grows to a height of 3 ft.; its basal leaves are irregularly white-blotched and narrow while young. Leaves have no endspine as agaves do.

ALOE VERA

BIDGEE

FERNTREE, JACARANDA

CASEY CLARK SUMALINOG

AFRICAN TULIP TREE

Ferntree, Jacaranda
PALO DE BUBA, GUARUPA

Jacaranda acutifolia
BIGNONIACEAE Trumpet-Creeper Family

This Peruvian native has been called the most beautiful of all blue-flowering trees. Flowers are soft lavender-blue, bell-shaped, 1½ in. long, somewhat fragrant; they appear a little before the leaves, around March, in upright clusters, as many as 40 to 90 in a cluster, each flower pendent. The foliage is lacy like a fern; it drops in late-winter or early spring, at which time the tree loses much of its charm in spite of the decorative light-gray bark. The tree may reach 60 ft. Now often included with *Jacaranda mimosifolia*.

African Tulip Tree
ARBOL DE FUENTE

Spathodea campanulata
BIGNONIACEAE Trumpet-Creeper Family

This tall evergreen tree is a favorite in tropical parks. Its great clusters of large, glowing-scarlet blossoms decorate the end of the branches; each is lop-sided, with five irregular, frilled lobes that break out of a yellowish-green split calyx. Pods are quite large and of an interesting shape, to 8 in. long. Leaves are 1 to 1½ ft. long, compound, with about nine dark green, leathery leaflets.

The tree is called "fountain tree" (**ARBOL DE FUENTE**) from the water secreted from its flowers. Blooming most of the year.

Mammee Apple
MAMEY

Mammea americana
CALOPHYLLACEAE Alexandrian-Laurel Family

Large, dense, evergreen, ornamental tree of compact growth, native to southern Mexico to Guatemala, and the Caribbean. Trunk up to 3–4 ft. in diameter, height 40 to 60 ft. or more. It is sometimes confused with the **Marmalade fruit** (see pp. 167, 168), also (erroneously) called **MAMEY**.

Leaves are a deep rich green, appearing as if varnished, opposite, roundish, 4–8 in. long. Fruit (in winter) is sometimes called **Santo Domingo apricot**; it is 4–6 in. in diameter, the surface russet-colored and somewhat rough. Its leathery skin is ⅛ in. thick covering yellow flesh, juicy but firm in texture, and containing 1 to 4 large, rough seeds.

MARCOARBO

MAMMEE APPLE

PAPAYA TREE

TROPICAL ALMOND TREE

It is mostly cooked or used in preserves and sweets; taste said to resemble apricot or peach. The small white, fragrant flowers are used for liqueur—creme de creole. In West Indies the season of ripening is in the summer. Cultivated especially in Veracruz and Tabasco. Wood is hard and durable.

Papaya Tree
PAPAYO

Carica papaya
CARICACEAE Papaya Family

It seems weird to many of us to see the massive yellow papayas of the table, weighing over 20 lbs., hanging down in trusses from the very trunk of the papaya tree—the female tree that is. Normally there are male and female trees; few of the former are allowed to grow; occasionally a tree has both male and female flowers.

The large, much-lobed and long-stalked leaves are in clusters at the top of the straight trunk. The tree is rapid-growing, unbranched and (kept) small. It starts bearing in 8 to 10 months, and continues for 3 or 4 years.

The entire tree has milky sap; it yields a valuable enzyme, like pepsin, aiding digestion; it is used as a meat tenderizer (papain). Even the primitive inhabitants of tropical America knew of this quality and used to wrap meat in papaya leaves.

Tropical Almond Tree
ALMENDRO

Terminalia catappa
COMBRETACEAE West Indies-Almond Family

With so many evergreen trees in the tropics having the same general "laurel" leaf shape, it is a relief to find the **ALMENDRO** with a different, broader pattern — and large, the leaves are 6 to 12 in. long. When the leaves turn a rich red before falling, they are

KEVIN FACCENDA
AIRPLANT

B.NAVEZ
VEGETABLE PEAR

very attractive, and make it possible to recognize the tree from a distance. Commonly used for street planting in the tropics; it has horizontal branches in whorls or tiers.

Bark is smooth, brownish gray. Flowers are small, white and delicate, in long racemes. Nuts angular, slightly winged, tasty; they have no relationship to the regular almond, *Prunus amygdalus*. India and southeast Asia is its original home.

Airplant
SANALO TODO
Kalanchoe pinnata
CRASSULACEAE Stonecrop Family

SYNONYM *Bryophyllum pinnata*
NATIVE RANGE Madagascar.

One of the most interesting tropical plants, originally from Africa, is now common in Mexico, not only as a cultivated perennial succulent, but also escaped into the forest. The old name, *Bryophyllum*, means "sprouting leaf", most appropriately. Even pressed in a herbarium this fleshy leaf may put out tiny plants, each ready to start life anew. That is why folks call it "life plant". Another less intriguing name is "flopper".

Early leaves are simple, later ones compound. A fleshy flower stalk may reach 3 ft. in height, and shows numerous pinkish-red hanging blossoms, protruding from an inflated calyx, yellowish-green with purplish base; this calyx remains after the inner flower drops, thus showing two types of "blossoms". The entire plant may take on a purplish tint as it matures. *Kalanchoe* belongs to the same family as *Sedum* and *Sempervivum*.

Vegetable Pear
CHAYOTE
Sicyos edulis
CUCURBITACEAE Cucumber Family

SYNONYM *Sechium edule*

Fast-growing vine, resembling a cucumber, with large perennial roots, formed the second season after planting. It may grow as much as 50 feet in one year, and yield 50 to 100 "vegetable pears".

Fruit smooth or corrugated, round or pear-shaped, surface sometimes covered with small soft spines—white to dark green. Tendrils are two- to five-branched.

Cultivated by Aztecs, Incas, and Mayas from time immemorial. All parts of the plant are useful: flowers and tender buds as greens; fruit cooked, stewed, candied, or as a salad; tuberous yellow roots cooked as potatoes. Infusion of leaves lowers blood pressure, and

ARAVINTH

INDIAN EBONY PERSIMMON

ERIC ALAN ISAACSON

CASTOR BEAN

is said to combat arteriosclerosis with positive results.

Other names are **CHOCHO, CHUCHU, XUXU, PIPINELLA, CHRISTOPHINE, MIRLITON, CHOUCHOUTE**. The woody stems furnish a fiber of good quality, called **PAILLE DE CHOU-CHOU**.

Indian Ebony Persimmon
ZAPOTE PRIETO

Diospyros ebenum
EBENACEAE Ebony Family

To begin with, both **PRIETO** and **NEGRO** mean black, referring to the inky-black color of the sweet pulp of the fruit. It can be eaten fresh or preserved; the natives make a brandy-like liquor out of it.

This medium-sized tree (up to 45 ft.) is cultivated in hot humid climates — particularly common in Morelos. Even the bark is blackish; leaves dark green, glossy, somewhat leathery, 3–6 in. long. The small whitish flowers are fragrant; groups of 3 to 8 form in the leaf axils. Fruit is rather common in Mexican markets in late winter; it is dark-green, roundish, up to 3 in. in diameter, with 5 to 10 large brown seeds.

This is a close relative of the American and Japanese persimmon, and also of the Old World ebony. In the Philippines the green fruits are said to be used as a **BARBASCO** for catching fish.

Castor Bean
HIGUERILLA

Ricinus communis
EUPHORBIACEAE Spurge Family

From its original habitat in northeastern Africa, the Castor bean has now become a familiar plant in many gardens, both north and south. In some parts of Mexico it is cultivated as a crop, for the production of castor oil. Growing to a height of 18 ft. or more, it is a beautiful plant in the tropics. It comes in different shapes and colors. Fruits are prickly, sometimes strikingly colored; they contain three seeds shaped like a large tick (*Ricinus* means tick in Latin).

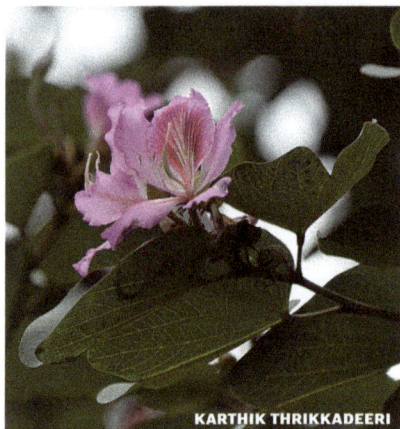

KARTHIK THRIKKADEERI

ORCHID TREE, MOUNTAIN EBONY

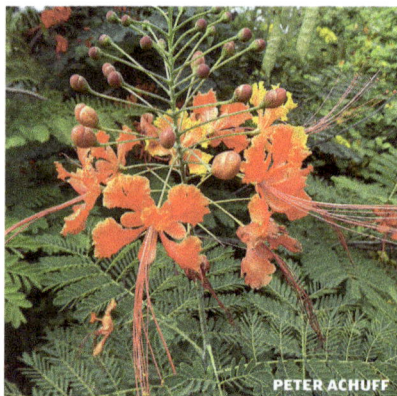

PETER ACHUFF

DWARF POINCIANA

Oil made from the seeds is used as a medicine, as a lubricant for airplane motors, etc., and for the fabrication of plastic material. It has even been advocated for preserving leather.

A related herbaceous shrub is **Manihot esculenta** from northern South America, the source of cassava and tapioca, widely cultivated in the tropics for its food value. **Manihot carthagenensis** is the **Ceara rubber tree** from Brazil.

Orchid Tree, Mountain Ebony
PATA DE VACA

Bauhinia variegata
FABACEAE Pea Family

You can't help but recognize *Bauhiania* by their "twin" leaves. **PATA DE VACA** refers to it: the leaf is cleft like a cow's hoof. Incidentally these twin leaflets are responsible for the botanical name, after the two brothers John and Caspar Bauhin, 16th century herbalists.

Commonly grown in parks, the Orchid tree (which isn't an orchid at all, but belongs to the Pea Family) is a beautiful small tree (6–20 ft.) when covered with spring flowers, pinkish-white marked with an orchid-colored feathery design. The flowers are scentless but as beautiful as an orchid. Leaves come a little after the blossoms.

Bauhinia variegata comes from India and China, where the bark is used for tanning and dyeing, and the flowerbuds (pickled) and leaves are eaten as a vegetable. There are additional Mexican species of *Bauhinia*, with white, greenish, pink, or purple flowers.

Dwarf Poinciana
CHINCHEMALINCHE, TABACHIN

Caesalpinia pulcherrima
FABACEAE Pea Family

A small tree or shrub, rarely over 10 ft. in height, widely cultivated and naturalized in the tropics of both continents. It is easily recognized by its large, red-and-yellow flowers with long-extended red stamens and style. Different from the **Royal poinciana** in that its flowers are fragrant, the seed-pods much shorter (4 to 5 in.) and in its intermittent blooming—richest in fall and spring. Not without leaves at any time; sometimes with scattered prickles.

The name **CHINCHEMALINCHE**, in the Nahua language, translates roughly as "curly red-head"; it was also the name given to Cortez' native sweetheart.

English names are Bride of Barbados, Flower-fence, Bird-of-paradise. The name **Paradise poinciana** is reserved for **Erythrostemon gilliesii**, cultivated in northern Mexico; it is

SUBHADRA DEVI

MANDARIN HAT

DARREN OBBARD

FLAMBOYANT TREE, ROYAL POINCIANA

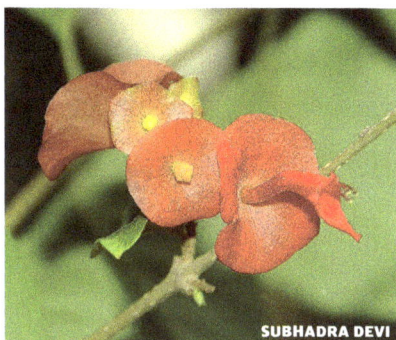

distinguished by copious hairiness and sticky flower clusters.

See also the yellow-flowered **Bird-of-paradise**, *Tara cacalaco* (pp. 63, 99, also known as **Mexican Caesalpinia**).

Flamboyant Tree, Royal Poinciana
FLAMBOYÁN

Delonix regia
FABACEAE Pea Family

This very showy flowering tree, with broadly spreading top, is from Madagascar originally, but it has found its way into almost all sections of Mexico as a highly favored ornamental shade tree. Fast-growing, and now well-known in all tropical regions.

The tree's fiery red blossoms, from April on, almost cover its surface, enhanced by the delicate, feathery, drooping leaves soon after. These flowers are glorious both in mass and individually (note the one ornately marked petal of each flower; it curls and falls in a day or two).

Unfortunately it is a deciduous tree, and for months, after both flowers and leaves are gone, the Flamboyant tree or "Flame of the Forest" is rather unsightly, with long, brown, curved pods (6 in. to 2 ft. long) hanging on. Its wood is so weak that breakage by wind is common. Its hard seeds are used in necklaces.

Mandarin Hat
SOMBRERO CHINO

Holmskioldia sanguinea
FABACEAE Pea Family

As intimated by the name, the blossoms are shaped like a Chinese coolie's hat, with a brick-red or orange larger calyx and a small tube-like corolla. They are not of large size, less than 1 in., but are showy with their color, bizarre shape, and quantities on the graceful branches.

The plant is a straggling shrub or tree, well over 10 or 15 ft. tall; it comes from the subtropical Himalayan region and is cultivated in Mexican gardens.

Avocado
AGUACATE

Persea americana
LAURACEAE Laurel Family

From early days the avocado has been cultivated in Mexico; it is one of the best-known of Mexican trees. The name **AGUACATE** comes directly from the Nahuatl **AHUACATL**, which has a double meaning. In Mayan dialects it is called **O, OJ, JU, UN**, and **ON**. The name "alligator-pear", sometimes used, is frowned upon by botanists.

AVOCADO

B.NAVEZ

CANNONBALL TREE

DEMIAN HISS

The avocado tree is not too easily recognized except by its long-stalked fruit of unusual shape, hanging down. Leaves are laurel-like, bespeaking the family to which avocado belongs. Flowers are small, greenish, produced in great abundance in loose trusses. Normally the tree is of great size, up to 60 ft. in height, but budded trees are dwarfed.

Three "races" of avocado are distinguished: the Guatemalan has rough or warty fruit and thick, brittle skin, ripening January to April; the West Indian race, ripening from July to November, has smooth-skinned, large fruit, strictly in hot countries; the Mexican race is the hardiest, but somewhat smaller; it has anise-scented leaves, smaller and narrower; its fruit is considered the choicest.

In addition to *Persea americana*, several other species are recognized, none as good for eating as *P. americana*; some have roundish fruit.

Avocado trees begin to bear when 4 or 5 years old, many continue for 50 years, and may produce as many as 500 fruits annually. Uses are not only for salads and desserts but for therapeutic purposes. The milky juice of the seeds is said to stain linen indelibly.

Cannonball Tree
BALA DE CANON

Couroupita guianensis
LECYTHIDACEAE Brazilnut Family

Here is one of those "never-never" trees — the unbelievable kind — for two aspects: both flowers and fruit are highly unusual.

At first sight the showy, scented, red-pink-yellow flowers, hanging down in 2 to 3 ft. strings, don't seem so unusual. They have three to six somewhat unequal petals. On closer inspection the peculiar "double-decker" stamens of their center draw attention to themselves: some are upright in a ring around the white pistil, others are suspended from a curious fleshy, white "awning" protecting the entire center; others again extend in a pink fringe from the awning. The whole intricate mechanism is evidently geared to cross-pollination by the appropriate insects.

Nine months later, the reddish, woody, 8 in. cannonballs ripen, with many seeds embedded in their pulpy interior, disagreeably odorous when ripe. The shell is used for

HEARTFLOWER TREE

CRAPE MYRTLE

household utensils by the natives; the pulp is eaten or used for making beverages. The untidy strings of these cannonballs and flowers hanging down along the straight trunk are in themselves an odd sight. The tree also has a peculiar habit of suddenly dropping its leaves several times a year.

Crape Myrtle
ASTRONÓMICA

Lagerstroemia indica
LYTHRACEAE Loosestrife Family

The "Lilac of the South" is a highly decorative shrub reaching 30 ft., a favorite in ornamental planting and used for roadside decoration, even in places with occasional frost. Huge clusters of pink, white or purple blossoms are present throughout summer and fall.

The petals are crinkled and crape-like; extending from a center calyx with numerous pale yellow stamens; total diameter is as much as 2 in. The bark is smooth and gray; leaves generally opposite but alternate toward the top, only 2 in. long.

Named for Magnus von Lagerstroem, a friend of Linnaeus; it is a native of China and southeast Asia in spite of the name indica. It sometimes escapes from cultivation in Mexico. The name **ASTRONÓMICA** is intriguing; so is another one, **ATMOSÉRICA**.

A number of other species of *Lagerstroemia* have come into cultivation from various tropical countries.

Heartflower Tree
YOLOXOCHITL

Magnolia mexicana
MAGNOLIACEAE Magnolia Family

SYNONYM *Talauma mexicana*

This "heartflower" used to be reserved exclusively for the nobility of the early inhabitants of Mexico; it is called by the Aztecs "Noble Lord Flower." Another name, **CHIPAHUAC**, means the "beautiful". A single blossom was considered enough to perfume a whole house.

It is a tall tree, up to 90 ft., over 3 ft. in diameter, native in evergreen forests of southern Mexico at mid-elevations, but also cultivated in gardens. Dried flowers can be bought in public markets; they and the tree bark are supposed to be good for the heart.

BREADFRUIT

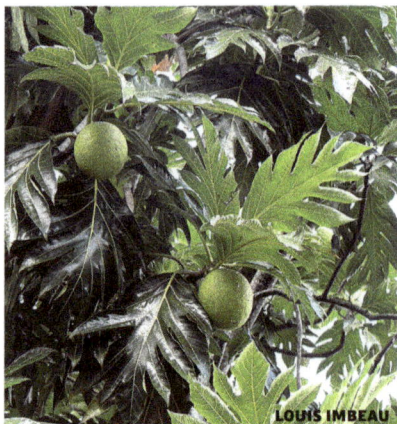

CHINABERRY

While it is similar to other cultivated magnolias, it differs in having non-opening fruit, and by its thick and leathery flower petals. Seeds are a brilliant red. Blooms from May to July. Strangely enough, its Himalayan relative (*Magnolia hodgsonii*) is better known in the United States.

Chinaberry
PARAÍSO

Melia azedarach
MELIACEAE Mahogany Family

This medium-sized tree (40 ft.) belongs to the same family as the mahogany, but its wood is soft and weak. With their lilac-purplish flowers and black stamens, the flower trusses are quite handsome; as are the yellow ball-shaped berries, containing large seeds; they are sometimes used as dress beads.

Even the foliage is attractive: no wonder the Spanish call it the paradise tree. It came from Tangiers originally, and has now escaped from cultivation all over Mexico. Partly on account of its sweet scent it is commonly planted in parks and gardens.

Other names are **CANELA** (meaning cinnamon) **LILA, ARBOL DE QUITASOL** ('sunshade), **PARAGUAS CHINO** ('Chinese rainshade') and **PIOCHA** (trinket for women's head dresses').

Breadfruit
ARBOL DEL PÁN

Artocarpus altilis
MORACEAE Mulberry Family

Captain Bligh, on his ill-fated trip in 1793, in H.M.S. *Bounty* tried to—and later did— introduce this fabulous Malayan tree into the Antilles. It may have reached Mexico one or two centuries earlier, via the Philippines.

One cannot fail to recognize it by its large glossy leaves and immense fruit (up to 12 in.). Even the milky sap is distinctive: it belongs to the Mulberry family, like the figs. Branches are quite fragile. The fruit is rough and yellow like a lemon; its taste is rather insipid but it is nourishing. Cultivated as food for people and for fattening swine. Another variety has numerous seeds, which are served like chestnuts.

ALEJANDROSG

COMMON FIG

JAGDISH SINGH NEGI

BANANA *Musa* × *paradisiaca*

Common Fig
Ficus carica
HIGO   MORACEAE Mulberry Family

The cultivated fig, introduced from Europe and Asia, is not as important in Mexico as many other tropical and subtropical fruits are. Wet weather interferes with the proper ripening. Easily recognized by the typical fig leaf and the well-known fruit. It has milky sap like the rubber plant (*Ficus elastica*) and other representatives of the genus. See also **Strangler fig** in Tropical Deciduous zone (p. 103) and other native figs in the Tropical Evergreen zone (p. 127).

Banana
Musa species
PLATANO, GUINEO   MUSACEAE Banana Family

Musa × *paradisiaca*, (**Fruit of the Wise Men**) — Eating banana
Musa × *paradisiaca* and **Musa** *troglodytarum* — Plantain for cooking
Musa *coccinea* — Ornamental
Musa *textilis* — Abacá, Manila hemp, — For fiber
Musa *nana*, **Dwarf banana** — Similar to *Musa* × *paradisiaca*.

Flower clusters of bananas are gorgeously beautiful, a great surprise to the uninitiated. At the bottom of the cluster is a huge bud with overlapping scales or bracts, purplish red on the inside (see photo). As they open up, the tiny flowers become visible; the upper ones develop into bananas, the lower ones furnish pollen, the middle ones drop off. Blue-gray, red, purple and brown may show at the same time with the yellow of the flowers. Only one bunch is produced on each stalk. Once the plant fruits it dies. New plants are grown from the underground stems. From planting to eating takes but 18 months.

Bananas, therefore, are not trees but perennial herbs, growing from shoots; seeds are formed only in the textile and ornamental species: **Musa** *textilis*, **PLATANO TEXTIL**, of the former and **Musa** *coccinea*, **PLATANO TUNO**. The latter produces brilliant scarlet red bracts, tipped with yellow; it is particularly showy and has become wild in some parts of the tropics.

MICHAEL BAKKER PAIVA

MUSA COCCINEA

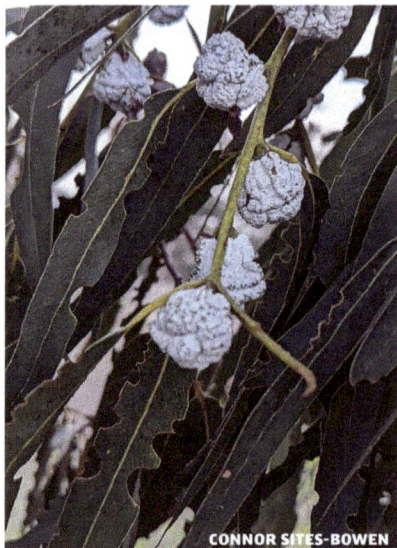

CONNOR SITES-BOWEN

EUCALYPTUS, BLUEGUM

There were no bananas in America originally; now three-fourths of the world production is in tropical America. A great many varieties are grown, both of the immediately edible banana, **Musa × paradisiaca** and the cooking banana or plantain banana, also *Musa × paradisiaca* and *Musa troglodytarum*. Some of the latter are of huge size, often a snare to the tourist shopping in the marketplace.

Abacá banana, *Musa textilis*, called **PLATANO TEXTIL** in Mexico, produces a most elastic and strong fiber, used particularly for rope and for Manila paper.

Bananas are best grown in a level plain where the underflow is at 3 ft. during most of the year: drainage is essential. In valleys among the hills they can be grown as long as there is enough water, either naturally or by irrigation. Frost must be avoided.

The name **PLATANO** is used in Mexico for the ordinary banana; another name is **GUINEO**. The cooking banana is called **PLATANO MACHO** (male). In Honduras and Guatemala, however, "banana" is the accepted word in Spanish as well as in English, and **PLATANO** is reserved for the cooking banana or plantain. In Chiapas the export banana is called **ROATÁN**, and the **BÁRBARO** is the variety for human use, even though it is of inferior quality; it can stand as many as 6 months of drought. Other names are **CRIOLLO, MORADO, MORADO AMARILLO, GUINEO DE SEDA**, and even **MANZANO** (apple).

Worldwide, about 80 species of *Musa* are recognized. Many of them have dozens of varieties and clones, propagated from rootstocks and by tissue culture.

Eucalyptus, Bluegum
EUCALIPTO

Eucalyptus globulus
MYRTACEAE Myrtle Family

Australia's gift to semi-tropical regions is hard to over-estimate. The bluegum is good for windbreaks and fuel. Its wood is used for flooring, tool handles, and furniture, being hard and durable. Oil of eucalyptus comes from the leaves. The common bluegum (there are a great many species) may reach 300 ft.; the trunk is smooth and grayish, the bark coming off in long thin strips. Leaves vary according to maturity; they all have the typical eucalyptus fragrance.

GUAVA

FLORO ORTIZ CONTRERAS

GLOSSY PRIVET

SAM KIESCHNICK

The angular seedboxes can generally be found under the trees. Often planted along Mexico's highways. A few related species have decorative flowers.

Guava
GUAYABA

Psidium guajava
MYRTACEAE Myrtle Family

NATIVE RANGE Southern tropical South America.

Frequently cultivated in Mexico and the tropics and distributed throughout the warmest regions of the globe, is the 25 ft. high tree, which furnishes the unusual-tasting roundish fruit, about 2 in. in diameter: it is of a characteristic sweet or slightly acid flavor, with a somewhat musky penetrating aroma. The pulp of this yellow fruit is white or pink; it surrounds a mass of more or less granular pulp in which are the small hard seeds.

The tree has a scaly, reddish bark, branchlets angular and somewhat felty; leaves opposite, 2 to 6 in. long, light green and smooth on top, with conspicuous veins underneath; flowers white, over 1 in. across.

Related are **Psidium oligospermum**, with smaller fruit and leaves, and two smaller-size trees with edible sweet fruit. Guava is among the best known tropical fruit.

Glossy Privet
TRUENO

Ligustrum lucidum
OLEACEAE Olive Family

A favorite ornamental small tree in Mexican parks and home grounds is this introduction from China and Korea. Its loose flower trusses of whitish blossoms, and its bluish-black berries are equally attractive, and not unlike those of the English privet, are a well-known hedge plant. Leaves are handsome as well: thick, glossy, evergreen with reddish leaf stalks; they are from 2 to 4 in. long.

In China the branches sometimes exude a white wax, caused by an insect.

Golden Bamboo
BAMBU

Bambusa vulgaris
POACEAE Grass Family

We are apt to associate bamboo with the tropical regions in Mexico: they seem to belong together. And yet, widespread as the plants are now, they were all introduced in

NAVANEETH SINI GEORGE

GOLDEN BAMBOO

LOUIS IMBEAU

SUGAR CANE

colonial days. We find them in deep, rich loam, in moist but well-drained soil, where they may grow to a height of 60 ft. or more under favorable conditions.

The golden or common bamboo is cultivated most, *Bambusa vulgaris*; it is used for home-building, furniture, fishing rods, conduits for irrigation, baskets, brushes, even manufacture of paper, in addition to its ornamental aspect. Variety *vittata* is the Green-stripe bamboo; its close relative *Phyllostachys* (now considered a sedge, *Carex*) also has decorative species and clones.

The fact is that there are dozens of other kinds of bamboo, difficult to distinguish. A thorny kind is called OTATE, *Bambusa bambos*; then there are LA JIMBA, EL PATAMBA, LA CHUSQUEA, etc.

Sugar Cane
CAÑA DE AZUCAR

Saccharum officinarum
POACEAE Grass Family

An annual rainfall of over 59 in. and a temperature of not less than 70° F. average is necessary for the profitable production of sugar cane. Look for it in the lowlands along the Gulf Coast or in the state of Sinaloa. It may well reach over 12 ft. in height and resembles an untidy, lush-green, corn field.

Short sections of cane are used as sweets by Mexican children, and are regularly for sale in market places. Harvesting is still often done by MACHETE, the sturdy Mexican knife, close to the ground, where most of the sugar is found.

Sugar cane was introduced by the Spaniards and Portuguese who got it during the Arab occupation; it was of importance in southeast Asia as long as four centuries before Christ. Different "races" of sugar cane are now adaptable to different climates and topography. Some production goes for the making of brandy and brown sugar (PANELA).

Coffee
CAFETO

Coffea arabica
RUBIACEAE Madder Family

Coffee shrubs can be recognized by their glossy evergreen, opposite leaves. Flowers are fragrant, pure-white, star-shaped, in clusters of one to four. Equally attractive are the brilliant red berries, half an inch in diameter. The plant may look almost as regular as a little spruce tree, with lateral branches in horizontal pairs.

It grows only in climates where the temperature stays above 45°F., in well-drained soils and protected from the scorching heat of the sun. Coffee beans come in pairs inside the crimson berry which takes 6½ to 7 months to mature.

Citrus fruits
Citrus species
NARANJA, MANDARINA, LIMON, LIMA, TORONJA
RUTACEAE Rue Family

ANNIKA LINDQVIST

COFFEE

Seeing so many citrus fruits in Mexico it is hard to realize that none are native; all came from the Far Orient: China, Burma, the Malay Archipelago (oranges appear in Chinese writings as early as 2200 B.C.). Practically all reached America via Spain. A few people claim they can tell the various citrus fruit trees apart on sight; most of us must wait until we see the fruit. The only indications we have are as follows: **grapefruit** is a large, round-topped tree with large, dark-green, glossy leaves. **Mandarins** are small trees with lance-shaped leaves, narrower than all the others. Sharp, short, stiff spines are found on **lemon** trees and **lime** trees, both are small trees. **Oranges**, **sour oranges**, and **grapefruit** all have interesting winged leaf stalks that are hinged both at the leaf blade and at the branch attachment. **Lemon flowers** are the only ones that have a bit of reddish-purple on the underside of the flower petals.

The following species are well established in Mexico. In addition there are others and a number of hybrids and trade names.

SWEET ORANGE, *Citrus* × *aurantium* form *aurantium* (synonym *Citrus* × *sinensis*), **NARANJA DULCE**, the well-known leading fruit, grown particularly in Nuevo Leon and Veracruz. Believed to have originated as a hybrid between pomelo (*Citrus maxima*) and mandarin (*Citrus reticulata*), also known as the sweet oranges, is a commonly cultivated species of orange that includes Valencia oranges, blood oranges and navel oranges.

SOUR ORANGE, *Citrus* × *aurantium*, **NARANJA AGRIA**, especially for marmalade, perfume (Eau de Cologne), and fruit stock for others.

MANDARIN, *Citrus reticulata*, **MANDARINA**, small fruit with thin, loose skin, including tangerines and Satsumas. Related is *Citrus nobilis*, delicious, with larger fruit, like King Orange.

LEMON, *Citrus* × *limon*, **LIMON REAL**, used especially for lemonade, and perfumery. Very sensitive to cold.

LIME, *Citrus × aurantiifolia*, **LIMON**, the well-known small, round-oval, acid fruit with greenish pulp, used for limeade and in soups, sauces, etc.; abundantly cultivated in all tropical countries: a poor keeper and shipper; least frostproof of all citrus fruits. Small tree with very sharp, short, stiff spines, small leaves with winged leaf stalks. Sweet lime has larger fruit, more like a lemon, and has been called *Citrus limetta* in Mexico.

GRAPEFRUIT, *Citrus maxima*, **TORONJA**, has been called the "aristocrat of the breakfast table", the largest of them all, both as to fruit and height of tree. **Pomelo** is one variety and the familiar **grapefruit**, another, more popular in the U.S.A. than in Mexico.

CITRON, *Citrus medica*, shrub or low tree, thorny, with large, pale-green leaves without wings or hinge; used for its thick, fragrant, almost spongy rind, used for candying in confectionery and in cakes; pulp scanty and acid. The **Etrog** or sacred Jewish citron is used at the Feast of Tabernacles, grown principally in the island of Corfu; quite expensive if of the prescribed size, form, and color.

KUMQUAT, *Citrus* species (sometimes placed in *Fortunella*), Chinese evergreen shrub, grown mostly for ornament and for preserving the small oblong fruit. *Citrus japonica* has bright orange-color fruit.

JEEVAN JOSE

LIME

White Sapote
MATASANO

Casimiroa edulis
RUTACEAE Rue Family

The tree, especially common around Guadalajara, may grow to a height of 50 ft. but is generally lower, with a short, stout trunk with warty excrescences around its base. Interesting glossy, bright green leaves, consisting of five leaflets, each 3–4 in. long; they are copper-colored when young. Small greenish flowers in January and February; fruit is greenish, quince-like, as large as a good-sized orange.

Delicious, sweet, cream-colored pulp, a little more bitter than the marmalade fruit. The fruit, and especially the three to four seeds inside are said to induce sleep two hours after taking it. It belongs to the same family (Rutaceae) as the citrus fruits.

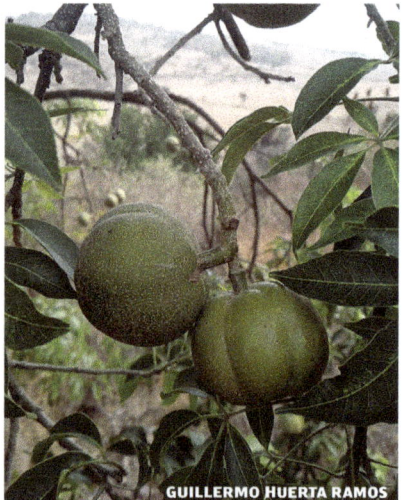

GUILLERMO HUERTA RAMOS

WHITE SAPOTE

SAPOTA, SAPOTE, SAPODILLA, ZAPOTE, ZAPOTILLO, MAMEY

The study of any cultivated fruit or ornamental is apt to lead into a maze of names, species, varieties and types. Tropical fruits are no exception. When, in addition, many kinds of people give the same name to a multitude of different fruits, the situation only worsens.

One of our dictionaries sagely skirts the difficulty in the definition of SAPOTA as "a general term employed in tropical America for widely differing fruits".

Below are some of the most prominent sapotas and their kin and acquaintances.

ZAPOTE COLORADO, *Pouteria sapota* (see pp. 167–168, synonym *Calocarpum sapota*), **Marmalade Fruit**. (Sapotaceae). Attractive large tree with large, obovate leaves and exquisite fruit, picked green to ripen in cool place. It is often wrongly called **MAMEY** (see *Mammea americana*).

ZAPOTE BLANCO (**MATASANO**), *Casimiroa edulis*, White Sapote. (Rutaceae). Medium-sized tree with short stout trunk, with warty bark, compound leaves, greenish fruit resembling a quince; soft, cream-colored pulp, sweet and delicious.

ZAPOTE BLANCO, *Morisonia americana*. Morisonia (Capparaceae, also spelled Capparidaceae). Low tree with simple, shining, leathery, oblong leaves, 6 in. long, of Sinaloa to Oaxaca and Chiapas where it may be called **CHICASAPOTE**. Its fruit, 1½–2 in. in diameter, with hard, rough shell, is fleshy inside but not edible. Flowers white and large. An illustration of added confusion: they call it **ARBOL DEL DIABLO** (tree of the devil) in Colima, south of Guadalajara.

ZAPOTE AMARILLO, *Lucuma campechiana* (synonym *Lucuma salicifolia*), Yellow Sapote, **Egg-fruit**. (Sapotaceae). Small tree in Morelos, Guerrero, Veracruz and Oaxaca, with long leaves, milky sap and yellow, fleshy fruit. The name **ZAPOTE BORRACHO** (drunk) indicates its sleep-inducing quality.

ZAPOTE NEGRO, *Diospyros ebenum*, Indian Ebony Persimmon, (Ebenaceae). Medium-sized tree, especially in Morelos, with lustrous leaves (8 in.) and olive-green fruit with almost black pulp. Related to Japanese and American persimmons. (**ZAPOTE PRIETO**).

MAMEY, **ZAPOTE DE SANTO DOMINGO**, *Mammea americana*, Maumee Apple (Calophyllaceae). Here is confusion compounded, since the name **MAMEY** or **MAMEY ZAPOTE** is often applied to *Pouteria sapota* (see above). incorrectly. The real **MAMEY** is a broad-crowned tree with thick trunk (3–4 ft.) and a rich shade of green leaves that appear varnished. Yellow, juicy fruit, particularly good for jam and preserves.

ZAPOTE DE AGUA, *Pachira aquatica*, Guiana chestnut or Shaving-brush tree (Malvaceae). Small or middle-sized tree, often with buttresses, of the Savanna, see p. 115. Fruit large, light-brown.

ZAPOTE DE MICO (monkey), **SONZAPOTE**, *Moquilea platypus* (synonym *Licania platypus*). (Chrysobalanaceae). Fruit large (5 in.), insipid.

ZAPOTILLO, species of **Sideroxylon** (**Jungleplum**), Sapotaceae; not too important.

CHICOZAPOTE, *Manilkara zapota* (synonym *Achras zapota*), highly important tree of the rainforest, described on p. 139. Also called **CHICLE** and **Naseberry**. (Sapotaceae).

Yellow Sapote
Lucuma campechiana
COZTICZAPOTL
SAPOTACEAE Sapodilla Family
SYNONYMS *Lucuma salicifolia, Pouteria campechiana*

Here is the "black sheep" of the sapotes, as indicated by the name **ZAPOTE BORRACHO** (drunk), showing that the fruit when eaten, induces a deep sleep with resulting "drunk-

JOSÉ BELEM HERNÁNDEZ DÍAZ

MARMALADE FRUIT

FLORENTINO FLORO

YELLOW SAPOTE

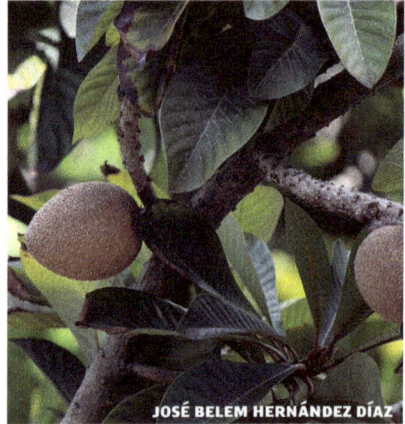

enness". This property was noted as far back as 1615 by Ximenez. The seeds had a reputation of being poisonous, and do have narcotic properties.

This is a small tree growing in Morelos, Guerrero, Veracruz and Oaxaca. Young branches are brownish; leaves are 4 to 11 in. long and about 2 in. wide; fruit yellow when ripe, unequally roundish, 3 to 4 in. in diameter; pulp reddish-yellow, with three or four dark brown seeds, 3 in. long and half as thick.

Marmalade Fruit
ZAPOTE COLORADO
SYNONYM *Calocarpum sapota*

Pouteria sapota
SAPOTACEAE Sapodilla Family

One of the most handsome tropical fruit trees, reaching 35 to 90 feet, both native and cultivated in fertile soils, with or without irrigation. Its fruit has been considered as the most exquisite of the tropics.

Even its leaves are beautiful: intense green above, paler or brownish below, leathery, 9 in. long, obovate and clustered at the tips of the branches. The tender twigs are covered with a reddish-gray down.

Fruit rusty brown, 4 x 6 in., ovoid, picked green to ripen in a cool place (and for better shipping). Since the oil from the seed was used as hair-oil from early days, the legend arose that it prevents falling hair. Mis-called **MAMEY**.

Angel's Trumpet
FLORIPONDIO
SYNONYM *Datura arborea*

Brugmansia arborea
SOLANACEAE Potato Family

Imagine a tall bush almost entirely covered with immense, pearly-white hanging trumpets, up to 12 in. long. They open at night and have an intense, musklike fragrance. Its leaves are somewhat hairy, with smooth edges; they occur in pairs, one a third shorter than the other, with inch-long stalks.

Originally growing from Ecuador to northern Chile, it is now widely cultivated as an ornamental, even though both leaves and seeds are poisonous like its relative the Jimsonweed. Another South American species, ***Brugmansia sanguinea***, with 8 in. long brilliant orange-red blossoms, is cultivated across Mexico.

ANGEL'S TRUMPET

Y. LIU

TREE TOBACCO

Tree Tobacco
CORNETÓN
Nicotiana glauca
SOLANACEAE Potato Family

Native of central South America, this small tree has become quite at home in the Thorn Forest and Tropical Deciduous zone, especially along streambeds and roadsides. Its bluish-green, smooth leaves on long stems are evergreen; flowers are pale yellow, tube-shaped, about 1½ in. long, blooming throughout the year. Bark is smooth and blue-green.

Attractive to hummingbirds, but not to cattle, horses, and sheep; deadly to insects.

Potato Jasmine
FLOR DE SAN DIEGO
Solanum laxum
SOLANACEAE Potato Family

SYNONYM *Solanum jaminoides*

A beautiful, rather delicate and fast-growing woody vine from Brazil, cultivated around the City of of Mexico and naturalized in Morelos and Veracruz. Flowers are star-shaped, in large trusses, white or bluish, nearly ¾ in. broad. It blooms almost continuously. Upper leaves are entire, lower leaves compound of three narrow leaflets.

Sandpaper Vine
Petrea volubilis
CAPITAN LILA, RASPA-SOMBRERO
VERBENACEAE Verbena Family

Showy vine, large and woody, with opposite leaves, the character of which is indicated by the names **Sandpaper vine** (**PAPEL DE LIJA**), **RASPA-SOMBRERO**, and **LENGUA DE VACA** ('Cow-tongue'). The beautiful, slender flower clusters, however, are responsible for such names as **Purple**

FRAN GONZALEZ

POTATO JASMINE

CHESTNUT DION

JOSÉ FRANCISCO COLORADO-DAPA

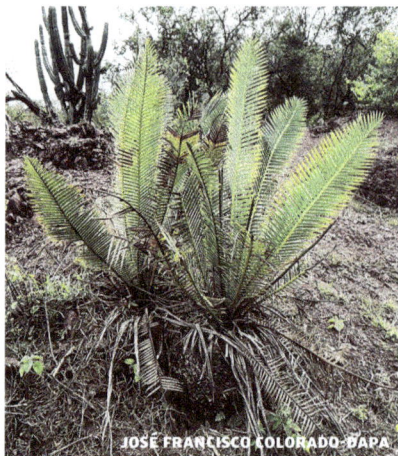

JUSTINE COBALEDA

SANDPAPER VINE

wreath, Queen's wreath, JASMIN AZUL (blue jasmine) and FLOR DE SANTA MARÍA.

Flowers are like a five-pointed purple-lilac star with a darker violet in the middle. The latter represents the corolla, which drops off while the lighter calyx remains, thus giving the impression of two shades of bloom on the same plant. Fruit is small and leathery. Tough stems are used as a substitute for rope.

Chestnut Dion
CHAMAL, PALMA DE LA VIRGEN

Dioon edule

ZAMIACEAE Sago-Cycas Family

It isn't a palm and it isn't a fern but a **cycad**, looking somewhat like either palm or fern. The Cycad family is fully as ancient as both; it is usually classified with the pine group under the Gymnosperms (naked seeds).

This genus is said to be the closest to the fossil forms of any living representative of the Cycad family. Two genera of this family, *Ceratozamia* and *Zamia*, are reported mainly from Veracruz.

Dioon edule, a native of Mexico, occurs naturally along the east coast and is commonly cultivated. Its beautiful leathery rigid leaves are 3 to 5 ft. long; they have about 100 linear to lance-leaved, sharp-pointed segments on each side, widest at the base. Its trunk may easily reach 3 ft. or more.

Male plants have cylindrical cones, 8 to 12 in. long. The pistillate cones, on female plants, are ovoid; they are pendent, sometimes nearly 2 ft. long, and remain hanging for several years; they contain edible, chestnut-like seeds, a favorite food of peccaries, bears, and domestic hogs. People roast them or boil them.

There is a huge related species, **Giant dioon** (*Dioon spinulosum*) in Veracruz and Yucatán, with 5–8 spines on each margin of the leaflets, which may reach 50 ft. in height. Dioon grows very slowly: tall plants indicate considerable age.

GIANT DIOON

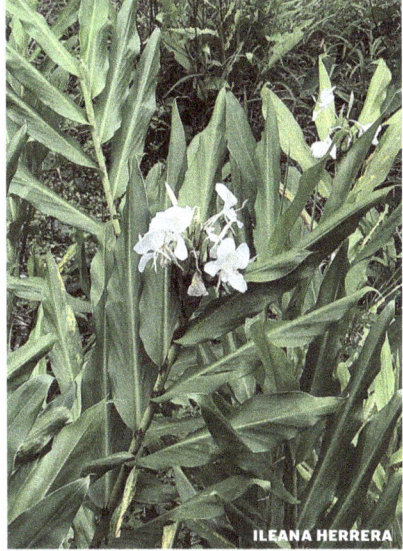

GINGER LILY

Ginger Lily
MARIPOSA

Hedychium coronarium
ZINGIBERACEAE Ginger Family

Tall, ornamental, strong-growing perennial with very sweet-scented beautiful white flowers, having a yellow spot on the large petal; the name **MARIPOSA** means butterfly and is not to be confused with the Mariposa lily, *Calochortus*, of northern climes.

Blooms are in a terminal cluster and continue throughout late summer and fall. Leaves are somewhat like a canna leaf.

Originally from India and other parts of tropical Asia, this member of the Ginger family is naturalized in portions of tropical America, where it is often cultivated in gardens and parks.

SANDPAPER VINE

Common Ornamental Plants

Even if you wanted to (which you certainly don't), you could not get away from the flamboyant **BOUGAINVILLEA**. Their flowers decorate patios, fences, and walls, highways, parks, and even in woody areas where they have acclimated themselves — different in color but always gorgeous, easily recognized by the "flowers" decorating the vine at almost any time of the year — flowers that are not really flowers but the colorful bracts around them.

So it is with the **POINSETTIAS**. If you are in Mexico around the Christmas holidays, you'll be intrigued by the variety of colors, some of them not yet seen in the United States. You don't need to be told they are poinsettias, and probably you are not too much interested in the fact that, here again, the colorful parts are bracts beneath the real flowers.

PINEAPPLES came from Brazil originally, but spread all over tropical America before colonial days, and all over the world after the Spaniards came to know them, and Columbus himself acted as their press agent. Note the tall stalk supporting the fruit.

CALLA LILIES are so closely associated in our mind with Mexican flower markets and with Mexican madonnas, it is hard to realize they came from Africa to begin with, relatives of Jack-in-the-pulpit and of Elephant's ear. Again, the "flower" is not the flower but a decorative leaf or spathe, surrounding the collection of flowers.

CANNAS are too well known to need an illustration; they are now cultivated in gardens all over the world. Originally, however, the Spanish conquistadors brought them from the New World for the use of their seeds for rosaries. The botanical name *Canna indica* is misleading; that particular species came from the West Indies, Mexico, Central and South America. Others are natives in Mexico, Brazil, Peru, and a few came from the Himalayas and the Malaysian tropics. They are grown for their beautiful flowers as well as for their lush foliage. The Mexican name **PLATANILLO** reminds us of the fact that it is a near relative of the banana.

FUCHSIAS are mostly of South American origin; they are grown in Mexican gardens where some grow to tree size (**Tree fuschia**, *Fuchsia arborescens,* up to 18 ft.). Flowers pink, red or purple.

TROPICAL HIBISCUS, which we are apt to associate with Hawaii, originated in tropical southeastern Asia. There are now numerous types and hybrids, one even more showy than the other. **Fringed hibiscus** has highly decorative, fringed, pendent blooms (an East African shrub).

There are a number of **TRUMPETVINES** in Mexico, many of them belonging to the Bignonia family. The most striking one, and a favorite of old Mexican gardens, is **Amphilophium buccinatorium** (p. 90), of a brilliant red color; it often climbs to the top of tall trees. It is also known as **LLAMARADA**. Longer, slender tubes and five small rounded teeth has **Pyrostegia venusta**, properly **LLAMARADA** or **Flame vine**. It is a great favorite in the warmer zones of Mexico.

POMEGRANATE is one of the ancient cultivated fruits; its flower quite beautiful. Theophrastus described it 300 years before the Christian era. The Moors in Spain named a beautiful city, Granada, after it. The scriptures use it as a favorite symbol of pulchritude. Black writing-ink is derived from the rind of the fruit. The acidic red pulp has been used on the table since time immemorial; the flowering shrub itself is a favorite in patios as a pot plant. Oh yes, of course, it must have therapeutic qualities, for instance as a "tapeworm remedy."

BOUGAINVILLEA
ROSALINDA MELENDREZ

TREE FUCHSIA
MUIR

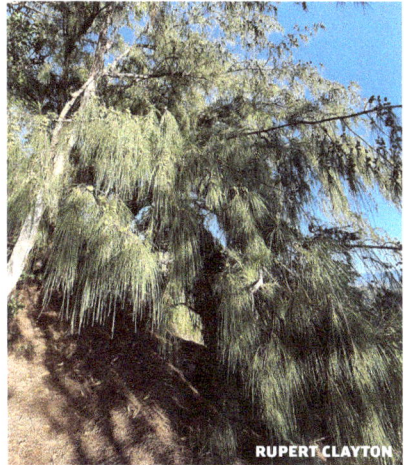
HORSETAIL BEEFWOOD
RUPERT CLAYTON

Both parks and roadsides feature a tree that goes under the descriptive name of **HORSETAIL BEEFWOOD** (*Casuarina equiseti-folia*), the wood is of a deep red color; the branchlets look like the horsetail plant). The Mexican name **PINO DE AUSTRALIA** indicates its origin. It isn't a pine, though somewhat resembling it. Height to 60 ft.; fruit conelike, one-half inch in diameter.

One of the anomalies in Mexico is the so-called **TRAVELER'S TREE** (*Ravenala madagascariensis*, Strelitziaceae), like the banana, a near relative, not really a tree, though it may reach 20 to 30 ft. in height. Its very large leaves grow in two ranks, creating a fan-shaped head. Clear watery sap collects in their concave bases, hence the reference to travelers.

The well-known **BIRD-OF-PARADISE FLOWER** (*Strelitzia reginae*, Strelitziaceae) with its beak-shaped orange-and-purple flower, is a favorite in flower arrangements.

AZTEC LILY or **JACOBEAN LILY** (*Sprekelia formosissima*) is native in a number of places in Mexico, and commonly grown as an ornamental summer bulb; brilliant scarlet, with slender petals. The bulb has an alkaloid, called **AMARILLIANA**, applied to the scalp to prevent falling out of the hair; Mexican name **AMACAYO**.

We should mention the fabulous **PASSION FLOWER**, *Passiflora caerulea,* and others, ranging from green, blue and yellow to red and purple. A native of New Spain, the Spaniards took it to be a clear designation by the great Creator that it might assist in the conversion of the heathen among whom it grew. The 10 colored parts of the flower were thought to represent apostles present at the crucifixion (without Judas and Peter); inside the corolla is a showy crown of colored filaments — the crown of thorns, or a halo —

TRAVELER'S TREE

AGNIESZKA KWIECIEŃ

BIRD-OF-PARADISE FLOWER

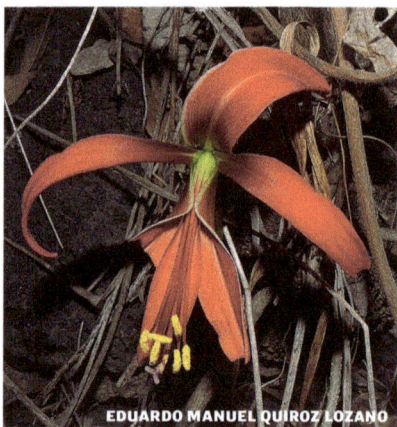

EDUARDO MANUEL QUIROZ LOZANO

AZTEC LILY

the five stamens suggest the five wounds, the three styles of the pistil are the three nails of the cross. The long tendrils stand for the cords or scourges, the five-fingered leaves are suggestive of the hands of the persecutors, or else the prongs of the lance or pike which "pierced the side of our Saviour, whilst they are marked beneath with round spots, signifying the 30 pieces of silver".

This account, by Jacomo Bosio, in 1610, eloquently attests the lively and devout imagination of the day. Surprisingly enough, no mention is made of the edible fruit of some of these passion flowers.

What other ornamental plants shall we mention? As you travel through this amazing plant paradise, one after another vies for attention. A few of the garden flowers, now in cultivation, that came from Mexico or thereabouts, have been mentioned before. There is the **Dahlia** (pp. 73–74), **Zinnia** (p. 74), **Pricklepoppy** (p. 70), **Shellflower** (p. 80), **Mexican star** (p. 73), **Zephyrlily** (p. 17), **Mexican coral drops** (p. 18), among others.

Sometimes we are suddenly transported to a garden scene of **Cosmos, Ageratum, Lantana, Mexican tulip poppy** (*Hunnemannia fumariifolia*) to mention just a few. We must remember that **Petunia, Nasturtium, Gomphrena, Marigold** (both "African" and "French") *Sanvitalia procumbens*, **Tithonia, Heliotrope**, and others came to us from Mexico or similar locations (not to mention **Tobacco, Vanilla, Pumpkin, Squash, Corn**, and **Beans**).

Vanilla brings to mind that we have (purposely) omitted the host of **orchids** found in Mexico. They have been treated in other books, and present a world of exotics, endless in variety. The Orchid family is one of the largest families of plants, with about 30,000 species currently recognized worldwide. Mexico alone has over 1,200 species, with an

MEXICAN TULIP POPPY

LANTANA

estimated 40% being endemic to that country. The greatest orchid diversity is found in the tropical areas and in temperate mountainous areas. However, many populations have been lost due to deforestation and illegal collecting; orchids should never be picked or collected.

In closing, we had to draw a line somewhere, as to what to include in this guide and what to leave to individual discovery. There is little more exciting than to come upon a new plant in a dramatic setting. We remain of the same opinion we expressed to begin with: for the plant lover, Mexico furnishes unending delight!

VANILLA ORCHID

NOTE: One of the few 'modern' guides to a portion of Mexico's plant life is: *Baja California Plant Field Guide* (3rd edition, 2012, Sunbelt Publications) by Jon P. Rebman and Norman C. Roberts. The following references are those cited in the 1962 edition of this book, and are arranged chronologically.

SAFFORD, WILLIAM E.. 1909. *Cactaceae of Northeastern and Central Mexico.* Washington, Smithsonian Report.

PITTIER, HENRY FRANCOIS, 1909-1922. *New or noteworthy plants from Colombia and Central America.* Contr. U.S. Natl. Herb. Vol. 13, 8 parts. Smithsonian Institution.

MAZA, MANUEL GOMEZ DE LA, 1914. *Flora de Cuba.* Habana. Imprenta y papelerias de Rambla. Bouza.

WOOTON, E. O. and STANDLEY, J. C., 1915. *Flora of New Mexico.* U.S. National Herbarium, Vol. 19.

STANDLEY, PAUL C., 1920-1926. *Trees and Shrubs of Mexico.* Contr. U.S. Nat. Herb. Vol. 23, 5 parts. (now out of print)

STANDLEY, PAUL C., 1930. *Flora of Yucatán.* Field Museum of Natural History, Botanical Series. Vol. III. Chicago.

GILL, Tom, 1931. *Tropical Forests of the Caribbean.* Tropical Plant Research Foundation. Survey of tropical forests including Mexico; 318 pp. Contains about 100 illustrations of trees and forest practices.

SMALL, JOHN K., 1933. *Manual of the southeastern flora.* Chapel Hill. University of North Carolina. Many line drawings. 1554 pgs.

MATSCHAT, CECIL HULSE, 1935. *Mexican Plants for American Gardens.* Boston, Houghton-Mifflin. 269 pages. Pen drawings. Has some valuable source material on Mexican plants.

MORTON, JULIA F., 1935. *Some Useful and Ornamental Plants of the Caribbean Gardens.* Caribbean Gardens, Naples, Florida. Souvenir booklet with 40 photos of striking plants, descr. Catalogo Alfabetico de Nombres Vulgares y Cientificos de Plantas que Existsen en Mexico. Mexico; Estudios Biologicos.

BRAND, DONALD D., 1936. *Notes to accompany a vegetation map of northwest Mexico.* U. of New Mexico, Biol. Ser., Vol. 4, No. 4, Albuquerque. 27 pp. Map shows 11 vegetation types. Small but handy.

MARTINEZ, MAXIMINO, 1936. *Plantas Utiles de Mexico.* 2d ed. Mexico, DF. Publ. by author. Describes a number of useful plants, illustr.

BRAVO H., HELIA, 1937. *Las Cactaceas de Mexico.* Universidad Nacional de Mexico. The standard authority on Mexican cacti, covering many aspects, with complete descriptions and fine illustrations.

PRESTON, RICHARD J., 1940. *Rocky Mountain Trees.* Iowa State College Press, Ames, Ia. A number of species extending in Mexico are included; pen drawings, exhaustive descriptions, distribution maps.

ARIAS, ALFONSO CONTRARAS, 1942. *Mapa de las provincias climatologicas de la Republica Mexicana.* Instituto geografica, Secretaria de agricultura y fomento. Maps and climate statistics of climate of Mexico and plant distribution.

GENTRY, HOWARD SCOTT., 1942. *Rio Mayo plants.* Carnegie Institution of Washington Publication 527. Washington, D.C. Exhaustive treatment of a small part of Sonora, showing geography, vegetation zones and plant lists. Photo illustrations.

KEARNEY, THOMAS H. and PEEBLES, ROBERT H., 1942. *Flowering plants and ferns of Arizona.* U.S. Govt. Printing Office, Washington, D.C. Many Arizona plants extend into Mexico.

MARTINEZ, MAXIMINO, 1944. *Las plantas medicinales de Mexico.* 3d ed. Mexico D.F. Published by author. Best known volume of Mexican plants. Exhaustive studies of medicinal properties. Illustrated.

BENSON, LYMAN and DARROW, ROBERT A., 1945. *A manual of southwestern desert trees and shrubs.* Tucson. Ariz. Univ. Biol. Sci. Bul. No. 6; 411 pgs., illust. Very useful flora with keys, distribution maps and illustrations; fits particularly the northwest portion of Mexico.

O'NEAL, CORA M., 1945. *Gardens and Homes of Mexico.* Banks Upshaw and Co., Dallas. Photos of old and new Mexican gardens. Reprint 1947.

STANDLEY, P. C. and STEYERMARK, J. A., 1946-1949. *Flora of Guatemala.* Fieldiana Botany Vol. 24, Part IV - VI. Chicago.

VON HAGEN, VICTOR WOLFGANG, 1948. *The Green World of the Naturalists.* Greenberg. New York. A Treasury of Five Centuries of Natural History in South America. Selections and biographies of authors.

LITTLE, ELBERT L. JR., 1950. *Native species of N. Mex. and Arizona.* U.S. Dept. of Agriculture; Agricultural Handbook No. 9. Quite useful for northern Mexico. Descriptions, drawings.

DODGE, NATT N., 1951. *Flowers of the Southwestern Deserts.* Southwestern Monuments Association, Santa Fe, N. M. A highly useful illustrated booklet including the Sonoran and the Chihuahuan deserts. Flowers arranged by color. 112 pp.

GOLDMAN, EDWARD A., 1951. *Biological investigations in Mexico.* Smithsonian Misc. Coll. Vol. 115. Early explorations by Nelson and Goldman; Physiography, Life zones. 70 photos of life zones.

LEON, HERMANO, 1951. *Flora de Cuba.* Four extensive volumes in Spanish.

McDOUGALL, W. B. and SPERRY, OMER E., 1951. *Plants of Big Bend National Park.* National Park Service, U.S. Dept. of the Interior. Flora, keys and pictures of the Park, which is across the Rio Grande from Mexico.

PATRAW, PAULINE MEAD, 1951. *Flowers of the Southwestern Mesas.* Southwestern Monuments Association, Santa Fe, N. M. Similar to its companion Deserts booklet, but less useful for Mexico.

WHITE, WILLIAM C. and PERTCHIK, BERNARD and HARRIET, 1951. *Flowering Trees of the Caribbean.* Rinehart and Co. Inc., N. Y. Thirty magnificent color paintings of the most striking trees, the majority of which are common in Mexico. Good descriptions.

MIRANDA, FAUSTINO, 1952. *La vegetación de Chiapas.* 2 vols. Sección autografica, Departmento de Prensa y Turismo, Chis. Mex. Splendid enumeration of plants of the region and plant zones with definite descriptions of both; pen drawings and photos.

WOMAN'S CLUB OF HAVANA, 1952, 1958. *Flowering Plants from Cuban Gardens.* Criterion Books, New York. In both English and Spanish. Full-page drawings and descriptions. 5 color plates.

ALLEN, PAUL H., 1956. *The rain forests of Golfo Dulce.* U. of Florida Press. Beautifully illustrated and carefully written. Plant index with keys, and ecological treatment of the flora of this part of Costa Rica; both practical and scientific.

BARRETT, MARY F., 1956. *Common Exotic Trees of South Florida*. (Dicotyledons). U. of Florida Press. 414 pp. illustrated, keys.

ERDMA N, WEST, and ARNOLD, LILLIAN E., 1956. U. of Florida. *Native Trees of Florida*. Description and sketches of 350 species.

SMILEY, NIXON, 1956. *Tropical Planting and Gardening*. H. F. Macmillan, by Director of Fairchild Tropical garden. Descriptions and small photos. Special reference to Ceylon.

BELVIANES, MARCEL, (Translated by HUXLEY, ANTHONY J.) , 1957. *Exotic plants of the world*. Hanover House, Garden City. Very beautifully done; 154 photos, 49 in color, short descriptions. Contains some Mexican plants.

BRUGGEMAN, L. (MARIE LOUISE ABRAHAM) , 1957. *Tropical plants and their cultivation*. Crowell, N. Y. This is a translation of TUINBOEK VOOR DE TROPEN. Colored drawings by OJONG SOER JADI. The 292 drawings and many more descriptions make it very valuable.

HARGREAVES, DOROTHY and BOB, 1958. *Hawaii blossoms*. Hargreaves Industrial, Portland, Ore. Over 100 fine color photos, with description of each. Many of the plants illustrated are in Mexico.

MENNINGER, EDWIN A., 1958 ed. *What flowering tree is this?* Stuart, Florida, published by author. Exhaustive enumeration of tropical trees, well-illustrated with photos, some colored.

O'GORMAN, HELEN, 1958. *Mexican Flower Engagement Calendar*. Mex. D.F. Ammex Asociados, Amazonas 90. A beautiful collection of 53 paintings in color of some of the most showy plants in Mexico.

GRAF, ALFRED B., 1959. *Exotica 2. Pictorial Cyclopedia for Indoor Plants*. Roehrs Co., Rutherford, N. J. A treasure house of information: 7600 illustrations, 231 in color. Mexico is given one page specifically; many plants of Exotica found there.

WRIGHT, NORMAN PELHAM, 1959. *Oriquideas de Mexico*. Editorial/Fournier, S.A. Mexico D.F. Attractive book, rich with 40 color plates, 105 pp. Written in both Spanish and English. Invaluable for orchid hobbyists.

HARGREAVES, DOROTHY and BOB, 1960. *Tropical blossoms of the Caribbean*. Portland, Ore. Over 100 color photos, with descriptions.

STORER, DOROTHY P., 1960. *Familiar trees and cultivated plants of Jamaica*. Institute of Jamaica, Macmillan and Co., London. About 70 good pendrawings and descriptions.

VINES, ROBERT A., 1960. *Trees, Shrubs and Woody Vines of the Southwest*. U. of Texas Press, Austin, Tex. 1104 pp. Numerous species are described with range and habitat, each with careful pen drawings by SARAH KAHLDER ARENDALE. An exhaustive guide to Arkansas, Louisiana, New Mexico, Oklahoma and Texas. A standard reference work.

AMERICAN HORTICULTURAL MAGAZINE, Special issue. Jan. 1961. *Cultivated Palms*. This journal of the Amer. Hortic. Society of Washington, D. C. has about 80 black-and white engravings, photos and pen drawings.

MUIRHEAD, DESMOND, 1961. *Palms*. Dale Stuart King, Publisher, Globe, Arizona. Excellent, modestly priced handbook on palms—their description, culture, and use in garden and landscape. 144 pp., many illus.

O'GORMAN, HELEN, 1961. *Mexican Flowering Trees and Plants*. Ammex Asociados, Mexico D.F. 228 pp. A beautiful reference book with 112 choice color-drawings by the author, selected on the basis of their attractiveness. Good description of each.

M. WALTER PESMAN

The widely known M. (Michiel) Walter Pesman (1887–1962), practicing landscape architecture in Denver for many years, was been responsible for many important projects, such as planning the grounds of the Denver Public Schools and Colorado State University and designing Colorado roadside developments. Born in Thesinge, The Netherlands, , he was educated there and at the University of Oklahoma and Colorado State University. He became a naturalized U. S. citizen in 1915.

He wrote *Meet the Natives*, a very successful guide to Rocky Mountain plants, as well as numerous pamphlets and magazine articles. He was a full-time instructor at Colorado State and teaches extension courses for the Universities of Colorado and Denver. Very active in public affairs of a conservation nature, he also speaks seven languages, and lived in Denver, Colorado, with his wife, the former Elizabeth Hyde.

STEVE CHADDE

Steve Chadde (b. 1955) is a botanist and plant ecologist who has degrees in Range Management and Plant Ecology from the University of Wyoming and Montana State University. In addition to his professional work as a botanist and ecologist for the U.S. Forest Service, the Montana Natural Heritage Program, and various consulting firms, he has published numerous books on plants, including state floras for Minnesota (2013), Wisconsin (2013), and for the Upper Peninsula of Michigan (2014). After a decade in the Philippines, he now resides in the Ozark Mountain region of Arkansas.

However original an author or an artist may be, he cannot produce on his own power alone. Knowingly or unknowingly he taps a reservoir of previous impressions, previous knowledge, previous experiences. Thus his work is, in a way, a culmination of "what the past has wrought in him."

Scientists are well aware of this, building as they do on all existing information. They welcome even a slight advance in a direction where further exploration is needed.

This little contribution, on my part, to the knowledge of Mexican vegetation is very definitely based upon previous work done by others. In some ways it is merely a compilation and a combination of earlier studies. I regret that I can only give full credit to some of the more obvious sources.

First of all should be mentioned the standard work on Mexican trees and shrubs by Paul C. Standley. What a treasure-house of information it has been ever since its publication!

Without A. Starker Leopold's vegetation map (pp. 4–5) my book would lose much of its meaning (originally published in his book *Wildlife of Mexico*, 1959).

For many years Dr. Maximino Martinez of the Instituto de Biologia, in Mexico City, has been the dean of present-day Mexican botanists. His books on useful and medicinal plants are standard works. Exemplifying the gracious Mexican courtesy, he was willing, at various times, to aid me in the identification of many plants I brought in to him, and to look over the manuscript in process.

Equally helpful and amiable was Dr. Faustino Miranda of the same Instituto, author of *La Vegetacion de Chiapas* and other works.

At the fine botanical garden at Tuxtla Gutierrez it was Professor Miguel A. Palacios Rincón who came to my rescue—botanically; in Guadalajara Professor Pablo G. Franco and Ing. Agustin Gómez y Gutierrez. The Sociedad Botanica del Estado de Jalisco was gracious enough to elect me to honorary membership.

Certain pamphlets and books on botanical aspects were helpful. I want to mention particularly *Las Cactaceas de Mexico*, the wonderful book by Helia Bravo H. of the Biological Institute.

A number of people in the United States have done recent work on Mexican plants (see **Bibliography**). In the early Powers' *Guide to Mexico*, which fell into my hands, a fascinating chapter on plant life of the Pan-American Highway showed the possibility of recognizing some of the typical representatives of Mexico's numerous plant zones. It was written by Dr. Leslie A. Kenoyer, now of San Antonio, Texas. In that way I was influenced in the decision to do my part in this direction. He was kind enough to let me re-draw some of his illustrations and slides.

During the earlier stages of my studies the following persons were very helpful in many ways: Dr. Mildred E. Mathias (University of California), Professor Harold E. Moore, Jr., (Cornell), Curator Rogers McVaugh (University of Michigan), Drs. Howard Scott Gentry and F. G. Meyer of Beltsville, Maryland, and Bernard W. Benson of the Boyce Thompson Southwestern Arboretum. Thanks to all of you!

If in this listing I have overlooked some, it is because these studies have represented untold hours of research from any sources available to me. So little systematized information is to be had!

It does not seem right to stop here. How many good people have contributed! How can I fail to mention the nice young student in Hermosillo who took me on a personally conducted tour of native plants? The **CAMPESINOS** in various parts of Mexico who knew the local names and medicinal properties of special plants? The friendly owner of the thatched cottage on the Isthmus of Tehuantepec who offered to show me the trees of the tropical jungle?

There were helpful, interested friends all over Mexico.

In Denver it was my wife who went through the arduous task of improving the manuscript and who is responsible for the title, *Meet Flora Mexicana*. Debts to other Colorado friends are hereby gratefully acknowledged.

In a way this book is the joint product of all you numerous folks interested in Mexico's plant riches.

About this Book

Sometimes it is interesting to know what goes on behind the scenes in any play. You may like to know some of the preliminaries of the writing of this book (or should I say compiling?). First there were a preliminary Mexican trip or two and "insatiable curiosity". Then came study of books wherever available. At the same time we made contacts with a number of botanists, such as Drs. Martinez and Miranda in Mexico, Prof. Kenoyer in Texas. It became apparent that a grouping by plant geography is possible and helpful.

Most exciting was the next step: the working technique, so to say. We realized that many other tourists would want information about the very plants that attracted our attention, mainly those along the highways. What more natural then than to gather plant material en route, sketch it while fresh, and then try to find out its name and all about it? I would walk ahead of the automobile, selecting plant parts; on being picked up I'd start sketching while the car moved on, keeping half an eye on new tantalizing plants I might have overlooked. Blessings on a wife who is a front-seat driver! About 200 sketches were thus made, some with "loose" waving lines and quaint angles due to a sudden swerving of the car. All were re-drawn on return and checked with other information.

Now for another confession. this book is suited particularly to winter tourists in Mexico. After all, December, January and February have special appeal, and these winter months show some of the most spectacular beauty in Mexican plants.

Later books, I am sure, will be written to cover the rainy season periods. Let us repeat again: this is a pioneering venture. The organization of the book itself is without much precedent, except in the author's *Meet the Natives*. Botany books have been expected to follow traditional taxonomic precepts, being neatly arranged by families, irrespective of where plants are found. This one is more or less on ecological lines.

After making these admissions concerning the book's acknowledged shortcomings we hope it will do something to make you feel more at home among the many, many interesting plants to be found in Mexico. We trust it may clear up a few puzzling questions about names, distribution, and growth habits. More and more tourists are finding plant knowledge one of the pleasures of travel.

Mexico's plants offer you a welcome and a challenge. The author wishes you **BUEN VIAJE!**

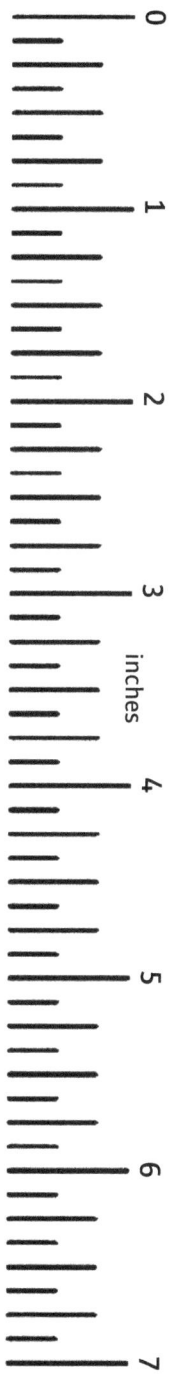

0

1

2

3

inches

4

5

6

7